WOMEN, CELIBACY, AND THE CHURCH

WOMEN, CELIBACY, AND THE CHURCH

TOWARD A THEOLOGY OF THE SINGLE LIFE

Annemarie S. Kidder

A Herder & Herder Book
The Crossroad Publishing Company
New York

The Crossroad Publishing Company
481 Eighth Avenue, New York, NY 10001

Printed in the United States of America

This book is set in 11.5/15 Goudy Old Style.
The display fonts are Bernhard Modern and Belwe Light.

Library of Congress Cataloging-in-Publication Data
Kidder, Annemarie S.
    Women, celibacy, and the church : toward a theology of the single life / Annemarie S. Kidder.
        p. cm.
    ISBN 0-8245-2110-2 (alk. paper)
    1. Celibacy – Christianity – History of doctrines. 2. Chastity – History of doctrines. 3. Women – Religious aspects – Christianity – History of doctrines.
    I. Title.
BR195.C45K53 2003
241.6'6 – dc21

                                                            2003008240

1 2 3 4 5 6 7 8 9 10   09 10 08 07 06 05 04 03

Contents

Acknowledgments

This book is the result of many people lending me support, encouragement, and direction along the way. Some I met only briefly, others I have known for years. I want to mention those, in particular, who have played key roles in the book's conception and development. For encouraging me to pursue the idea of constructing a tentative theology of the single life, I thank Freda Gardner, professor emerita of Christian Education and former moderator of the Presbyterian Church (USA). For providing me access to research material, offering input, and allowing me to present my findings to seminarians studying for the priesthood, I am indebted to the library staff, faculty, and president of Mt. St. Mary's Seminary at the Athenaeum of Ohio, Cincinnati. For moral and spiritual support, I thank the spiritual directors Donna Steffen, SC, of Cincinnati, Ohio; Mary Bea Keeley, IHM, of Monroe, Michigan; and the sisters of St. Walburg Monastery. And for the eagerness of fleshing out and guiding me in the methodology of research and in Roman Catholic theology and history of doctrine, I thank Professor Robert Hater of Mt. St. Mary's. My gratitude also goes to members of The First Presbyterian Church of Ann Arbor, who have listened to portions of the manuscript and made helpful suggestions. I especially thank Gwendolin Herder of The Crossroad Publishing Company for her enthusiasm in making possible the publication of the manuscript and to the editors for their concise suggestions and trimmings. Above all, I wish to thank those women and men living the single and celibate life who have readily availed themselves in sharing with me their struggles, hopes, and longings as they seek to live out the Christian faith in service to their Lord. It is to them, along with all willing and unwilling celibates in Christ, both now and then, that I dedicate this book.

Introduction

A Personal Journey

This book results from a hunger to understand myself as a single woman in relation to her faith, her God, and the Christian church. It comes from wondering about my role in the framework of the created world, my gifts and passions and creativity in the community of other believers, and my responsibilities in service to others and to a loving and merciful God.

My questions about celibacy and the single life have been with me for a long time. They go back, as far as I can tell, to innocent play with neighborhood kids in the backyard of my childhood home, where we often busied ourselves playing family, complete with its intricate housekeeping duties. Who gets to play Mom, who Dad, who the children? I would often opt to be one of the children, not because I liked to be bossed around, but more because I wanted no part of the role of parent or of marriage in general. In elementary school I wondered why many of my female classmates wanted to marry some day and have children. I had no desire in that regard, either in finding a partner, building a home, or having children of my own. By the time high school came around, I dated like everyone else.

But the thought of becoming permanently bonded to another human being seemed strange and out of the question. Either my dating relationships were not "marriage material" or I was subconsciously picking dates who would never lend themselves to a committed lifelong relationship within the bonds of marriage. By the time I was in college I felt I had seen and experienced whatever there was to know about dating. Subsequently, after breaking up with my boyfriend of four years, I vowed that it would be the last time I experimented with the coupled life. I made my resolution known to my mother, who, realizing I meant

1

what I said, urged me to seek psychological counseling, as if my lack of interest in marriage was aberrant behavior that needed to be cured. To please her and to explore my own motives, I went several times, but stopped because the psychologist attributed my lack of interest in a partner to stress at work and a "confused psychological state." I was not sure that I wanted to be "cured."

Feeling on the fringe of normalcy, I continued my work at a publishing house and my studies in mass communications at the Hochschule der Künste in Berlin, graduated, and moved to the United States to study journalism. To my surprise I found the climate much more congenial toward the single life. The country seemed concerned with moral living, chastity, and religious endeavor; churches were mushrooming at every corner. Unlike in my own country, Germany, where churches were mainly filled with tourists or people who had cultivated a sophisticated appreciation for organ and choral music, American churches were filled on Sunday mornings with people who were keenly listening — or at least appeared to be — to interpretations of the Bible and exhortations to live a holy life. I was quickly drawn into Christian fellowship and Bible study groups. My friends were active in Campus Crusade for Christ and the local church, and our spare time was absorbed by church activities. All of my friends on campus were single, though some were dating and then engaged to be married. I was told that you didn't date unless you had every intention of getting married at some point. This made complete sense to me. Since I had no intention of marrying, I carefully avoided the term "dating" when it came to my own social interaction with the opposite sex. I didn't "date," but forged friendships with men instead. And I felt totally accepted in this climate conducive to the single life. Rather than being viewed as the oddball, I was now not only accepted, but, moreover, was considered to be living a life in line with Christian teaching — hence with God.

Following graduate studies in journalism, I enrolled in seminary. The majority of my classmates were male and married. The few females in the School of Theology were for the most part single. In light of my sheltered life on campus, I couldn't help but feeling that God had established a serious connection between the study of theology and being single and female. I viewed my singleness as a sign of my utter devotion to the study of God and to God in general. While it was acceptable for my male classmates to be married, something I never really questioned back then, it was less acceptable for me as a female — the underlying assumption being that a woman simply could not handle the marital distraction and remain faithful to God at the same time. It did not take me long to convince myself of the truth of this assumption. And as if to emphasize my love of and devotion to God in public, I made it known to my classmates and professors that I would never get married. I suspect that all I wanted was a pat on the back, which, on occasion, I got. But never did I dream that it would also produce hostility. One of my professors took issue with the very idea of singleness and read me the riot act. I was limiting God and what God had planned for my life, he said, scolding me for the narrowness of my thinking, my lack of trust in God, and my primitive belief that I could regulate my life as I saw fit, when it was to be left up to God's design and good mercy. Subsequently, I avoided him as far as that was possible in the close-knit life of a seminary. A year later I ran into the professor again while serving for a summer term as a chaplaincy intern in Hamburg, Germany, at a hospital that was owned and operated by a Protestant group of female religious and in whose motherhouse I was staying. He was doing research at a seminary in Hamburg and asked me to be shown the grounds of the motherhouse and to be introduced to the mother superior and the community of sisters, who called themselves deaconesses. I couldn't help but feel a sense of satisfaction as I introduced him to this community of faith, women who had pledged themselves to a life of service to God and others through communal living and the celibate life. Little was said about their commitment following our return to the States. But I had to face him once more when, two years later, and to my own great surprise, I married and had to endure his I-told-you-sos in the course of a seminar he taught, along with his repeated New Testament exegesis on the beatitudes and the gift of the marital bond.

Eight years later, I was single again. I felt the I-told-you-so was on me, but I have not had the opportunity to share it since our professional lives and denominational affiliations have not intersected. Still, I sometimes wonder what I would tell the professor were we to meet again. Would I have an exegetical thesis ready to present to him that upholds my point of view? Would my argument be informed by carefully researched theological tenets that would corroborate my personal view of the single life in relation to God? Could I argue from biblical precepts and historical antecedents? I am not sure that I could. But I am sure of this much, that my personal experience as a woman who has been single for most of her adult life and in service of the church, both as a volunteer and in ordained ministry, has shaped my thinking and the questions I have concerning the single life and its relation to my spiritual walk with God in Christ.

The guiding questions that have resulted in this book, then, are largely intertwined with my own journey as a Protestant and as a woman. In the course of my work in the church over the past fifteen years, I have found that these questions are also those that many of my friends, colleagues, and fellow believers have asked at one point or another. Can we as Christians expect and anticipate the development of the spiritual gift of celibacy for service in the church? If so, what is its connection with human sexuality? What is the biblical tradition on celibacy, and how have the Old and New Testaments informed the early church? What was the status of celibacy in the early church and among the Church Fathers? How has the rise and fall of monastic communities in the West, and how have the Reformation and subsequent theological movements within Protestantism influenced the status and the practice of the celibate life today? And finally, can one formulate a theology of the single life that draws on Scripture, early church practice, the Church Fathers, and the reformers and be relevant for today?

This book is written for Christians, both Protestants and Roman Catholics, men and women, laity and clergy, single and married, who want to find theological underpinnings for the celibate life in Scripture and Christian tradition. It is for pastors who want to come to a greater appreciation of and increased sensitivity toward those members of their congregations who have never married or are single or widowed or divorced. And it is to give those of us who are single or may have committed ourselves to the single and celibate life an affirmation, a sense of empowerment, and the resolve to tap into the spiritual riches of this life in community with others and with God. I write from a woman's perspective, to be specific, a white, middle-class, Western, Protestant, heterosexual, and post-Enlightenment woman's perspective. It has been shaped by my personal experiences and struggles in making sense of the divergent voices of biblical scholarship, church authorities, praxis, and sociological and psychological trends. This means, above all, that many of my observations will give special attention to women's issues. I hope that this perspective will not deter, but invite both men and women to an honest personal reflection on their own sexuality and to increased engagement with the issue of celibacy. In particular, it is my hope that the principles addressed will benefit readers regardless of sex, sexual orientation, and denominational affiliation, and will open up greater dialogue among Christians and allow for a more tolerant, hence more honest and affirming, appreciation of God's moving among us.

Celibacy or Singleness?

Initially, I had intended to write a theology on the single life from a Christian perspective by examining both those who were single either by choice or circumstance, regardless of sexual activity. This would have included people living alone in an unmarried state. They might be in a committed monogamous relationship, either heterosexual or homosexual, and they might be sexually active. It would have included singles not sexually involved with one particular person, though open to the prospect. And it would have included all those singles not in a dating or sexual relationship with a partner and living a celibate life.

This approach proved wrong for two reasons. First, it would have placed greater focus on Christianity's programmatic attempts to minister to the particular needs of singles, instead of on the underlying spiritual and faith dimension. Over the last thirty years, churches have devised specialized singles ministries in an effort to meet the social and psychological needs of their increasing number of single members through Christian fellowship and like-minded exchange. Churches have sought to accommodate single members because nearly one fourth of all households in the United States are currently occupied by a single person.[1] They are aware that many factors have contributed to the trend toward singleness, including longer life expectancy, a rising divorce rate, marriage at a later point in life, greater educational and economic advantages and opportunities for women, a growing individualism, a cultural emphasis on one's self-realization through career and work instead of raising a family, and increased societal acceptance of the single status at large. As a result, singles' ministries in churches seek to address the issues related to the single life, including loneliness, lack of a partner, and dating. However, these ministries generally do not encourage lifelong singleness, but ultimately aim at marriage. Years of being part of diverse singles groups in churches and attending their gatherings and activities have confirmed this impression. I have found that the singles ministries in many churches tend to continue to promote the theological assumption based on Genesis 2:18 that "it is not good that the person should be alone" and that he or she needs a helper. Once we graduate from our own immaturity and brokenness toward a whole, read marriageable state, these ministries seem to imply, we are ready to look for a mate again, and the church becomes the ever-willing helper. Since my interest was to explore the spiritual aspect of the single life, studying the churches' ways of aiding single people in finding a mate was beside the point.

My initial approach proved wrong also for a second reason. Singleness defined as the state of not being married makes marital status the defining moment and characteristic of a person's life.[2] It defines the single person by a negative, the *not* being married. Moreover, it only describes a sociological, but not a spiritual dimension in a person's life. Such a sociological definition does not readily invite a deeper theological reflection in a Christian context. Although a good many books have been published highlighting the positive side of singleness[3] from a Christian perspective or affirming people in their journeys,[4] the direct theological or spiritual link remains elusive.[5]

It is precisely because of this elusive link between the single life and spiritual development that I have adopted my approach: Instead of examining the single life, I shall focus on the celibate life. This orientation has resulted from my readings on the traditional "counterpart" of singleness, namely, marriage, and its theological presuppositions.

From a Christian theological perspective, in marriage two people commit themselves to each other before God, a commitment illustrating God's empowering love lived out through an intimate relationship with each other. Translated to the single state, a committed, celibate person lives out God's empowering love not through an intimate relationship with another person, but through a relationship with God in Christ. In this way, celibacy can be linked theologically with a person's spiritual development and growth.

Chapter 1

Celibacy, Sexuality, and Wholeness

================

Toward a Definition of Celibacy

Celibacy is commonly defined as a state of nonmarriage in tandem with a state of sexual abstinence. While most people would describe themselves as single, divorced, or widowed, they would hesitate to describe themselves as celibate, though by definition they might be. Protestants particularly might hesitate to refer to themselves as celibate when Western Christianity has most commonly reserved the word for the Roman Catholic clergy, along with members of religious communities, who have vowed lifelong sexual abstinence. Instead, Protestants prefer to talk about chastity or living a sexually "moral" or upright life without specifically addressing sexual activity or abstinence. My own denomination illustrates the point. In 1997, the Presbyterian Church (U.S.A.) adopted by a narrow majority vote of its 173 presbyteries the so-called "fidelity and chastity" amendment as part of its constitution. The discussion that gave rise to the new clause involved the question of whether practicing gays and lesbians should be ordained to the office of deacon, elder, or minister of Word and Sacrament. Many felt that this should never happen and were quite clear on what their vote would be. However, the amendment was redrafted by the Committee on Ordination and Sexuality of the 1996 General Assembly under the leadership of the Rev. Roberta Hestenes of Solona Beach, California, and sent to the presbyteries for vote, where it was approved by a majority of the presbyteries the following year. In its new form, it caught many by surprise, especially those who would have liked to place the requirement of sexual abstinence for single people only on the gay and lesbian community. It asked that all officers, both gay and straight (a distinction that was not made explicitly by the amendment), either live in singleness and chastity or in fidelity within the bonds of marriage (the latter obviously not a choice for gays under Presbyterian polity). With that, the amendment shifted its exclusive focus from a minority (the gay and lesbian community) toward inclusion of a significantly larger body of the denomination's constituents, namely, its heterosexual leadership as well. Ordained deacons, elders, and clergy both homosexual and heterosexual were told to identify with and conform to either of two distinct sexual lifestyles: either to be chaste and single (with the implication of practicing sexual abstinence), or to be married and faithful to one's spouse.

Of particular interest for this discussion is the requirement of sexual abstinence for single officers, called the chastity-in-singleness clause. According to Hestenes, the clause proposes that single elders, deacons, and ministers of Word and Sacrament exercise "restraint from engaging in sexual intercourse outside the bonds of marriage between a man and a woman."[1] But refraining from sexual intercourse apart from marriage actually is identified as celibacy, if celibacy is the state of nonmarriage and sexual abstinence. In fact, when the first version of the "fidelity and chastity" amendment surfaced at the 1994 General Assembly in Wichita, Kansas, the word "celibacy" was used at the place where the amendment now reads "chastity." Kathleen Norris, a Presbyterian author, poet, essayist, and Benedictine oblate, has written on celibacy as a spiritual discipline. About the amendment she says that her sense is that the "people might have meant celibate" in the amendment, rather than chaste.[2] Thus, the amendment actually prescribes for its single officers the practice of celibacy.

The 1997 ratification as church law of the "chastity-in-singleness" clause leaves many Presbyterians wondering whether it is reasonable to expect the practice of celibacy from the church's single officers. Two questions need to be raised in this regard: First, can celibacy be expected from or imposed upon the individual by law — without, for example, the presence of a particular grace gift or calling from God? This question was answered with a resounding "no" by members of the 1997 General Assembly Committee on Ordination and Sexuality when they proposed changing the "fidelity and chastity" amendment to instead require officers "to demonstrate fidelity and integrity in marriage or singleness, and in all relationships of life." While the proposed amendment — called Amendment A and commonly referred to as the "fidelity and integrity" amendment — passed General Assembly, it was defeated the following year by the presbyteries with a 57–114 vote. Second, Protestants have not generally defined their own sexual behavior as celibate; nor have Protestants been encouraged to reflect on the practice of the celibate life as a possible spiritual discipline or as a spiritual gift. References to celibacy would be a rare occurrence in a Protestant church, either as part of its adult education classes, new member orientation, officer training, confirmation, spiritual gift inventories, retreat ministry events, or as a reference in a sermon. Perhaps our Protestant heritage prevents us from using the word because the Roman Catholic Church has laid claim to it. Still, the Presbyterian Church (U.S.A.) constitution requires celibacy of its single officers and clergy. The discussion is likely to continue; each General Assembly since 1996 has dealt with the issue in some form.[3] To judge from the debate in the Presbyterian Church (U.S.A), celibacy is likely to remain a subject of discussion in all Protestant circles. But not until participants are willing to call celibacy by its proper name, and move beyond a discussion of what constitutes "chaste" and "moral" Christian behavior, can they begin to address the issue of sexuality and its connection with the spiritual life.

The word "chastity" should be abandoned in the context of Protestant discussions on sexual abstinence of single people, and the word "celibacy" adopted. Not only may our hesitation to use "celibacy" prevent church members from considering a celibate lifestyle and exploring celibacy as a potential spiritual gift or discipline,[4] but the word "chastity" has an archaic ring to it that implies transgression and sinfulness. A. W. Richard Sipe, one of the leading authorities on the psychological and spiritual aspects of celibacy, says that he refuses to use the word "chastity" because it is "aligned with sin rather than with a process of growth and is usually used to designate the absence of sexual activity of someone else or a state free from sexual sin."[5] This places on the single person the double negative of *not* being married and *not* sinning sexually — hardly an incentive to develop a healthy spiritual attitude that honestly grapples with one's sexuality. The word "chas-tity" when intended to denote a celibate lifestyle is ambiguous, and the term "celibacy" should be used. This usage invites us to explore con-temporary views of celibacy as a spiritual gift in the Protestant tradition, along with psychological and sociological observations on human sex-uality, and the particular connection between human sexuality and the spiritual life.

Celibacy as Spiritual Gift

In recent years, church leaders and laity have been encouraged to dis-cover their spiritual gifts and to use them in service to the body of the church. One of the first books to relate gifts to the well-being and growth of the church was C. Peter Wagner's *Your Spiritual Gifts Can Help Your Church Grow,* which was published in 1974. Wagner, pro-fessor of church growth at Fuller Theological Seminary, identifies and discusses twenty-seven spiritual gifts, based on New Testament passages and their interpretation. One of them is celibacy.[6] As a Protestant theologian and church growth expert, Wagner directed attention to an area of spiritual development that Protestant churches have tended to neglect. He writes, "The gift of celibacy is the special ability that God gives to certain members of the Body of Christ to remain single and enjoy it; to be unmarried and not suffer undue sexual tempta-tions."[7] Wagner says that women and men with the gift of celibacy have tremendous advantages because they "can serve the Lord better than those without it because they don't have to worry about how to please their husband or wife or family." But he also makes it clear that it is a spiritual gift that cannot stand alone. In his interpretation, there is no merit whatsoever in being unmarried unless it allows the believer to be more effective in the use of other gifts for the benefit of the church.

There are various views[8] on the emergence and development of these spiritual gifts. According to Wagner, they are given at conversion, so that we have them throughout our Christian life and are called to use them faithfully and be careful not to abuse them or let them fall into disuse. Other authors believe that the spiritual gifts, for example, those listed in 1 Corinthians 12 and 14, are given in worship only at the discretion of the Holy Spirit, so that people may not have them in a lasting sense.[9] A third view maintains that the gifts gleaned from the New Testament are only a sampling and a reflection of their time but not all-encompassing and fully representative of the complete range of gifts available to God's people.[10] The common theme of these views on spiritual gifts is that they are given to be used to serve others, with God as both the giver and in the persona of the people of God, the ultimate recipient of these gifts. In the case of celibacy this would mean that, as a spiritual gift, it cannot be legislated or prescribed by outside authority in the form of sanctions or constitutional directives, but will be given by God either in particular situations or for a lifetime with the ultimate purpose of uplifting, serving, and benefiting the body of the Christ, the Church.

Celibacy and Marriage

It is surprising that in his spiritual gift inventory, Wagner does not list marriage as a spiritual gift. In his section on the gift of celibacy he notes: "Notice that no special gift is necessary to get married, have sexual relations, and raise a family. God has made humans with organs and glands and passions so that the majority of people, Christians included, need to get married and they do just that."[11] Arguing from the viewpoint of what the majority enjoys, he included[12] (and with the example of the Shakers, who "made the mistake of universalizing the gift of celibacy, and now have all but died a natural death as a denomination," as a deterrent), Wagner makes marriage look simple, "natural," commonplace, even secular. But the question is, If marriage does not require a special gift, why would a life of celibacy? Can we take for granted that people are gifted for a life of marriage, but that it takes a special gift to enter into a life of sexual abstinence in singleness? I believe not. Perhaps we have been taking for granted that most people "automatically" are qualified to enter the state of marriage simply because of their "organs and glands," instead of first asking whether they might not be gifted with the ability to live a celibate life instead.

Several similarities exist between the life of celibacy and that of marriage in terms of spiritual giftedness and personal consecration.

According to Susan A. Muto, author of *Celebrating the Single Life: A Spirituality for Single Persons in Today's World* and a celibate herself, the committed celibate and the faithful couple see "their sexual needs in the context of their spiritual commitment to God, to the Church, and to one another." In that regard, she sees no distinction between Christian celibacy and Christian marriage since both states of life represent human responses to a calling from God. Both are "vocations requiring commitment to people entrusted to one's care as members of Christ's body."[13] God summons, and the Christian responds concretely, either to the call of marriage or to the celibate life. Moreover, both ways are demonstrations of a call to holiness. What distinguishes them may be their way of drawing people closer to God, as well as their way of showing love to members of the Christian community. Ultimately, though, says Muto, both celibacy and marriage enjoy benefits and attractions, and both states share in the joy of resurrection and the lonely sadness of Christ's agony and death. According to this view, both marriage and celibacy can be considered spiritual gifts.

Celibacy and Sexuality

Humans are sexual beings by definition. But sexual involvement and sexuality are not the same thing. Sex is a biological urge intended for pleasure, the release of tension, recreation, and procreation. Sexuality involves the totality of our being, our body, mind, feelings, spirituality, sensuality, dreams, and attitudes concerning our own bodies and those of others. Sex is aimed at genital activity culminating in orgasm, while sexuality is part of the intricate fabric of what makes us human and finds expression in various channels other than sexual activity — including creativity in the arts. Sometimes people equate sexuality and sexual activity, and assume that since we are all sexual beings, we cannot be whole and healthy without ongoing sexual activity. I still remember a professor of sociology at a university in Berlin remarking in a lecture twenty years ago that she did not see how anyone could function as a whole person without sexual activity. It makes me wonder whether this assumption is not more widespread than we might like to admit. Dorothy Payne, a Presbyterian pastor and executive director of the New Berith Women's Center in White Plains, New York, has worked with thousands of single women and listened to their problems and concerns. She concludes that "cues from all sides keep many women insecure about their sexual lives," so much so that "one of the most confusing — and incorrect — common beliefs is that women need regular sexual intercourse to be healthy, normal people."[14] Much work remains to be done to dispel the mistaken notion that people need sex to be complete. At the same time, while many would concur that one can be a wholesome, fully developed human being without sexual relations, the challenge remains for the celibate person to learn how to fully embrace and live out his or her sexuality apart from an intimate sexual relationship.

One of the concepts helpful toward this end is the idea of self-love. In constructing a theology of sexuality, James B. Nelson points out that "our sexuality is both the physiological and psychological ground of our capacity to love."[15] In other words, human sexuality is "God's magnificent and ingenious gift to implant within us the desire for intimacy and relationship." Such a desire for intimacy and relationship finds expression in a healthy acceptance and love of self. Self-love differs from narcissism or selfishness in that it affirms one's personal worth. It is reflected in Jesus' injunction to love our neighbor as ourselves. Self-love then is a prerequisite for one's ability to affirm others. If we don't love ourselves, we will most certainly have trouble loving and affirming anyone else. In the sexual area of one's being, according to Nelson, such positive self-regard and self-affirmation may find genital expression, as in self-touch or masturbation, or it may not.[16] The important thing for single people to do is to acknowledge, rather than deny, repress, or malign, their sexuality, and to embrace it as the seed for both relationship and intimacy.

The celibate life may also open up an aspect of sexuality that might go unnoticed otherwise, or may not come to fruition, namely, conviviality. According to Thomas Moore, "the withdrawal of a certain kind of sexuality can elicit another kind of eroticism, the kind that emanates from and sustains conviviality" as a quality of relationship. In this sense, the celibate life is not a repression of eros or one's sexuality, but "a form of soulful sublimation, a spreading of eros throughout life." Through the celibate life, one's sexuality may be transformed into "a way of letting others into your life that is not limited by a relationship to a single individual."[17] At the same time, it increases one's sensitivity for pleasure and beauty, which might otherwise get drowned in lust or be ignored altogether. In this view, celibacy can further the quality of an individual's experience in community and the sheer erotic pleasure of another person's company apart from the sexual act.

Celibacy can then free people for a life of love for self, others, and God. They remain alone for others, which translates into remaining single so as to better focus on the kingdom of God. But their sexuality requires particular coping mechanisms. In discussing the psychological aspect of sexuality in the life of the celibate, William F. Kraft explores in particular genital sexuality.[18] He defines it as "behavior, thoughts, fantasies, desires, feelings that involve or promote directly or indirectly genital behavior," with intercourse and masturbation as two explicit examples. Kraft contrasts genital sexuality with one's primary sexuality, such as being a man or a woman, and with affective and esthetic sexuality. While Kraft considers the primary, affective, and esthetic sexuality of a person as more important than genital sexuality, he acknowledges that genital sexuality often presents the "most pressing problems" to the celibate person.

Kraft identifies five psychological coping mechanisms for dealing with genital sexuality in the celibate lifestyle: repression, suppression, gratification, sublimation, and respectful integration. He finds that genitality has probably been disassociated from spirituality more than any other kind of sexuality, and he attempts to demonstrate how the two can be interwoven. In repression, the person tries to exclude certain sexual experiences and feelings from conscious awareness. By so doing, these experiences can increase in strength and promote pressure for expression. Concretely, repression could lead a person to project or displace his feelings by blaming others for immodesty or becoming the community's "sex-censor." In suppression, on the other hand, sexual experience is acknowledged but kept from overt expression. Instead of acting upon one's acknowledged feelings, the celibate both accepts and affirms her sexuality and freely chooses to control overt genital gratification. In sublimation, the person redirects energy from sexual activity to another that is judged to be culturally, socially, physically, functionally, esthetically, or spiritually "higher" or better or more acceptable. Rather than holding sexuality in check as in suppression, a person rechannels that energy into another activity. While such a mode of behavior is positive, it can also impede healthy and holy growth when based primarily or exclusively on repression. This is the case in overeating, or in overly paternal or maternal behavior, where genital feelings may be repressed and sublimated into other activity excessively. The fourth coping mechanism is gratification, in which the celibate actually engages in genital behavior, treating another person, either in reality or in her fantasies, primarily as a physical being, as though both were only genital beings. There may be various reasons for doing so, including loneliness, escape from anxiety and depression, boredom, and a desire for embodiment, but the fulfillment that abates these emotions will only be temporary and does not promote a wholesome life or psychospiritual growth.

So what, then, is the preferred way of dealing with one's genitality in the celibate life? Kraft suggests respectful integration. Instead of seeing sex as an enemy or impediment, the celibate is challenged to experience sex as a friend and a help, to promote authentic integration. Rather than viewing genital functions, such as feelings and fantasies, as physical functions, a person can listen to them as genital articulations that say something about self and others as integral people. In this sense, "respect" means to see again or to take a second look, thus looking through and beyond genitality to the deeper dimensions of a person's makeup and, at the same time, one's own. In this case, genital sexuality can help a person become more alive and in tune with the finer and deeper aspects of herself and others, thus enhancing her own spirituality.

Another aspect of celibacy and sexuality is based on family systems theory. This theory says that our perceptions and responses are closely linked with the type of family system with which we are associated. Kenneth R. Mitchell has explored this aspect of celibacy in an article entitled "Priestly Celibacy from a Psychological Perspective."[19] While the article is about priestly celibacy, I believe it offers helpful perspectives on the celibate life in general. According to Mitchell, everyone has the possibility of belonging to three family or family-like units. The primary family unit is the family of infancy and childhood, the one you were born into and brought up in, where you received love, criticism, care, nurture, support, and education from a variety of adults. The secondary family unit is the one created in adult life through marriage and possibly by having children, of which you are the head. The tertiary family unit consists of a work associates. The biggest issue for the celibate is that the secondary family is severely altered, so that the celibate is deprived of its gratifications, including sex, touch, closeness, warmth, and deep personal involvement. This may mean that the celibate seeks to re-create the secondary family unit either by drawing closer to the primary family and overemphasizing her relation to it, or by creating a secondary family unit within the tertiary family unit.

The second case, in which the celibate may re-create the secondary family unit by drawing on the tertiary one, can result in complicated work relationships. For example, fellow workers may be viewed as children to be disciplined or reared, or bosses may be regarded as mates or parental authority figures. Drawing on research conducted on multiple-staff ministries in Presbyterian churches,[20] Mitchell observed that one characteristic of the stable, long-term, productive multiple-staff relationships was that the men in them socialized with each other very little and that even their spouses did not choose their closer friends from other staff spouses. It is helpful to recognize the need of the celibate for a secondary family unit and to seek alternatives. While these alternatives will exclude sexual intimacy, they can meet the celibate's need for touch, closeness, warmth, and deep personal involvement through a close network of intimate friendships that are not directly drawn from one's work associates and one's primary family unit.

Women and Sexuality

Sexuality moves beyond physical and biological aspects of the body and toward social expectations and cultural ideals that influence women and men. One important aspect of sexuality is gender. According to Evelyn Eaton Whitehead and James D. Whitehead, gender is about masculine and feminine behavioral patterns. Our awareness that we are a woman or a man is central to our sexuality. To a large degree, this awareness is shaped by cultural expectations. Mature sexuality challenges us to be confident and comfortable with the way in which we are women or men. This means recognizing both how our experience fits the social norm and how it contradicts it.[21] While both sexes are responsible for developing mature sexuality perceptions, there is growing evidence of a fundamental difference between men and women in the way their sexuality finds expression in relationship. This difference has been demonstrated most convincingly by Carol Gilligan's study on the development of women and men in regard to moral education.[22] In exploring various theories of development of boys and girls, she concurs with Nancy Chodorow that a child's personality formation is, with rare exceptions, firmly and irreversibly established by the time the child is around three. Given that for both sexes the primary caretaker in the first three years of life is typically female, the interpersonal dynamics of gender identity formation are different for boys and girls. Female identity formation takes place in a context of ongoing relationship, since mothers tend to experience their daughters as more like, and continuous with, themselves. In contrast, boys, in defining themselves as masculine, separate themselves from their mothers, thus curtailing their primary love and emotional tie. According to Chodorow, this means that for boys — not girls — issues of differentiation have become intertwined with sexual issues. As a result, relationships, particularly issues of dependency, are experienced differently by women and men. For boys and men, separation and individuation are critically tied to gender identity since separation from the mother is essential for the development of masculinity. For girls and women, on the other hand, issues of femininity or feminine identity do not depend on the achievement of separation from the mother or on the progress of individuation. This then is responsible for differing gender-related patterns in relationship, where males tend to have problems with relationship and females with individuation. But Gilligan goes beyond that by showing how earlier developmental theories, such as Lawrence Kohlberg's six stages of moral development, favor a "right-and-wrong" perspective, derived from the ideal of male individuation, over against the "relational care" perspective prevalent in women.

These findings have several consequences for women and their sexuality. First, based on women's accounts of the crucial dimensions of sexuality, one finds that intimacy as trustworthy friendship is very important. In fact, in writing on women and sexuality, Lisa Sowle Cahill observes that feminist theologians and ethicists characteristically establish the context of intimate friendship first, and only afterwards proceed to the question of sexual expression. They virtually never begin with the fact of sexual acts, then ask after their moral meanings, permissibilities, and limits.[23] Instead, women's literature on sex and theology, for example, centers its content much less on sexual desire and its culmination in intercourse than on the relational potential. The result is that sex as an act or activity tends to be subsumed within a more holistic and relational view.

Second, the moral evaluation of sex by men is based on a "right-and-wrong" approach, with much focus given to the culmination of the sex act and its specifics. Women, on the other hand, evaluate sex morally in light of its underlying and contextual aspects, such as relationship, friendship, and care. The focus is less on the sex act than on the nature of closeness and the intimacy of the relationship. Based on their pastoral and counseling experience, the Whiteheads outline additional typical male and female approaches to sexuality. For instance, they say that while women find close personal relationships a source of security, men derive emotional security from independence, so that relationships can be threatening to men. In friendships, women seek self-disclosure, while men seek camaraderie, which spills over into their sexual expectations. Women value emotional connectedness and only then are open to the possibility of sexual intimacy, while men experience sexual attraction first and only later may open up to emotional connectedness.[24]

In light of these observations, a maturing experience of sexuality for women may mean developing a sense of autonomy and separateness, a setting oneself apart from others that creates room for self-exploration and a redefinition of identity. Examples of such redefinitions of female identity can be seen in the women's liberation movement of the sixties and seventies and in recent feminist theologies and writings. One feminist theologian, Virginia Mollenkott, points out that many women are beginning to realize that their claims to individualism have been denied in the name of a biological or spiritual determinism, so that in their effort to maintain connectedness to everybody else, women tended to consider everybody else's needs except their own.[25]

Another redefinition is apparent in the trend evolving over the last three decades for women of marrying age to remain single.[26] While such a redefinition of female identity may initially appear as a discarding of the feminine self, along with the risk of losing relationships, it will help women grow beyond the automatic responses to traditional gender definitions and toward an exploration of their sexual identity, integrity, and love of self.

In addition to sexual response, women's embodied sexuality figures differently from that of men's in the area of parenthood. Since women have been primarily responsible for infant care, the nurturing behavior may appear to be determined by biological roles and then be social-ized through complementary responses. The question arises whether human mothers are biologically destined or socialized into exhibiting characteristically nurturing, feminine traits. Social science and anthro-pological studies suggest that the culture is at least as influential as biology in determining "appropriate" models and behavioral traits for parenthood.[27] Regardless of whether nature or culture is responsible for the gender differences in personality and sexual identity, women will need to continue to explore and exercise previously underdeveloped skills directed at their own bodies, spirituality, and self to complement the orientation of nurturing others.

It may be helpful to explore the gender-related dualistic nature in-nate in the psyche of the human being. This dualism presupposes that people are androgynous, that is, that they are born with both mas-culine and feminine traits. The Swiss psychoanalyst Carl Gustav Jung was the first to describe this characteristic of the human psyche. Jung called the masculine side the "animus" and the feminine side the "an-ima." People embody both animus and anima; no one exists with either purely masculine or feminine traits. Women then will exhibit their an-ima more prominently in their behavior, with traces of animus emerging on occasion. Men, conversely, operate on the basis of the animus, with

traces of emerging anima. In an impulse toward mature sexual identity, women will begin to befriend and to start integrating their animus,
men their anima. The job of befriending this androgynous behavior is
to achieve a balanced wholeness in sexual identity. Exercising androgynous behavior is never completely achieved. It is unlikely that we
will see women or men showing both traits of animus and anima to
equal extents. Androgynous behavior is not like ambidextrous behavior, where we can use the left hand or the left brain to the same extent
as the right. But it will encompass a greater facility in moving back and
forth between the animus and the anima and in exercising behavioral
patterns commonly ascribed to the opposite sex. When presenting this
view to church groups, I have sometimes encountered resistance to it,
particularly from men. The argument runs that if we do not capitalize
on our natural tendencies and preferred modes of behavior, we will
sacrifice our strengths and land ourselves in a sea of mediocrity. Why
not be proud of our sexual identity and capitalize on what we do best?
I reply that we cannot be our best unless we develop a more wholistic approach to self. Furthermore, the less developed side, the animus
in women, for example, has a tendency to take over when we least
expect it or when we seem powerless to control its emergence. The
saying that we are as sick as our secrets could be adjusted to, We are as
sick as our undeveloped side. Androgynous behavior liberates us from
surprise takeovers by the animus (or anima in men) and opens up a
greater freedom in consciously responding to outside stimuli.

Based on opinions coming from the areas of psychoanalysis and pastoral counseling, women may be better at androgynous behavior than
men. Jungian analyst and counselor John A. Sanford says, for example,
that women are better at it than men because they needed to expand their "maleness" so as to survive in a male world.[28] Men tend
to fight the development of "femaleness" possibly because they already
control the power structures in society for the most part and find no
immediate advantage in giving up this "birthright." In addition, according to John R. Landgraf, men may not feel that they need to develop
androgynous behavior because there are plenty of women out there
"who are willing to submerge their identity into that of a big, brave,
manly patron." Or they may be afraid to get in touch with fears, tears,

and helplessness — feelings and vulnerabilities "real men" have been carefully taught to avoid.[29] The implied advantage women may have in developing their animus has several consequences for their sexuality.

First, if men are more resistant or slower in developing wholeness than women, women who are actively growing toward androgynous behavior will become less tolerant of male immaturity. For single women in midlife, this may mean that developing an intimate relationship with a man based on mutual respect, emotional reciprocity, and sexual intimacy may become harder to achieve. It could explain why, in the view of a sarcastic critic of the cultural milieu, it is more likely for single women between the ages of thirty and fifty-five to become the victim of a terrorist attack than to get married. Second, women will become more of a threat to men as a result of their ability to move back and forth between the anima and the animus nature, which allows them greater flexibility in responding to crisis, which might spell greater professional competency in the world of business and industry, and hence may constitute a power threat to male authority and structure.[30] Third, rather than settling for less than an equal partner, single women may begin incorporating several men into their lives collectively,[31] such as the professional colleague, the friend, the playmate, who do not demand to be the only one in a woman's life, and allow for intimate relationships that are not necessarily genital.

Women, Intimacy, and Self-Love

The model of animus and anima in the development of the human being toward psychological and spiritual wholeness is only one example of a couplet of apparent opposites. Other couplets come in what Jung calls archetypes, or personality patterns that are common to human existence and form universal phenomena. According to this model, each of us has two modes of being in, perceiving, and evaluating the world: the preferred personality mode and the shadow or dormant personality mode. The preferred personality mode describes our personality type, while the shadow personality mode is the unfamiliar, unknown, sometimes threatening, sometimes exhilarating experiences one encounters. To close off or to deny these experiences is to become stuck, rigid, one-sided, and closed. Commonly, one begins to experience one's shadow side at midlife, around age forty. At that point, the person has a choice of embracing it or rejecting it. According to Janice Brewi and Anne Brennan, who have done research on over twenty thousand people in midlife, rejecting this shadow side "is to die at forty and to not get buried until ninety." Embracing this shadow side too enthusiastically, however, is to throw off and demolish all that has been built in the first half of life. Integration and individuation require bearing the tension until these apparently irreconcilable opposites come together into one.[32]

Some of these couplets are described in Jung's important work *Psychological Types,* which was first translated into English in 1923.[33] He felt that human beings could be divided into conscious types according to how each of us gives preference to some behavioral patterns, while leaving others in a less developed state. Jung identified such couplets of psychological type as extraverted/introverted, intuitive/sensing, and thinking/feeling. These couplets formed the basis for the work of Katharine Briggs and Isabel Briggs Myers, who subsequently added a fourth couplet, the judging/perceiving, and developed in the 1930s into what has today become the most widely used personality type indicator and psychological instrument in the world, namely, the Myers-Briggs Type Indicator.[34] While this instrument has frequently been misused in pegging and predicting stereotypical behavior depending on one's type, its great value lies in helping us uncover our undeveloped potential, i.e., our shadow side. It is when we are willing to bear the tension between operating in our preferred mode and seeking to engage our shadow side that psychological and spiritual growth will occur. This growth is manifested in a sense of self-intimacy and a greater appreciation for and love of self.

What then is self-intimacy? According to the Whiteheads, self-intimacy begins with the realization that each one of us is not singular, but plural. We combine within ourselves not one but a variety of ambitions, potentials, motives, and ideals. The challenge of self-intimacy is to better understand this plural self and to better love it.[35] Self-intimacy begins as a paying attention to the information coming from within. As we listen, we learn about the shadow side and the contending voices that seek to get our attention. We become more aware, for example, of why we overwork, overeat, get angry or depressed, or are self-negating. We become emboldened to enter into dialogue with the other side in us and to establish contact with our demons and the dark driving forces we have sought to ignore, deny, or repress. While this may sound a bit morbid, we need to keep in mind that the ultimate goal of befriending our plural self and of exploring the shadow side is self-possession and the ability to be in the world without feeling the need to defend our preferences, opinions, and choices. Once we have begun this process of developing a greater intimacy with self, we can allow ourselves to live in the present and to accept ourselves the way we look and feel and act right now. This may mean that we see no need to deny or conceal our age, for example, because we have now come to like ourselves the way we are.

The practice of self-intimacy sounds like a private endeavor, but mostly it is not. Community and family usually are the arenas that teach us about our shadow and disclose to us valuable insights about ourselves. Many times, it is colleagues, partners, close friends, and even enemies who reflect back to us information about who we are and what we are becoming. Again, these insights are helpful because they restore to us the possibility for personal and spiritual growth, and certainly its need. The ability to be intimate with self will result in a joy in being alone. This uncluttered solitude is possible and regenerative. It needs no background noise or busyness or outside activity because we know what we are left with in solitude is good — namely, ourselves. Greater intimacy with self encourages acceptance of oneself, which could also be called self-love. It assumes that we are becoming more and more aware of our strengths and weaknesses, and instead of defending our weakness to others and exploiting our strength in relation to them, we begin the process of integration.

While I have touched upon the developmental issues for women in the process of self-integration and sexual identity, I want to address the issue of self-love in relation to women's increased consciousness of themselves as victims of patriarchal oppression. Simply put, the question is, How can I love myself as a woman when society and our male-oriented, patriarchal system loves me only in relation to how well I fit the prescribed gender role? According to the Whiteheads,[36] many women are at a particular stage of conventional thinking when they first hear about "women's issues." At this stage, a woman experiences congruence between her own experience and the culture's definition of her. The generally accepted description of the good woman reflects the norms by which she judges her own conduct. In cases of disparity, she holds herself accountable, even when she herself is not to blame for digressing from the cultural expectation of her. The second stage of a woman's consciousness is not one of congruence, but one of dichotomous thinking. Here, the woman has come to sense that her experience of herself does not fit "the way things are supposed to be." Initially, she may judge that she is the problem and try to modify herself so as to fit in again. But as her experience of being different grows, she may well begin to question not herself but the cultural definitions that no longer fit. She may feel she has been misled and betrayed. It is at this stage that dichotomous thinking emerges.

According to the Whiteheads,[37] women in the dichotomous stage feel much anger: against the culture that has lied to them, against the institutions that have failed them, against the norms that continue to constrain them, and often, and unwittingly so, against the men with whom they live and work. Newly aware of the many ways in which women have been oppressed, they are alert to oppression and chauvinism everywhere, in part because it is so widespread, in part because of their increased sensitivity. Women gain strength to affirm their experience through their anger. But while this anger may be useful in defining and maintaining her position and concerns, a woman may also undercut her relationship with those men she is close to because frequently this anger will be directed at them. Not all women move beyond this point. Their sharp dichotomous thinking continues to describe the world of their experience, clearly dividing good and evil along gender lines. But many make the shift and move on to what could be described as the stage of integrated thinking. As a woman makes this move, she does not leave her anger behind, for the oppression and injustice that generate her anger still remain. But her experience of anger is now accompanied by control. At this stage, women can be more objective in evaluating their feelings of hostility and determine their cause and proper object. They can decide when and how to express anger. In this way, anger, which is often an alien emotion for women, can be accepted as part of herself and can become an important resource in her commitment to social change. Concomitantly, the woman comes to realize that the line dividing good and evil along gender differences does not neatly separate, but cuts through the heart of each person, including her own.[38] Through this self-awareness — having worked through and come to use their anger intentionally — women are defining themselves less in light of patriarchal culture and gender definitions, but more in light of the freedom from their own oppression. It is when women are able to view themselves as liberated from their dichotomous thinking and have moved toward integrated thinking that they are practicing a love of self.

What then can we conclude from the above observations about women and celibacy in particular, and about the connection between celibacy and spirituality in general? On the one hand, we find that women are increasingly aware of their role as the oppressed and of the subsequent anger issues, of their relational and nurturing capabilities, and of their willingness to explore growth areas on the opposite end of their personality type or archetypal spectrum. On the other hand, we have a growing number of single women living in the United States, with a nearly 20 percent increase over the last thirty years. Both women's increased self-awareness and the rise in the number of single women may suggest a correlation between spiritual exploration, its resulting sense of freedom and independence, and the choice to remain single and celibate.

Reasons vary why many women today do not marry. Some simply have not found the right partner to meet their standards — i.e., matching their own level of education or economic rank. Others are financially secure enough on their own. Some do not want to be bound by a marriage partner, but want to engage in sexual relationships. Still others prefer to remain single and to practice sexual abstinence. Those who remain single and practice sexual abstinence may do so for two reasons: One, they may seek to abide by the external principles of a faith tradition such as Christianity that approves only of two lifestyles, namely, monogamous marriage and celibacy; a few may even have taken private vows of celibacy, or be a part of a religious community requiring celibacy of its members. And two, they may practice sexual abstinence — individually or as part of a religious community of celibates not primarily because their religious tradition expects it of them, but because it is internally motivated and has emerged out of self-awareness, inner autonomy, and spiritual transformation and growth, all of which continue to inform and enforce their celibate practice. This second point suggests a correlation between celibacy and spirituality among both men and women.

In seeking to construct a gender-inclusive theological framework for celibacy within the Christian tradition, the next task will be to explore the scriptural references to the celibate life in both the Old and New Testaments. Particular attention will be given to the notion of conversion to the Christian faith, and the transformative aspects of celibate Christian discipleship.

Chapter 2

Celibacy and the Bible

A cursory glance at a topical Bible commentary reveals only a few passages directly dealing with the issue of celibacy. *Roget's Thesaurus of the Bible,*[1] for example, provides three subheadings under the entry celibacy, namely, "virginity," "chastity," and being "unmarried." Under the last subheading, the reader is referred to "eunuchs" as a separate entry elsewhere. While we find examples from both the Old and New Testaments under "virginity" and "chastity," the subheading "unmarried" only contains references to the New Testament, which may give an indication that the practice of being or remaining unmarried was uncommon in Old Testament times, but more common and perhaps even socially acceptable beginning with Jesus' time. Instead of jumping ahead, I propose to examine both the Old and New Testament passages pertaining to celibacy, using Roget's subheadings as an initial guide.

Celibacy in the Old Testament

The word "celibacy" is never mentioned in the Old Testament. We will therefore consider passages and narrative accounts in the Old Testament that refer to the three categories of virginity, chastity, and the unmarried state. All Scriptural passages quoted will be from the New Revised Standard Version of the Bible. Particular attention will be given to the issues relating to women.

Virginity

In the Old Testament, the words "virgin" and "virginity" both relate exclusively to women, though the words are found in later manuscripts referring to men.[2] The words appear particularly in the context of virginity being a preparatory step for marriage. In Genesis 24, Abraham sends out a servant to go back to Abraham's home land, Haran, "to get a wife for my son Isaac" (4), where at a well the servant chances upon Rebekah. And "the girl," the account reads, "was very fair to look upon, a virgin, whom no man had known." The Hebrew word for virginity is also found in the context of marriage preparation in Deuteronomy 22:13–21. Here we have an example of the importance of virginity prior to marriage, and its legal ramifications. For example, if the husband is tired of his wife, he may bring charges against her for not finding evidence of her virginity in order to be able to divorce her. In that case, the Mosaic law advises that "the father of the young woman and her mother shall then submit the evidence of the young woman's virginity to the elders of the city at the gate" and "then they shall spread out the cloth before the elders of the town" (15, 17b). This piece of blood-smeared cloth serves as evidence that the husband's charges are untrue. Moreover, he is fined "one hundred shekels of silver (which they shall give to the young woman's father) because he has slandered a virgin of Israel" (19) and is to remain married to his wife. However, if no evidence can be produced, which is to assume "that evidence of the young woman's virginity was not found, then they shall bring the young woman out to the entrance of the father's house and the men of her town shall stone her to death" (20, 21). Unless a woman was tired of her life, she did well to remain celibate until marriage and retain visible proof of her premarital virginity.

The custom of only marrying a woman that is a virgin is also found in the book of Esther, written possibly six hundred years later than Genesis and Deuteronomy, either in the fourth or third centuries B.C. After Queen Vashti refused to expose herself and dance before her drunken husband and his cohorts and was subsequently disenthroned, King Ahasuerus went looking for a queen. Yielding to the advice of his servants to "let beautiful young virgins be sought out for the king" (Esth. 2:2), he had commissioners sent out in all the provinces "to gather all the beautiful young virgins to the harem in the citadel" (3a), and then began sampling them one by one. About each of the virgins we are told that "in the evening she went in; then in the morning she came back to the second harem" and did not go in again, "unless the king delighted in her and she was summoned by name" (14). It is reasonable to assume that the women gathered by the royal commissioners were virgins, that is, had never had sexual intercourse with a man prior to the king. But because they had been sexually "sampled" by the king, they forfeited the privilege of entering into marriage as an "honorable woman" under Jewish law, hence were left to remain as captives in the king's harem.

The king making the woman a part of his harem seems to be the equivalent of marrying her, hence of taking care of her. Jewish law prescribed that whoever seduced a woman and had intercourse with her had to "give the bride-price for her and make her his wife" (Exod. 22:16). In the case of rape, the man had to marry her as well and was not permitted to divorce her "as long as he lives" (Deut. 22:29). The only exception was when the father of the woman refused to give her in marriage, in which case the man had to pay "an amount equal to the bride-price for virgins" (Exod. 22:17) to the father, and the woman was left to live at home under her father's roof with only a marginal chance of ever being married.

Priests in particular needed to be careful only to marry a woman who was a virgin, according to Leviticus 21:13. "A widow, or a divorced woman, or a woman who has been defiled, a prostitute" in short, would not do. For a priest would otherwise "profane his offspring among his kin" (14, 15).

Women who had never slept with a man were considered precious chattel to the Hebrew mind. During times of war and battle, women and children were to be killed, but "virgins who had never slept with a man" were spared (Judg. 21:10, 12). This fact is illustrated by an episode in the Israelites' war against the Midianites. After all the adult males had been killed in battle, Moses commands that the women and male children be killed as well, along with "every woman who has known a man by sleeping with him" (Numb. 31:17). "The young girls who have not known a man by sleeping with him," Moses advises, the Israelites are "to keep alive for yourselves" (18).

Virgins were used as sacrifices to compensate for the shortcomings, transgressions, and foolishness of others, and to bring honor to those who protect or revenge them. Four stories in particular illustrate this point. The first one involves Tamar, King David's daughter, who is raped by her brother Amnon. She pleads with him in the struggle. "No, my brother, do not force me, for such a thing is not done in Israel; do not do anything so vile! As for me, where could I carry my shame?" (2 Sam. 13:12, 13). But Amnon will not listen and proceeds to rape her. Afterwards, he projects his disgust with himself on to Tamar and orders his servant to throw her "out of my presence and bolt the door after her" (17). Tamar in turn puts ashes on her head, tears her robe, puts her hand on her head, and goes away weeping. She seeks refuge with her brother Absalom, with whom she was staying, who advises her "to be quiet for now" since, after all, Amnon was her brother, and not to take the matter to heart (20). Tamar obliges, remaining "a desolate woman, in her brother Absalom's house" (20b). Two years later, Absalom kills Amnon in a conspiracy to avenge his sister's rape, and gains honor for himself.

The second story involves Lot, who had welcomed two angelic visitors to his house in the city of Sodom. Despite the visitors' protests, Lot convinces them to be hosted and entertained by him and to spend the night. But before they lie down, "the men of the city, the men of Sodom, both young and old, all the people to the last man, surrounded the house," ordering: "Where are the men who came to you tonight? Bring them out to us so we may know them" (Gen. 19:4, 5). But Lot went outside, shut the door after himself, and said: "I beg you, my brothers, do not act so wickedly. Look, I have two daughters who have not known a man; let me bring them out to you, and do to them as you please; only do nothing to these men, for they have come under the shelter of my roof" (7–8). Lot is willing to sacrifice his two virgin daughters to protect his own honor and pride, especially after having insisted on providing hospitality against the wishes of his two guests.

The third story describes how Lot's two virgin daughters had sex with their father to ensure the family lineage. Both of his daughters were engaged to be married, in fact, their husbands-to-be were already called "sons-in-law" (19:14). The sons-in-law did not believe Lot's warning to "get out of the city" (14), hence were left to suffocate and die in the subsequent rain of sulfur and fire that swept the city.

Lot's wife, on the other hand, while fleeing, disobeyed the command not to look back (17) and was turned into a pillar of salt (26). This meant that Lot was left without a wife and the two daughters without husbands-to-be. And so, to compensate for the foolishness and disobedience of both their mother and their future husbands, the virgins take turns making their father drink wine and then having sex with him. Their argument is voiced by the older daughter, who says to the younger, "Our father is old, and there is not a man on earth to come in to us after the manner of all the world" (31). Their efforts to ensure offspring through their father bear fruit when both daughters become pregnant and each gives birth to a son. But the redactor makes it clear that the daughters' efforts are considered shameful,[3] while Lot not only comes off looking innocent because of his drunken state, induced by the daughters for the purpose of intercourse, but also is rewarded with two sons to continue his lineage.

The fourth story is of Jephthah, "the son of a prostitute" (Judg. 11:1), who became known as a mighty warrior. His father was Gilead, who was married to a woman with whom he had children. Eventually Jephthah's half-brothers denounced his inheritance and drove him out of the house (2). Jephthah settled in the land of Tob and collected around himself a band of outlaws with whom he raided the land (3). As word spread of Jephthah's battle skills, he was summoned back to Gilead to help the townspeople fight the Ammonites. After an initial protest, Jephthah agreed to help. Prior to the battle, though, Jephthah uttered a prayer and a vow, promising the Lord, in exchange for victory over the Ammonites, "whoever comes out of the doors of my house to meet me . . . as a burnt offering" (31). Jephthah wins the battle, returns to his home, and the first one to come out of his house is his daughter, his only child (34). To allow her father to save face and not to lessen his military acclaim, despite his foolish vow, she agrees to be killed and offered up to the Lord. Only "grant me two months, so that I may go and wander on the mountains, and bewail my virginity" (37). After the two months were over, the daughter, who "had never slept with a man," returned to her father, "who did with her according to the vow he had made" (39).

Based on this brief overview of Old Testament passages relating to virgins and virginity, we can make the following observations. First, women were to keep their virginity until marriage at the threat of losing their life. Even after marriage, they had to maintain the visible proof, tucked away, as it were, of their premarital virginal state in case their husband sought to divorce them on grounds of sexual activity prior to marriage. Second, women were considered valuable chattel if they were still virgins during times of war. Third, women who had lost their virginity at the hands of a man who had no intention of marrying them, either through rape or seduction, were likely to end up having to live under their father's roof, with a relative, or in a servant-master relationship (i.e., as a mistress or slave), and were unlikely candidates for subsequent marriage. Fourth, the virginity of women often served to compensate for the foolish, reckless, or violent behavior of others; women would suffer disgrace and dishonor while advancing the grace and honor of others, mostly men, by virtue of their virginity or its untimely loss. In all the passages examined, no mention is made of a woman intentionally remaining a virgin or unmarried.

Chastity

Chastity in the Old Testament refers to men temporarily abstaining from sexual intercourse with women. Before Moses goes up to Mount Sinai, he instructs the people to consecrate themselves, to wash their clothes and to be careful not to ascend or to touch the mountain. And, as a preparatory rite for the third day, the men are not to "go near a woman" (Exod. 19:15). Another reference is made in the context of eating holy, consecrated bread. On his flight to Nob, David stops at the temple at Nob to beg some food from the priest. Pretending that he needs food for his companions as well, he presses the priest. "Give me five loaves of bread, or whatever is here" (3), to which the priest replies that he has no ordinary bread, "only holy bread — provided that the young men have kept themselves from women" (4). David assures the priest that "indeed women have been kept from us as always when I go on an expedition; the vessels of the young men are holy" (5). According to Mosaic Law, "if a man lies with a woman and has an emission of semen, both of them shall bathe in water, and be unclean until the evening" (Lev. 15:18). A menstruating woman also was considered unclean for seven days, "and whoever touches her shall be unclean until the evening" (19b). If a man has intercourse with a menstruating woman, he shall be unclean for seven days (24). This injunction was particularly important to priests of whom levitical codes demanded cultic purity. Hence, they were to refrain from sexual intercourse with their wives prior to presiding at religious services. The sacred donations of the people of Israel, for example, were not to be touched by "a man who has had an emission of semen" (Lev. 22:4). The practice of chastity, or of sexual abstinence from intercourse with a woman, was intended to keep a man holy.

The Unmarried State

The Old Testament prescribes marriage as the norm. To marry was more or less a duty because preserving the male lineage through children was paramount, and children were to be born only within marriage. Remaining unmarried was a sign of disgrace, even disobedience to the order ordained by the Lord. In the patriarchal and matriarchal stories, people get married. Abraham marries Sarah, Isaac marries Rebekah, Jacob marries Leah, then Rachel, Moses marries Zipporah. Men are eager to find themselves women, and women make sure they end up properly betrothed. The older Leah is safely placed in the marital bond with Jacob through trickery, with her father acting as the cunning accessory to the nuptial deception. Voluntary singleness is not a desirable state in a culture that places primary importance on procreation, which was to happen only in the state of marriage, or, as in the case of female servants, in the relationship of ownership by their masters.

It is true that we find some women and men in the Old Testament who are not explicitly identified as married, and so could have been single. Was Miriam, the sister of Moses, or Aaron, Moses' brother, married? What about Samuel, the first judge of Israel, or Samson? And the prophets? While the Old Testament does not give us conclusive answers, partly because their marital status may have been irrelevant to the redactor, we find one example of a prophet who was ordered by divine injunction to live in the single state. In the sixteenth chapter of the book of Jeremiah, the Lord orders the prophet: "You shall not take a wife, nor shall you have sons or daughters" (16:2). But this injunction is neither to ensure greater holiness and ritual purity on the prophet's part, nor to provide for his undivided attention to prophetic duties. Instead, Jeremiah's unmarried state is to be a symbolic and grotesque illustration of Israel's sorry state of barrenness. The people are barren because they had been unfaithful to the Lord, because they had been deprived, through their deportation to Babylon, of their homeland and uprooted from their religious and cultic activity, because both children and parents will die in the land of captivity of deadly diseases (Jer. 22:26–30). They are barren because the dead will not be lamented, or even buried. And they are barren because battles and famine will decimate their numbers, and their dead bodies will become food for bird and beast (16:4). Thus, Jeremiah's unmarried, or even celibate, state is to reflect Israel's declining strength and virility and the people's inability to prosper and multiply as a nation. In this sense, being unmarried means the end of one's lineage, so that instead of living on through offspring, one is remembered no more.

Jeremiah's example illustrates the Jewish mind-set that being unmarried is a curse because it precludes procreation. Being unmarried is the equivalent of childlessness and, more important, barrenness. The word "barrenness" refers mainly to a woman's inability to conceive, not so much to the man's inability to procreate. Whenever a couple is childless, the Old Testament finds the culprit in the woman who is "barren." Sarai, who was married to Abram, was "barren" and "bore him no children" (Gen. 11:30; 16:1). The wife and female servants of King Abimelech are barren until Abraham prays to God on the king's behalf "and God healed Abimelech, and also healed his wife and female slaves so that they bore children. For the Lord had closed fast all the wombs of the house of Abimelech" (Gen. 20:17, 18). Rebekah was "barren" so that "Isaac prayed to the Lord for his wife" (Gen. 25:21). Rachel was barren (Gen. 29:31), and "she said to Jacob: 'Give me children, or I shall die!'" (Gen. 30:1), which causes Jacob in turn to become "very angry with Rachel" and shifting the blame back to her, to say, "Am I in the place of God, who has withheld from you the fruit of the womb?" (2). Manoah's wife was "barren, having borne no children" (Judg. 13:2) until she is "careful not to drink wine or strong drink, or to eat anything unclean" (4) and subsequently gives birth to Samson (24). Hannah "had no children" (1 Sam. 1:2) and "the Lord had closed her womb" (5), until she made a vow to the Lord to give her son as a nazirite until the day of his death (11), then she gave birth to Samuel. And Michal, the daughter of Saul, and wife of King David, who makes fun of his dancing before the Lord as the Ark is being brought into Jerusalem, "had no child to the day of her death" (2 Sam. 6:23). In all but Abimelech's case, it is the woman who is held responsible for the couple's childlessness, not the man. In fact, the redactor often introduces other women into the story, usually concubines or female servants or slaves, to give evidence of the husband's virility. Abraham had a child with the Egyptian slave-girl Hagar (Gen. 16:4) before he has one with Sarah. Jacob had four sons with Leah, one son with Rachel's maid Bilhah, then two sons with Leah's maid Zilpah, then two more sons and a daughter with Leah, until finally Rachel "conceived and bore a son" (30:23). Elkanah had "sons and daughters" (1 Sam. 1:4) with Peninnah, one of his two wives, long before he had children with Hannah (7; 2:21). And David had children with Bathsheba, Maacah, Haggith, but not with Michal. Conversely, Jewish custom did not allow women to have intercourse with men other than their husbands and thus "prove" their fertility with another man, in the same way that men could "prove" their fertility by being allowed to impregnate other women. Another way of ensuring that the woman is held accountable for the lack of children is to make certain requirements of her that she needs to heed in order to become pregnant, as in the case of Manoah's wife (Judg. 13:4) or Hannah, who first has to promise to dedicate her son to God (1 Sam. 1:11) before she conceives. A woman may also be delivered from "her barrenness" if the husband prays "to the Lord for his wife" (Gen. 25:21), as in the case of Isaac and Rebekah, or in the case of Elkanah offering to the Lord "a double portion" at the temple on behalf of his barren wife Hannah (1 Sam. 1:5), compared to the single portions he allots to his fertile wife, Peninnah, and her children.

For a woman of childbearing age to seek voluntary singleness and celibacy at the time would have been an act of outright rebellion, a refusal to continue the male lineage, a presumptuous waste of her fertility, and the robbing of God's blessings from men of the generations yet to be born. A desire for celibacy would have been an especially severe affront if the woman was still a virgin, that is, had never had intercourse with a man, and was neither widowed nor divorced.

Eunuchs

Throughout the Old Testament, from Genesis to Esther and on to Isaiah and Jeremiah, we find references to eunuchs. Although the modern meaning of the word refers to a man who has been emasculated or castrated, the Old Testament uses the term primarily in reference to a high court official. Eunuchs are employed mostly by the Egyptian pharaohs and the Persian and Babylonian kings. Joseph, for example, was sold by the Midianites into Egypt, to Potiphar, a eunuch of Pharaoh and the captain of the guard (Gen. 37:36). Later we learn that the eunuch Potiphar is married and that his wife is attracted to Joseph and "cast her eyes on Joseph and said, 'Lie with me'" (Gen. 39:7). Other officers of Pharaoh's are also called eunuchs, such as the chief cupbearer and the chief baker (Gen. 40:2), whose dreams Joseph comes to interpret while in jail for being falsely accused by Potiphar's wife of attempting to seduce her. Eunuchs also appear in the service of Babylonian kings, such as in the prediction of Isaiah to Hezekiah, King of Judah. "Some of your own sons who are born to you shall be taken away," Isaiah says. "They shall be eunuchs in the palace of the king of Babylon" (2 Kings 20:18; Isa. 39:7). Eunuchs are also ascribed to King Nebuchadnezzar's court (Jer. 39:3; 13). In fact, the first chapter of the book of Daniel describes the three-year training of "some of the Israelites of the royal family and of the nobility, young men without physical defect and handsome, versed in every branch of wisdom, endowed with knowledge and insight, and competent to serve in the king's palace" (Dan. 1:3–4), Daniel among them.

Other references to eunuchs as court officials are found in the era of Israel's kings. When the people clamor for a king, for example, the prophet Samuel warns them, saying, a king "will take one-tenth of your grain and of your vineyards and give it to his officers [eunuchs] and his courtiers" (1 Sam. 8:15). They designated court officials, or eunuchs, under the kings of the Northern Kingdom, such as King

Ahab (2 Chron. 18:8), the king who restored the Shunammite woman's land (2 Kings 8:6), and King Joram and his mother Jezebel (2 Kings 9:32). Other court officials, called eunuchs, served under King David (1 Chron. 28:1), and under King Josiah (2 Kings 23:11) and King Jehoiakin (2 Kings 24:12), both of Judah. The NRSV translates all above-mentioned references to eunuchs as court or palace officials, except for three instances: 2 Kings 20:18, which threatens that the king's sons will become eunuchs, though the king would prefer that to rivalry over his throne (19); 2 Kings 23:11, which refers to Josiah's removal of the horses that had been dedicated to the sun in the temple precincts, near the "chamber of the eunuch Nathanmelech"; and 2 Kings 9:32, which is a reference to the "two or three eunuchs who looked down" from the window and consented to Jehu who was on the ground to throw Jezebel out the window. The other times the Hebrew word is translated into English as eunuchs is in the book of Esther, where eunuchs, who were court officials under the Persian King Ahasuerus, were guarding the king's harem (Esth. 1:10, 12, 15). Thus, the NRSV uses the term "eunuch" only when referring to court officials who were directly charged to oversee or protect women, i.e., Jezebel and the women of the harem, once in reference to exporting the troublesome sons of King Hezekiah, and once in reference to a defiled temple precinct. These English translations are based on today's meaning of the word "eunuch" as a castrated or emasculated man. The Hebrew word "eunuch," on the other hand, is mostly used so as to designate high court officials in direct service to the king and has no implication of sexual abstinence, celibacy, or the unmarried state. Eunuchs then were not necessarily sexually abstinent or castrated or unmarried. Their role as guards over women is marginal in the Old Testament, whereas their role as high court officials figures prominently.

However, two Old Testament references in light of today's understanding of what a eunuch is are puzzling. The first one is found in Deuteronomy 23, which seemingly prohibits eunuchs from attending public worship (23:1). The passage says that "no one whose testicles are crushed or whose penis is cut off shall be admitted to the assembly of the Lord." The word "eunuch" is nowhere mentioned. Instead, the passage suggests that there were men who had suffered permanent injury to their male organs, either through mutilation in battle at the hands of others or from birth, so that they could no longer procreate. The implication is that since they were no longer, or never were, eligible to have their lineage continue through offspring, they did not need the Lord's blessing in the context of public worship. The second passage is found in Isaiah 56, where the prophet promises blessings to eunuchs. "I am just a dry tree" (Isa. 56:3), the eunuch says, which means that he fully recognizes and acknowledges his barrenness. In light of the Jewish emphasis on procreation, it is all the more surprising to hear that now the Lord promised enormous blessings to those "eunuchs" who faithfully kept the Sabbath and held fast to the covenant. The blessing promised to them is "a monument and a name better than sons and daughters" "in my house and within my walls," in short, a name and a lineage that was "everlasting" and that "shall not be cut off" (56:5). This is a crucial turning point of Old Testament thought concerning infertility and barrenness. The old order of receiving blessing and salvation only through procreation and male offspring is transcended. In its place moves blessing and salvation through one's faithfulness to the Lord's covenant and by choosing things that are pleasing to the Lord. It is reasonable to assume that not just men, but women also, who considered themselves "dry trees" would be remembered by the Lord and be blessed on account of their faith, rather than the number of male descendants they bore.

Celibacy in the New Testament

We will now explore virginity, chastity, the unmarried state, and eunuchs as they are found in the New Testament.

Virginity

The term "virgin" is used in the New Testament in several ways. A virgin could be a woman who has never had intercourse with a man. A virgin could also be a young woman of marriageable age or a recently married woman. The word, which is neuter in the Greek, can also apply to both men and women who either have given their undivided attention to God or who have never had intercourse, regardless of their age.

We will begin our examination with Paul's writings, as the oldest documents in the New Testament. The Apostle Paul makes two separate
references to virgins, in the First and Second Letter to the Corinthians.
In 1 Corinthians 7:25–35, Paul appears to answer a question raised by
the Christians in Corinth in a letter they had written him (7:1), asking, How then should we live once we have been called by Christ into
discipleship? The answer begins in the first verse of chapter 7, where
Paul refers to "the matters about which you wrote" (1) and extends
through chapter 14:40, addressing such issues as marriage and the unmarried state, food sacrificed to idols, spiritual gifts, and worship. The
entirety of chapter 7 addresses the issue of marriage and the unmarried
state. Apparently, the church in Corinth felt that, possibly in light of
Christ's perceived imminent return, "it is well for a man not to touch
a woman" (7:1), hence to remain celibate. Paul agrees with this view,
which stands in contrast to the usual Jewish view favoring the married
state. But he also makes room for the individual believer's gifts in that
regard. "Each has a particular gift from God, one having one kind and
another a different kind" (7), he says, so that "to the unmarried and
the widows I say that it is well for them to remain unmarried as I am.
But if they are not practicing self-control, they should marry. For it is
better to marry than to be aflame with passion" (8–9). Remaining unmarried, hence celibate, is recommended to those who have the gift to
do so. But for those who cannot control their sexual passions, marriage
is the better, and only, alternative.

Throughout chapter 7, Paul insists that Christians should attempt
to remain in the state they were in when they experienced their call
in Christ. If they are uncircumcised, they should remain so (7:18); if
they are slaves, they should not be too much troubled by it, but should
seize the opportunity for freedom if it presented itself (21–22); if they
are married, they should remain married (10–13; 27a) if at all possible;
and if they are unmarried, provided they possess the gift of controlling
their sexual passions, they are to remain so (8; 27b) as well.

The call to remain unmarried, if possible, applies to both men and
women. On three occasions, Paul balances his argument by alternating
his references to the unmarried state between men and women. "Are
you free from a wife? Do not seek a wife" (27b), he says, "but if you

marry, you do not sin, and if a virgin marries, she does not sin" (28). Similarly, he says that "the unmarried man is anxious about the affairs of the Lord" (32) and "the unmarried woman and the virgin are anxious about the affairs of the Lord" (34), in contrast to "the married man [who] is anxious about the affairs of the world, how to please his wife" (33) and "the married woman [who] is anxious about the affairs of the world, how to please her husband" (34). And finally, he says that the man "who marries his fiancee [virgin] does well; and he who refrains from marriage will do better" (38). Likewise, if a woman's husband dies, "she is free to marry anyone she wishes" (39). But "she is more blessed if she remains as she is" (40). Paul then suggests that remaining unmarried for those who are unmarried at the time of their call in Jesus Christ is advisable to both men and women, given the ability to control their sexual passion, since it allows them to concentrate more on "the affairs of the Lord." This advice applies to unmarried men in the same way as it does to the widowed and virgins. Paul's thoughts on the issue of virginity stand in sharp contrast to Old Testament thinking. For in Christ, men no longer need to be redeemed and saved by continuing their lineage through offspring; in fact, they are now encouraged to remain unmarried, hence without offspring. Women no longer find their redemption by bearing children, preferably sons; and virgins are no longer considered precious chattel on account of their potential to bear "undefiled kin," but are allowed, and even encouraged, to remain single and, hence, childless.

In chapter 7 of 1 Corinthians, Paul uses the word "virgin" for women about to be married (37) and, by implication, for young women who have never had sexual intercourse. To Paul, virgins then are those who have never been married (28), and they are to be distinguished from those who are widowed (8) and those who are unmarried on account of divorce.[4] But eventually Paul uses the word "virgin" in an even broader sense. In 2 Corinthians, Paul tells members of the church in Corinth of his hope of presenting the Corinthians "as a chaste virgin to Christ" (2 Cor. 11:2). He is aware that he is speaking in a metaphor that may appear like "a little foolishness" (1), but he employs it nonetheless to explain his "divine jealousy" (2) in light of other prophets and teachers — "superapostles" (5) and "false apostles, deceitful workers" (12) whose teaching may have become attractive to the Corinthians but is incongruent with that of Paul and his co-workers' teachings. "For I promised you in marriage to one husband," he says. Here, Paul plays on the Jewish tradition that prescribes virginity as a preparatory state for marriage. Only now, virginity is not bound up with the physical and sexual, but the transcendent. What characterizes the Corinthians as "virgin" is that they follow Paul's teachings and show "a sincere and pure devotion to Christ" (3). This virginal state does not apply to the individual, but the faith community at large. And, though the Corinthians may have become enticed by these other teachers and even lost their "virginal" state, it appears that it may be recovered by their returning to the orthodox faith advocated by Paul. In this sense, virginity applies to both men and women who hold on to Paul's teachings and demonstrate "a sincere and pure devotion to Christ."

The Synoptic Gospels use the word "virgin" mostly to describe a woman who has not had sexual intercourse with a man or a woman of marriageable age. The Gospel of Matthew records Jesus' parable of the ten virgins (Matt. 25:1–12), who are waiting to meet the bridegroom. These virgins are waiting to accompany the bridegroom in a procession to the house of the bride, to bring her to his home for the wedding banquet. The invited guests, among them the ten virgins, were allowed to accompany the bridegroom and the bride to the marriage feast. But without a torch or lamp they could not join the procession, nor enter the bridegroom's house. The term "virgin" in this parable does not qualify these women's sexual state or their virginity, but simply refers to young women of marriageable age who are part of a bridal procession and wedding party, and who could best be described as "bridesmaids."

A second reference to a virgin in the Gospel of Matthew is a quotation from the prophet Isaiah in reference to Mary, the mother of Jesus. Matthew's quote from Isaiah is part of his ongoing effort throughout his Gospel to prooftext from Old Testament passages the fulfillment of the messianic expectation in the birth of Jesus Christ. Matthew translates Isaiah as saying, "Look, the virgin shall conceive and bear a son, and they shall name him Emmanuel" (Matt. 1:23). The Greek word used here is virgin without qualifying whether it means a woman who has never had sexual relations with a man or simply a woman of marriageable age. The Isaiah passage clarifies the meaning here; it does not use the term "virgin" in the sexually pure sense (as it was used in the Old Testament passages discussed above), but it employs the term "young woman." The Hebrew word then stresses the woman's youthfulness and implies, at the same time, that she is sexually ripe and of marriageable age, or already married.

The Gospel of Luke uses the term "virgin" both times in reference to Mary, the mother of Jesus. The two occur in v. 27. Six months after Elizabeth, a relative of Mary's, had finally conceived "in her old age" (Luke 1:36), the angel Gabriel was sent by God "to a virgin engaged to a man whose name was Joseph, of the house of David. The virgin's name was Mary" (27). As in Matthew, the word "virgin" does not qualify her sexual relations with a man, but simply asserts that she is of marriageable age, as indeed Luke tells us. Only later does Luke make it clear that Mary is a virgin in the sense that she has not had sexual relations with a man. In response to the angel's announcement that Mary would conceive and bear a son, she exclaims, "How can this be, since I am virgin?" (34). But Luke does not use the word "virgin" in this exclamation; instead, he has her say, "How can this be, since I do not know a man?" The only time the word "virgin" is used by Luke in his Gospel is in reference to a woman of marriageable age.

If one assumes that Acts is the companion work to Luke's Gospel, written by the same author, then Luke uses the word "virgin" one other time. In reporting on Paul's journey to Caesarea, Luke mentions Philip the evangelist, who "had four unmarried daughters [virgins] who had the gift of prophecy" (Acts 21:9). Based on Jewish tradition it is most likely that the daughters lived in the house with their father, since they were not married. The very fact that Luke mentions them in connection with Paul's and his own stay at Philip's house indicates that these daughters were of marriageable age. Their age is not of interest to Luke, only the fact that they are not married and have the gift of prophecy. Luke then links here the unmarried state with the exercise of particular spiritual gifts as a result of being called in Christ, which in the case of all four daughters of Philip is the gift of prophecy.

Chastity

Whereas the Old Testament viewed chastity in the context of men temporarily abstaining from sexual intercourse with women, in the New Testament we find a reference to both men and women temporarily abstaining from sexual intercourse. This reference occurs in 1 Corinthians 7, where Paul discusses the marital state and matters of sexual morality and abstinence. The reference is preceded by a discussion in chapters 5 and 6 of sexual issues of immorality. Based on these two previous chapters, it appears that the Corinthians were continuing to engage in the same sexual practices as prior to their call in Christ. Paul mentions some of these practices, including "a man living with his father's wife" (1 Cor. 5:1), a man having married his stepmother, sexual intercourse outside of marriage, adultery, and male prostitution (6:9). Paul tells the Corinthians that these practices have to cease because "you were washed, you were sanctified, you were justified in the name of the Lord Jesus Christ" (6:11). To help resolve the issue of sexual immorality, Paul suggests that "each man should have his own wife and each woman her own husband" (7:2). From now on sexual intercourse is to take place only within a monogamous marriage relationship. Rather than attempting to satisfy their sexual needs outside of marriage, the marriage partners are to fulfill these needs in the context of their marital bond and they are to make an effort to satisfy each other's sexual passions. "The husband should give to the wife her conjugal rights, and likewise the wife to her husband" (7:3), Paul writes. "For the wife does not have authority over her own body, but the husband does; likewise the husband does not have authority over his own body, but the wife does" (4). The marriage partners are responsible for finding sexual fulfillment through their spouse alone and are expected to meet their spouse's sexual needs as well. The only exception is when both partners have agreed to abstain from sexual relations for a set time. According to Paul, this sexual abstinence on the part of both marriage partners is for the purpose of prayer. But it is only temporary and the partners are "to come together again," meaning to resume sexual intercourse "so that Satan may not tempt you because of your lack of self-control" (5). Paul views chastity within marriage for both men and women as mutually agreed-upon temporary sexual abstinence from their marriage partner so as to allow for deeper concentration in prayer on the part of both individuals.

One other reference to chastity as sexual abstinence is found in the book of Revelation and refers to the Lamb and the 144,000 faithful followers of Christ worshiping Christ as the Lamb in song before the heavenly throne. Their song is reserved for them alone, for "no one could learn that song except the 144,000 who had been redeemed from the earth" (Rev. 14:3). The next verse specifies them as those "who have not defiled themselves with women, for they are virgins" (4). At first sight, the passage seems to refer to men who have been sexually chaste. But the following two verses give further details about them: they are those who "follow the Lamb wherever he goes. They have been redeemed from humankind as first fruits for God and for the Lamb, and in their mouth no lie was found; they are blameless" (4–5). The term "virgin" in this context does not suggest sexual virginity, or permanent or temporary sexual abstinence, on the part of the 144,000, but implies exceptional Christian discipleship, particularly one that is ritually undiluted by idolatry and lies. In this passage, chastity relates only to men — not women — who practice faithful Christian discipleship, who adhere to proper Christian doctrine, i.e., the truth as opposed to lies, and who abstain from idolatrous practices.

The Unmarried State

In his first letter to the church in Corinth, as we have seen, Paul suggests that Christians do well to maintain the state they are in at the time of their call in Christ — either as married or unmarried believers. But if they cannot practice sexual self-control, the unmarried should marry since "it is better to marry than to be aflame with passion" (1 Cor. 7:9). Paul would prefer that believers remain as they are and "in the condition in which you were called" (7:20). Those who are married ought to remain married; those who are unmarried ought to remain unmarried. In light of Jewish thought that favored marriage over divorce, the advice to the married to remain married is not surprising. But the advice to the unmarried to remain unmarried is, since it runs counter to traditional Jewish practice. Paul's advice is revolutionary, particularly when he suggests the unmarried state not just to men, but to women as well. In fact, Paul would wish "that all were as I myself am" (7), that is unmarried, and gifted "to remain unmarried as I am" (8).

Paul lists three reasons why remaining unmarried if one is unmarried at the time of one's call is advised. First, marriage involves distress in the flesh. Paul says that "those who marry will experience distress in this life, and I would spare you that" (1 Cor. 7:28). It is possible that Paul is referring to the "distress" of having a marriage partner who is sick and requires care, in contrast to the unmarried person who only needs to care for himself or herself. Distress "in the flesh," as the Greek has it, may mean the extended responsibilities toward the children resulting from marital intercourse. Or it might imply the energy expended during marital intercourse that, in the case of the unmarried — thus sexually inactive — could be redirected toward serving the Lord. The unmarried, according to Paul, are spared from the distress in the flesh particularly related to married life. Second, marriage involves anxiety concerning worldly matters and pleasing one's spouse. The married person "is anxious about the affairs of the world" and "how to please his wife" (33) and "how to please her husband" (34). Conversely, the unmarried's anxiety is directed toward "the affairs of the Lord, how to please the Lord" (32) and the practice of being "holy in body and spirit" (34). The unmarried state allows for greater, more single-minded devotion to the Lord and a more unequivocal practice of cultivating personal holiness before the Lord. It is interesting that the reference to being "holy in body and spirit" is only made in the context of the unmarried woman and the virgin, not the unmarried man. This is especially surprising since throughout his letter Paul has been careful to balance his statements concerning sexual morality by alternating between men and women. Here, unmarried women are viewed as becoming "holy in body and spirit" on account of their unmarried state, whereas no further qualifications are added for men who remain unmarried. It may mean that the practice of celibacy for women was held in particularly high regard, more so than for men, and that in the case of women celibacy was more easily correlated with holiness. Thirdly, Paul says that remaining unmarried makes particular sense in light of the present circumstances and "the impending crisis" (7:26). It is not clear what this crisis involves, whether it is related to the crisis of sexual immorality among the Corinthians or to Paul's view of the imminent second coming of Jesus Christ — which meant that there was no time to waste on secular matters such as marriage. It appears that Paul is more concerned with the latter, since he goes on to refer to his perceived imminence of Christ's return by saying that "the ap-pointed time has grown short," so that "from now on, let even those who have wives be as though they had none" (29). Paul then advises the believers in Corinth to use the interim time until the Lord's return to promote "good order and unhindered devotion to the Lord" (35).

In one of the later epistles, the so-called pastoral epistles, it ap-pears that a Christian sect had taken the practice of celibacy to the extreme by forbidding marriage among their members. First Timothy identifies the leaders of the sect as "liars whose consciences are seared with a hot iron" (1 Tim. 4:2). Adherents of the sect are those who have renounced the true faith "by paying attention to deceitful spirits and the teachings of demons" (1). The invectives used in the passage against such an imposed state of singleness indicate that the Christian community preferred freedom of choice in matters of marriage over against a legislated mandate to remain single, which is linked with "hypocrisy" (2).

In the same epistle, the author distinguishes between two types of widows: those "who are really widows" and have "set their hope on God and continue in supplications and prayers night and day" (1 Tim. 5:3, 5) and the widow "who lives for pleasure" but is "dead even while she lives" (6). Only the former are to be included on the list of widows who would receive alms from the church, but only if they had no rel-atives who could take them in (16). The other type of widow, the one "who lives for pleasure," seems to be younger. They are not to receive alms and subsidies from church members. In fact, the author says it is likely that their "sensual desires alienate them from Christ" which makes them "want to marry" (11). This sensual desire on their part, along with other unpleasant conduct, such as idleness, gadding, gos-siping, and acting like busybodies (13), will "incur condemnation" (12) and make a bad name for the Christian community and an "occasion to revile us" (14). Therefore, the author advises that these younger widows "marry, bear children, and manage their households" (14), which is especially advisable since "some have already turned away to follow Satan" (15). The language used is strong, almost accusatory, and advocates marriage over the unmarried state. Not unmarried men, but unmarried women are accused of ruining the community's reputation because they cannot remain truly celibate, but instead give free reign to their sensual desires, which will eventually lead them to marry. Since chances are that they will get married anyway, they might as well do it quickly, so they can begin to "bear children, and manage their households." Both passages from 1 Timothy show a radical reorientation from Paul's previous view of the unmarried state. While Paul advocates the unmarried state for greater devotion to doing the Lord's work, the author of 1 Timothy advocates marriage by hurling invectives against those who teach celibacy and by encouraging widows, especially those of childbearing age, to remarry as quickly as possible.

Eunuchs

There are only two references to eunuchs in the New Testament, one in the Gospel of Matthew, the other in the book of Acts. The Greek word literally means a "bed-keeper" or chamberlain, hence a man in charge of the sleeping quarters in the courts of oriental monarchs who support numerous wives. In contrast to the Old Testament in which eunuchs are identified by their position as high court officials, the passage in Matthew shifts the emphasis to their sexual activity, that is, their ability or inability to procreate, or their desire for or interest in sexual intercourse and marriage.

The context of the reference in the Matthew passage is a discussion concerning marriage and divorce. Some Pharisees had sought Jesus out and, to test him, asked whether it was lawful for a man to divorce his wife for any cause (Matt. 19:3). Jesus tells them that it is unlawful for a man to divorce his wife, except in the case of unchastity on her part, but that if he does nonetheless and subsequently marries another woman, he commits adultery (9). The point Jesus seeks to make is that divorce not only becomes more difficult in his interpretation of marriage, but that the internal motives of the one seeking the divorce are exposed and translate into sinful behavior if the intent of the divorce was to subsequently marry someone else. In light of this interpretation, the disciples, not the Pharisees, are beginning to wonder whether it is worth getting married at all. They conclude that "if such is the case of a man with his wife, it is better not to marry" at all (Matt. 19:10). But Jesus replies that the decision on whether or not to marry is not necessarily up to the individual, "for not everyone can accept this teaching, but only those to whom it is given" (11).

On the issue of remaining unmarried, Jesus provides three distinctions among people (12), all using the word "eunuchs." The first type are eunuchs "from birth." These are people who are either not eligible or able to be married because they are unable to engage in sexual intercourse and hence to produce offspring. The second type are those who "have been made eunuchs by others," which means that they have been injured or cut so that they have lost the ability to procreate and/or engage in sexual intercourse. Just like the first group, these people would have no need to be married, since the married state, according to Jewish law, was first and foremost for the purpose of procreation through sexual intercourse. The third are "eunuchs who have made themselves eunuchs for the sake of the kingdom of heaven." These are people who have voluntarily renounced the marital state so as to better serve the kingdom of heaven. Though they have the ability, and most likely the desire, to procreate and to engage in sexual intercourse and are potential marriage candidates, it "has been given to them" to remain unmarried, and by implication, to abstain from sexual intercourse, for the kingdom's sake. In Matthew's Gospel, Jesus proposes that people may remain unmarried, hence celibate, not because they choose to, but because they have been given the gift of doing so. This gift does not exist as an end in and of itself, but is given to the believer in the context of faith and for the purpose of advancing the reign of God on earth.

The second and only other reference in the New Testament to a eunuch is found in the book of Acts. Philip, the deacon and evangelist, who has four unmarried daughters with the gift of prophecy and later hosts Paul and Luke in his home (Acts 21:9), is prompted by the Lord to take the wilderness road leading from Jerusalem to Gaza (Acts 8:26).

There he encounters "an Ethiopian eunuch, a court official of the Candace, queen of the Ethiopians, in charge of her entire treasury" (27). Luke tells the reader that the eunuch had come to Jerusalem to worship and is now returning home. Prompted by the Spirit, Philip is told to approach the man, who is reading from Isaiah, and is invited to sit next to him and explain the Scripture passage concerning the suffering servant prophecy. Philip interprets the passage by proclaiming to the man "the good news about Jesus" (35), and the man asks to be baptized at the sight of a pool of water along the road. "What is to prevent me from being baptized?" he asks Philip rhetorically, who in turn baptizes him.

Based on his request for help in understanding the Isaiah passage, his apparent unfamiliarity with the idea of the expected messiah as suffering servant, and his nationality as an Ethiopian, it appears that the man was a proselyte, or convert, to the Jewish faith. As would befit his status as a high court official, he was riding in a chariot. The term "eunuch" then identifies the man as a high court official, not as someone who was unable to procreate or who was castrated. The fact that Luke shows that this man is converted to Christ could well mean that Luke sought to indicate the fulfillment of Isaiah 56:3–8, where not only those who are "dry trees" (Isa. 56:3) but more important "the foreigners who join themselves to the Lord" (6) are gathered next to "those already gathered" (8) into the family of God in Christ Jesus.

New Developments

A comparison between the Old and New Testaments on the issue of virginity, chastity, the unmarried state, and eunuchs shows significant differences in development, particularly for women. In the Old Testament, the issue of virginity involves only women, not men. Women in the Old Testament were required to keep their virginity until marriage. If the woman's virginity was questionable following marriage and the woman could not prove her premarital virginity, she could be stoned to death. Women who were raped, seduced, "sampled," or had lost their virginity prior to marriage had only a marginal chance of being honorably married later. In contrast, the New Testament uses the word "virgin" to identify both men and women. Both men and women are encouraged to maintain, if possible, their current single or marital status at the time of their call in Christ, which meant virginity and lifelong celibacy for those who had never been married.

On the issue of chastity, the Old Testament interprets it as referring only to men abstaining from sexual relations with women at certain times, mostly in preparation for worship and ritual activity. Men were also to abstain from intercourse with menstruating women because of purity regulations that applied to men. In the New Testament, chastity means temporary sexual abstinence for both men and women in marriage.

The Old Testament is clear in its rejection of the unmarried state. Men are to continue their lineage through offspring, and women are to bear their husbands sons so the male lineage will continue. Since procreation is to occur only within marriage, not to marry is considered a violation of the divine blessing and a deprivation of blessings from future generations. In contrast, the New Testament, particularly Paul, encourages those who are single at the time of their call in Christ to remain so, just as he is. In addition, the freely chosen unmarried state is praised for allowing the individual undivided attention to the affairs of the Lord.

Regarding eunuchs, the Old Testament refers to them only as males. The term is primarily used to denote high court officials, who could even be married, not men who are emasculated or castrated. On rare occasion, eunuchs appear to denote castrated men who serve as harem keepers. The prophetic passage of Isaiah, written probably during the period of Israel's exile, predicts a reversal of the law that blessing only comes to those who bear and produce offspring and continue the male lineage. Now blessing is predicted for eunuchs, that is the barren and childless, which will come not through sons and daughters, but on account of their righteousness before the Lord. In that sense, the Isaiah passage forms a transition to the New Testament, where eunuchs are identified by their sexual inactivity. Some have intentionally renounced sexual activity for the sake of the kingdom of heaven, sacrificing the sexual act, marriage, and procreation. With that, celibacy is encouraged as a high and honorable calling for both men and women, who have become "eunuchs," that is, court officials in the heavenly court. This new development in Judeo-Christian tradition in regard to celibacy would have had significant consequences for women. To find out if this was so, some passages depicting possibly celibate women shall be explored in Luke's writings, the Gospel of Luke and the Acts of the Apostles.

Luke-Acts

The Gospel of Luke features women more frequently than any of the other Gospels. The theory most commonly accepted, based on source criticism, is that the author of Luke used the Gospel of Mark (with some omissions) — often called Q (from the German word *Quelle*, meaning "source") — and sources that were probably both oral and written that are unique to Luke. These sources shall be called L. Much of the L material apparently was available only to Luke and is not found in the other Gospels featuring women. Such sections include the infancy narratives, portraying Elizabeth, Mary of Nazareth, and Anna the prophetess; the raising of the son of the widow of Nain (7:12–17), the forgiven prostitute who anoints Jesus (7:36–50), the Galilean women followers of Jesus (8:1–3); Mary and Martha (10:38–42), the woman crying out from the crowd (11:27–28), the bent woman (13:10–17); the parable of the sweeping woman (15:8–10), the parable of the persistent widow (18:1–8); the daughters of Jerusalem (23:27–32), women at the cross (23:49), and women preparing spices (23:56). While some of the material appears to make the point of placing women in submissive roles, other material bears traces of women's increased involvement and leadership roles. The technique that brings women into greater focus in Luke's Gospel is known as pairing. One version of a story or teaching may refer to a man, while the next may refer to a woman. This pairing occurs most frequently in the discourses of Jesus — for example, the man who plants a mustard seed and the woman who takes leaven (13:18–21), the man who searches for the lost sheep and the woman who searches for the lost coin (15:4–10). Also, there are healings that come in pairs, and two lists of the names of Jesus' followers, one of the male apostles (6:12–19) and one of women (8:1–3). In addition, there is a noticeable tendency to defend, reassure, and praise women. For example, Luke refers to widows more frequently than do the other Gospels. Widows are of particular interest here since they are expected to remain celibate following the death of their husband in accordance with Jewish laws. Since Luke has more material about women (forty-two passages, of which twenty-three are unique to Luke), it is important to consider his references to women who are widowed, hence celibate, and those women mentioned who are actively engaged in Christian discipleship.

The first reference to a widow in the Gospel of Luke is to Anna (or Hanna), the daughter of Phanuel of the tribe of Asher (Luke 2:36). Anna is called a prophet. Her prophetic role consists in identifying the child Jesus as someone worthy of praise and thanksgiving to God. Upon seeing the child, she "began to praise God and to speak about the child to all who were looking for the redemption of Jerusalem" (2:38). Thus, she views the child of importance to those who longed for the coming of the long-awaited Messiah to deliver the Jews from captivity and oppression. Her prophetic role is validated by the details describing her long widowhood and old age. She was "of a great age," had "lived with her husband seven years after her marriage," and "then as a widow to the age of eighty-four" (36–37), thus implying her long life of celibacy. Then the state of her celibacy is linked with her exceeding piety. "She never left the temple but worshiped there with fasting and prayer night and day" (37), Luke says. Anna then represents a woman whose life embraces both long-standing celibacy and great piety. Perhaps as a result of her celibate and devout lifestyle, she has become endowed with the gift of prophecy and, in particular, with the gift of identifying the child Jesus with "the redemption of Jerusalem." In the preceding passage about Simeon who also acts as a prophet concerning the child Jesus, we see another example of pairing in Luke. But, in contrast, no mention is made of Simeon's marital status or celibate lifestyle, only that he "was righteous and devout" (25).

The other four explicit references to widows in the Gospel of Luke portray them all as women who are experiencing economic hardships and deprivation. In the passage where Jesus reads from the scroll of Isaiah in the synagogue in Nazareth and tells the people that no prophet is accepted in the prophet's hometown (4:16–24), we have Luke pairing widows and lepers. "There were many widows in Israel in the time of Elijah...yet Elijah was sent to none of them except to a widow at Zarephath in Sidon" (25–26), Jesus says. Likewise, "there were also many lepers in Israel in the time of the prophet Elisha, and none of them was cleansed except Naaman the Syrian" (27). The three remaining passages on widows depict them in similar ways, highlighting their hardship and deprivation. The woman of Nain bemoaned the death of her only son, and "she was a widow" (7:12), which prompted Jesus' compassion for her. A widow kept coming to a judge to be granted "justice against my opponent" (18:3), and finally receives it. And the houses of widows are repossessed and "devoured" by the scribes and the outwardly religious (20:47). Only the persistent widow is portrayed as a model of Christian discipleship.

There are two passages in Acts that make explicit mention of widows. The first depicts them as needy, referring to the Hellenistic widows as those who were neglected "in the daily distribution of food" in favor of the Jewish widows (Acts 6:1). But in the following paired narrative, when seven men of good standing and full of the Spirit and of wisdom are selected, we are not told that the unjust situation is remedied, only that now the twelve apostles are freed up to devote "ourselves to prayer and to serving the word" (6:4), instead of having "to wait on tables" (2). The second mention of widows in the book of Acts shows again women in a situation of need, rather than in a position of leadership and strength. It describes the death "of a disciple[5] whose name was Tabitha, which in Greek is Dorcas" (9:36), who "was devoted to good works and acts of charity" (37). Through two male disciples word was sent to Peter, who was staying nearby in the city of Lydda, to come without delay. Upon Peter's arrival, "they took him to the room upstairs" and "all the widows stood beside him, weeping and showing tunics and other clothing that Dorcas had made while she was with them" (39). Peter had all of them leave, and then prayed for her to come back to life, which she did. And "calling the saints and widows, he showed her to be alive" (41). It is noteworthy here that Luke distinguishes between saints and widows, probably referring to other male disciples, including the two messengers, as "saints," while to all others as "widows." Also, it is likely that Tabitha had been a widow herself and had built a ministry of "good works and acts of charity" (36) toward other widows in her community, particularly by providing them with bare necessities, such as articles of clothing. But while her service to the community of women, particularly widows, is highly valued by them, exemplified by their being the first allowed to see her alive again, Luke does not connect her possible widowhood, hence celibacy, with her discipleship. In fact, her particular position of leadership among the other women is downplayed. As a result, Tabitha the benefactress, along with the other widows she had served out of her abundance and sense of call in Christ, continues to remain a needy woman who depends on charity — in this case Peter's and that of the two male disciples.

Except for the prophet Anna and Philip's four virgin daughters who possessed the gift of prophecy, we find no other concrete example of Luke linking female celibacy, either in widowhood or virginity, with increased spiritual activity and more focused dedication in service to God's reign. Where such a link exists, as it well may in Tabitha's case, it is downplayed. This leaves us with a host of women in Luke and Acts who were faithful and active in the early stages of the Christian movement, but whose station in life as unmarried, hence whose celibacy, remains unknown and can only be presumed.

There are several women mentioned only by Luke and not found in the other Gospels who were faithful disciples of Jesus and may have been unmarried. The Gospel of Luke identifies them as the women traveling with Jesus (8:1–3), the sisters Mary and Martha (10:38–42), and the women at the cross and empty tomb (23:49; 24:1–12). As for the women traveling with Jesus and who accompany Jesus and the twelve through cities and villages, they are identified as those "who had been cured of evil spirits and infirmities" (8:2). Their reason for following is not bound up with Jesus' ministry and teaching, but purely with their own personal needs and the experience of being healed by him. Thus, discipleship for these women is not portrayed as resulting from their devotion to Jesus as a great teacher and healer per se, or as suspecting him of being the long-expected messiah, but from their personal and, one might presume, selfish need to be made well. Their discipleship appears inferior to that of the male disciples. Moreover, their discipleship consists in providing "for them[6] out of their resources" (8:3), leaving the reader with the impression that these women were wealthy and gave out of their fortunes. Only three women of the "many others" in the group of female followers are mentioned by name: "Mary, called Magdalene, from whom seven demons had gone out" (8:2) and whose description in the other Gospels do not depict her as wealthy; "Joanna, the wife of Herod's steward Chuza," and Susanna (3), who is not further identified. Joanna is the first of many women of wealth and status mentioned by Luke, but she is married. This leaves only Mary Magdalene and Susanna who could have been single, along with the unnamed "many others." While their discipleship is depicted as consisting of service, possibly domestic, and providing Jesus and his disciples with resources, it could have been more than that, such as the ministry done by the seventy(-two) in Luke 10:1–20. Furthermore, the passage suggests the possibility that women traveled with Jesus in an itinerant ministry for longer periods of time, or that, since the area was small, women left their homes for ministerial day trips, which would have been more feasible if they were single, widowed, or divorced.

The sisters Mary and Martha are mentioned also in the Gospel of John (11:1–46) in the account of their brother Lazarus's resurrection. But Luke's story of Mary and Martha at their home (Luke calls it Martha's home, but the reading is ambiguous) entertaining Jesus is unique (Luke 10:38–42). While Mary sits attentively at Jesus' feet, Martha "was distracted by her many tasks" (10:40) and complains to Jesus that "my sister has left me to do all the work by myself." Jesus' response commends Mary for having "chosen the better part, which will not be taken away," while Martha is downgraded for being "worried and distracted by many things" (10:41). Mary's role as listener and student of the word of the Lord is praised, while Martha's role of domestic table server is downgraded. The passage appears to give women a choice concerning the nature of their discipleship. But this choice does not extend to the ministry of the proclaimed word, thus is limited. They can either study the word in quiet, or tend to household duties that serve Jesus' ministry. Mary's choice of listening and study, in contrast to household duties, is praised, but it is doubtful that she would have had this choice at all had she been married with children. More likely is that her unmarried, hence celibate, state, in the context of living with her sister and brother, afforded her this opportunity of discipleship.

The women mentioned by Luke during Jesus' crucifixion and resurrection are rather sketchy and later on disappear altogether. In contrast to the Gospel of Mark, which names the women who are witnesses to the crucifixion, burial, and resurrection a total of three times (Mark 15:40, 47; 16:1), Luke only makes one reference to them by name (24:10), and then only in the context of other women who are said to have been with them. The named women are among "the women who had followed him from Galilee" (cf. Mark 15:41) and stood watching his death from a distance (23:49), had followed Jesus' burial and had seen "the tomb and how his body was laid" (23:55), and "prepared spices and ointments" (23:56) to take to the tomb after the Sabbath observance. In naming the three women, Luke seems to draw on Markan material which lists two of the three women, i.e., Mary Magdalene and Mary, the mother of James (Mark 15:40; 16:1), whereas Luke adds Joanna, who had appeared earlier as the wealthy benefactress of Jesus' and the Twelve's ministry and as the wife of Herod's steward Chuza (8:3). Thus, apart from women whose names had been transmitted to him by Mark, Luke has no new women appear at the foot of Jesus' cross or by his tomb apart from the wealthy, married Joanna.

Other women who distinguished themselves through faithful discipleship and may have been unmarried, hence celibate, appear in Luke's account of the Acts of the Apostles. Among them are the women gathered in the upper room in Jerusalem, "certain women, including Mary the mother of Jesus" (Acts 1:14). The mention of Mary may serve a theological purpose for Luke because it shows continuity between Jesus' birth and the birth of the church. However, the mention of her without her husband, Joseph, may also indicate that Mary was widowed at the time. Joseph makes his last appearance in Luke's Gospel when Jesus is twelve years old and he and his parents travel to Jerusalem for the Passover festival (Luke 2:41–51). The Gospel of Matthew mentions Joseph only up to the family's return from Egypt to Nazareth (Matt. 2:19–23), and Mark and John do not mention Joseph at all. Following Jesus' Passover celebration at age twelve, Joseph disappears from the Gospels and only Mary, his mother, remains. She is present when Jesus carries out his ministry, once at a wedding in Cana (John 2:1–12), which she had attended along with her son, his "brothers and his disciples" (2:12), and once while Jesus is found surrounded by a crowd of followers and "his mother and his brothers came to him" (Luke 8:19–21; cf. Mark 3:31–35; Matt. 12:46–50) but could not penetrate the crowd. All three Synoptic Gospels agree that his mother and brothers were present, whereas Joseph has disappeared. While the Gospel writers may have taken Joseph out of the picture for theological reasons to allow them to focus on the relationship between Jesus and his heavenly Father, Joseph's absence from the Gospel narratives may still point to the fact that Mary was widowed by the time Jesus began his earthly ministry, and most likely at the time the eleven remaining disciples and she and other women were gathered in the upper room in Jerusalem. Her widowhood and consequently her celibacy would make her then a prime example of a celibate female disciple in the emerging Christian movement.

Other references to women who may have been single and celibate include the servant woman Rhoda and her mistress "Mary, the mother of John whose other name was Mark" (Luke 12:12), and the women at Philippi who had gathered "outside the gate by the river" along with "a certain woman named Lydia, a worshiper of God" (Acts 16:13–15). The story of Rhoda is part of the larger story of Peter's imprisonment by King Herod under maximum security. After Peter is rescued by "an angel of the Lord" (12:7–10), he goes to the house of Mary, the mother of John. Many believers had gathered at her house in prayer (12:12) when he knocked at the outer gate and was greeted by Rhoda (12:13). Rhoda is so overjoyed that she leaves him standing there, instead of opening the gate, to report to the others who was at the door. They do not believe her and so they go to the gate themselves, "and when they opened the gate, they saw him and were amazed" (12:16). We do not know whether Rhoda was part of the inner circle of believers and a believer herself and was perhaps hired by Mary because of that, or whether she was converted as part of Mary's household while in her employment, or whether she was simply familiar with Peter and the others because of her position as servant. Even if she was a believer, the nature of her discipleship is downplayed by Luke. Not only does she bungle her custodial duties, but her announcement is not well received by the inner circle — much like the women's resurrection announcement labeled as "an idle tale" by the eleven in Luke 24:11 — who question her mental state, saying "You are out of your mind!" and then insist she has seen only Peter's vision or "his angel" (12:15). On the other hand, Mary, the mother of John, is depicted by Luke as being among the wealthy female benefactors of the early Christian movement. Since Mary is identified by her son, not by her husband, as is Jewish custom, it could mean that Mary was a widow. But more important than her marital status to Luke is her wealth. Mary distinguishes herself as reasonably wealthy on account of a home large enough to have "many" gather there, one that was costly enough to need securing by a gate, and one that had a servant to tend to the gate. Thus Mary is presented by Luke not primarily as a faithful disciple who may have been widowed, but as a benevolent benefactress who operates from the sidelines by silently offering her home in support of the Christian cause.

Another example of a possibly single, hence celibate, woman as disciple is Lydia, who is among the women gathered at Philippi for worship. These are women that Paul and his companions encounter on the Sabbath while looking for a "place of prayer" outside the gate by the river (Acts 16:13). They "sat down and spoke to the women who had gathered there." Among them is Lydia, a Gentile woman, who worships God but is not a member of the Christian movement (16:14). After listening "eagerly to what was said by Paul," "she and her household were baptized" (16:15). Afterward, she urges Paul and his companions to stay at her home and use it as the center of their missionary activity in Philippi (see Acts 16:16, 40). Again Lydia is portrayed by Luke as a wealthy woman, in this case "a dealer in purple cloth" (16:14), which was a luxury item. As evidence of her wealth, we find that she is the head of her household and owns a home large enough to readily accommodate Paul and his companions and to open it up as a gathering place for the newly formed Christian community in Philippi (16:40). This contrasts with her prior attendance at a meeting for prayer with other women in the rather modest and sparse setting outside the city gate by the river. One wonders why she did not make her home available earlier to other "worshipers of God," presumably Gentile converts to Judaism, and only now opens it up to the Christian movement.

Lydia deserves further attention because her house, located in the "leading city of the district of Macedonia and a Roman colony" (Acts 16:12), becomes the early center of the newly founded church in Philippi and its gathered community, which later is the recipient of Paul's Letter to the Philippians. Furthermore, Lydia is the first European convert of Paul and his companions, which possibly included Luke. Her story parallels the story of Peter and Cornelius, in which the latter, along with "his relatives and close friends" (10:24), becomes the first Gentile convert to Christianity (Acts 10). Cornelius is identified as "a centurion, an upright and God-fearing man, who is well spoken of by the whole Jewish nation" (10:22) and "who feared God with all his household" and "gave alms generously to the people and prayed constantly to God" (10:2). But in contrast, Lydia is only described as "a worshiper of God" and "a dealer in purple cloth" (16:14). Her religious character and piety prior to and following baptism remain marginal, while her offer to use her home as a missionary base has prominence. As in earlier examples, Luke again portrays women as wealthy benefactors of the Christian cause. However, underlying this portrayal a different picture emerges, which can help shed light on the role of women in the early Christian community. For example, this home was not necessarily, as is often presumed, that of a successful merchant, but was probably the modest living quarters of mostly women who labored along with her and possibly under her supervision in the textile industry.[7] We are told that Lydia was originally from Thyatira, a city that formed the center of the purple-dying industry. Hence, she was a foreigner and had come from the East, like many purple dyers, most likely together with other women, who may have been the same women with whom she was worshiping by the river. Also, women constituted a majority in the textile business because it was labor-intensive and low-paying, hence unattractive to men. Thyatira was located in the region of Lydia, so that her name indicates the region she comes from, not her proper name. The use of a regional name, also called an *ethnicon*, indicates that she may at one point have been a slave who had then been freed, but who then retained her regional name as a personal name.[8] Furthermore, the purple-dying business was dirty, smelly, and lowly labor, with the majority of its employees being slaves, freed persons, and women. Since employees worked both in the dye-house and in sales, it is likely that Lydia was an employee, not the owner or sole dealer, in one of the many dye houses in Thyatira and had been sent to Philippi, along with other co-workers, as part of a larger operation.[9] On the question as to whether Lydia was single our biblical text remains silent. It is true that she is identified as the head of her household, but this could also mean that her husband had remained in Thyatira, and that she would later return there. This possibility is further emphasized by the fact that Paul's letter to the Philippians nowhere mentions Lydia, unless she had assumed a different name, such as Euodia or Syntyche (Phil. 4:2) — the only two women mentioned in the letter, but in the negative context of being at odds with each other. It seems unlikely that her husband lived in the same house as Lydia without exercising his role as *pater familias* and that Lydia had rights and freedoms over their living quarters independently from her husband's. Hence, we do not find here a clear connection between Lydia's faithful discipleship and her status of being single, hence celibate. At the same time, her conversion and subsequent involvement with the Christian movement, including her insistence on making her house a missionary base and hosting the first house church in Europe, may have opened up new rights and privileges previously withheld from women by a patriarchal society.

On the issue of celibacy in relation to Christian discipleship it is worth noting two more passages that are unique to Luke. In Luke 18:29b–30, the Gospel writer has Jesus say that "there is no one who has left house or wife or brothers or parents or children for the sake of the kingdom of God, who will not get back very much more in this age, and in the age to come eternal life." In contrast, Matthew omits the word "wife" from this saying of Jesus (see Matt. 19:29) and so does Mark (see Mark 10:29–30). The parallel texts agree on an enumeration of family relations, i.e., "brothers or sisters or mother or father or children or fields" (Mark) and "brothers or sisters or father or mother or children or fields," but they do not mention how male disciples are to relate to their wives. Luke makes the same point in the second passage, when Jesus says that "Whoever comes to me and does not hate father and mother, wife and children, brothers and sisters, yes, and even life itself, cannot be my disciple" (Luke 14:26). In the parallel text in Matthew, Jesus says that "Whoever loves father and mother more than me is not worthy of me; and whoever loves son or daughter more than me is not worthy of me" (Matt. 10:37). It is unlikely that Luke intended the injunction to "leave" one's wife quite literally, allowing male followers of Christ were to shirk their responsibilities as husbands and fathers and pick up and leave their children and wives so as to be free to do "full-time" ministry. Such an interpretation would run counter to Paul's thoughts on marital responsibility. Since Luke travelled with the apostle Paul on one of his missionary journeys to Philippi (see the "we" passages in Acts 16:11–16), and possibly knew Paul's Letter to the Corinthians, it is unlikely that he would have intended a literal meaning. Paul's thought on this matter as expressed in his first letter to the church in Corinth helps to interpret the Lukan passage. Here, Paul argues that "from now on, let even those who have wives be as though they had none ... and those who buy as though they had no possessions, and those who deal with the world as though they had no dealings with it. For the present form of this world is passing away" (1 Cor. 7:29b–31). Based on Paul's view then, Luke's advice is not that the male disciple is to "leave" his wife or to "hate" her, but to keep in perspective the larger context of Christian discipleship, whereby wife, children, mourning, rejoicing, possessions, and dealings with the world are secondary activities and attachments, not to take precedence over one's personal attachment to and fellowship with Christ. While it is true that Luke only refers to male disciples in relationship to their wives, and not wives in relationship to their husbands, the same principle could apply to wives as well. Not that they are to "leave" or "hate" their husband, but they are "to deal with the world as though they had no dealings with it" (1 Cor. 7:31), hence not allow their family responsibilities to take precedence over their attachment to and fellowship with Christ.

Chapter 3

Celibacy in the Early Church

═══════════════════

Beginning with the second and third centuries, several documents emerge that are patterned after Luke's Acts of the Apostles. These documents, titled the Apocryphal Acts of the Apostles,[1] were probably written from approximately A.D. 160 to 225. Though they did not become part of the canon of Christian Scripture, they enjoyed great popularity, particularly among the more literary-minded.[2] Among their protagonists are the apostles Peter, Paul, Barnabas, Philip, Andrew, Matthias, Matthew, Thomas, Bartholomew, Thaddaeus, and John. The purpose of the Apocryphal Acts appears to be the telling and retelling of early apostolic activity. Rather than seeking to convert the pagan and Gentile world by describing the life of Jesus and urging readers to recognize him as the promised messiah and Son of God, the Apocryphal Acts, much like Luke's Acts, appear to have been written for an audience that was already Christian and enjoyed tales of successful conversions and missionary activity. The stories report the apostles' work, trials, and frequently their subsequent martyrdom. But even though the apostles are martyred in the end, the stories convey the idea that they did not labor in vain, because they left behind perfect and exemplary Christian converts, many of them women.

Acts of the Apostles Peter and Paul

The first book, titled the *Acts of the Apostles Peter and Paul*, opens with Peter and Paul being involved in a dispute between the Jews and the Gentiles in Rome. The Jews claimed to be "a chosen race, a royal priesthood" while "you of the Gentiles are no great thing in your lineage" (479). Paul was able to appease the Jewish opposition, but subsequently the Jews accused Peter "of having renounced their synagogue." Peter then delivered a sermon about Christ, resulting in the conversion of the majority of the people, including two women. One was Nero's wife, Libia, the other the yoke-fellow of Agrippa the prefect, Agrippina. Because of their conversion to the Christian faith, "they went away from beside their own husbands" (479), resulting in Simon, a magician, accusing Peter of being "a wizard and a cheat" (480), probably because he felt threatened at his own trade. The book launches into an extensive discourse among Paul, Peter, Simon, and Nero, and it ends when Nero, in consultation with Agrippa, orders Paul to be beheaded and Peter crucified. Even though the discourse before Nero never makes mention of Libia's and Agrippina's decision to discontinue sexual relations with their husbands, the book implies that Nero and Agrippa, the husbands, took revenge on Peter and Paul for encouraging their wives to do so.

Acts of Paul and Thecla

The second book is the *Acts of Paul and Thecla*. It begins with Paul being offered hospitality by Onesiphorus and his wife, Lectra, and their children in the city of Iconium. Immediately, there was conversation about Christian doctrine, including "the word of God about self-control and the resurrection" (487). Paul began praising the advantages of sexual abstinence and virginity in the form of a set of beatitudes. "Blessed are they that have kept the flesh chaste," he said, "for they shall become a temple of God; blessed are they that control themselves, for God shall speak with them; blessed are they that have kept aloof from this world, for they shall be called upright: blessed are they that have wives as not having them, for they shall receive God for their portion . . . blessed are the bodies of the virgins, for they shall be well pleasing to God, and shall not lose the reward of their chastity" (487). Overhearing the "discourse of virginity and prayer" was a certain virgin Thecla, engaged to Thamyris. After three days of intent listening, Thecla's mother sent word to Thamyris to talk sense into her daughter, which Thamyris attempted to do. During the conversation, it became clear that Thecla had made up her mind not to marry Thamyris, so that Thamyris "wept for the loss of a wife, and Theocleia of a child, and the maidservants of a mistress," while Thecla "did not turn round, but kept attending earnestly to the word of Paul" (488).

The story indicates that Paul's teaching on sexual abstinence and celibacy was directed to both men and women. The dejected fiancé Thamyris accused Paul of "leading astray the souls of young men, and deceiving virgins, so that they do not marry, but remain as they are." The same is charged by the two travel companions of Paul's confirming that "he [Paul] deprives young men of wives, and maidens of husbands." Both young men and young women were attracted to Paul's teaching, illustrated by Thecla's mother saying to Thamyris, "all the women and the young men go in beside him" (488), meaning Paul. After Thecla's fiancé involved the civic authorities, Paul was bound and imprisoned. At night, Thecla gained entrance to the jail by bartering her bracelet with a guard so she could continue listening to Paul's teaching about "the great things of God." When she was discovered, the trial continued before the proconsul. He asked Thecla why she did not "obey Thamyris." But when she remained silent, her mother cried out demanding "her that will not marry" be burned (489). The verdict resulted in Paul being flogged and driven out of the city; Thecla was to be burned. As she was led up to the pyre, the governor wept "and wondered at the virtue that was in her." But when the fire was lit and Thecla stripped of her clothes, a heavy thunderstorm arose, and the fire did not touch her, and she escaped unharmed.

In the meantime, Onesiphorus and his wife and children "had left the things of the world" and joined Paul's itinerant ministry, which had taken him from Iconium to Daphne. Sent on an errand, one of Onesiphorus's children chanced upon Thecla, who was searching for Paul in the countryside and led her to him. She told Paul that she was determined to follow him wherever he went. But Paul was concerned about her attractiveness to men and the possibility that she might not withstand their approaches. Thecla protested, saying that Christ's seal would protect her from temptation — meaning her baptism, which she was yet awaiting. But Paul did not baptize her; instead he took her with him on his next missionary journey to Antioch after he had sent back Onesiphorus and his household.

At Antioch, Paul's concern about Thecla's attractiveness was confirmed when a man named Alexander became enamored with her and, assuming Paul to be her next of kin, showered him with gifts. When Paul denied having the authority to give Thecla away in marriage, Alexander went to Thecla and forcefully embraced her. Thecla was furious by his disregard of "a servant of God" and "one of the chief persons of the Iconians." And she "tore his cloak, and pulled off his crown, and made him a laughing-stock" (489). Out of shame, Alexander had her brought before the governor, who condemned her to the wild beasts, while the women of the town protested the "evil" and "impious" verdict.

Until her fight with the beasts, Thecla was allowed to stay with a wealthy widow who had lost her daughter. When Tryphaena had to release Thecla to be taken to the arena, she mourned Thecla's impending death as if it was that of a daughter's. In fact, her loud cry scared away Alexander who had come to take Thecla to the fight — a fight he himself was coordinating and for which he was supplying the wild beasts. At the arena, the crowd was in an uproar, and the women once again sided with Thecla, shouting, "Let the city be raised against this wickedness. Take off all of us, O proconsul! Cruel sight! evil sentence!" (490). In the course of the fight, a lioness was brought in, but she did not harm Thecla, instead tore to pieces a bear and a lion so as to protect Thecla. More wild beasts were led into the arena, but Thecla sought refuge with the seals in a ditch of water, which did no harm to her either. Thecla considered her immersion in the waters of the ditch her baptism. Meanwhile, the women were weeping and wailing and throwing sweet-smelling herbs and nard in the rink. As a last resort, Alexander decided to bring in fierce bulls. The guards tied Thecla to the bulls and heated the bulls' testicles to make them more ferocious. At the sight of this spectacle, Tryphaena fainted and was presumed dead. The governor stopped the fight and Alexander, out of fear of Caesar's hearing about Tryphaena's death, pleaded to have Thecla released. Upon a last examination by the governor during which Thecla testified to the presence of the living God whom she served, she was set free. In turn, the "women shouted aloud, and with one mouth returned thanks to God, saying: There is one God, the God of Thecla" (491).

For a while, Thecla returned to Tryphaena's house and began teaching and preaching so that Tryphaena and "most even of the maid-servants believed." Then, donning a man's cloak and taking with her "young men and maidens," she set out to find Paul. She found him preaching in Myra, and told him of her self-baptism, of Tryphaena's conversion, and of her call from God to return to her native Iconium. She left behind many of Tryphaena's gifts, such as clothing and gold, to be used by Paul for the service of the poor. Upon her return, she found her former fiancé Thamyris dead, but her mother alive. After she testified of Jesus Christ to her mother, "she departed to Seleucia, and dwelt in a cave seventy-two years, living upon herbs and water. And she enlightens many by the word of God." The last two paragraphs of the story briefly mention an attempt by Greek physicians to corrupt her, her subsequent escape, and her burial place near Paul's in Rome.

Another manuscript expands on the last two paragraphs. As in the first manuscript, her trials are mentioned, but we also hear of her min-istering to other women, particularly the well-born. Having heard of the virgin Thecla, they came "and learned of the oracles of God. And many of them bade adieu to the world, and lived an ascetic life with her" (492). Apart from preaching and teaching, Thecla's ministry en-compassed the healing of the sick and the exorcism of unclean spirits. Because of her powerful healing ministry, the physicians of the town, "having lost their trade" and no longer well-regarded, resolved to enlist some scoundrels "to defile her [so that] neither the gods nor Artemis would listen to her in the case of the sick." However, the men were unable to rape her, because Thecla prayed to the God who had pre-served her virginity until then, and was able to escape unscathed into the opening of a rock which closed shut behind her. Thus Thecla remained a virgin to the end.

Throughout the story, Thecla prays and converses with God in lengthy exchanges. Her gifts of preaching, evangelizing, and healing can be directly attributed to her devotion to and intimate relationship with Jesus Christ. Because of her faith, she renounced her impending marriage, remaining in her station of life at the time of her Christian conversion. Thecla is a virgin, but it is not her virginity that imbues her with spiritual gifts and powers. Only the Greek physicians mistakenly assume that they are derived from her virginity. They do not realize that these powers come from her connectedness with Christ and her faith in the living God. This faith first helps her discern the call to celibacy and then unleashes in her the particular gifts of ministry. Once she has discerned the call to celibacy, despite the heavy opposition from her fiancé and mother, Thecla is freed to engage in itinerant ministry and mission work, until she settles in Seleucia. Moreover, she is free to leave the area that had been her home, find Paul, accompany him on his missionary travel, and then settle in a place of her choice. Thecla's freedom comes from her faith, not her virginal state. Still, her decision not to marry and to remain celibate open up for her doors to exercise ministerial gifts that might otherwise have remained closed, or would not have opened up to the degree the story reports.

The second manuscript calls Thecla an apostle. She shared the apostolic privileges of someone like Paul by proclaiming the word of God as God's servant and witness to Christ's resurrection. As in the case of the apostle, her proclamation was accompanied by signs and miracles of healing and exorcisms. Like an apostle, she was persecuted. A central theme is that both Paul and Thecla suffer on account of their celibacy. But while both practiced a celibate life, the sources of their trials differed. Paul suffered because he promoted celibacy as an option to marriage, especially among young single men and women. Thecla suffered because she practiced celibacy as a woman by fending off sexual advances from men and, implicitly, by refusing to bear children. While Paul's trials resulted from his teaching, Thecla's resulted from remaining single and celibate. Paul's problem was the mind, Thecla's the body. No one in the story appeared to take issue with Paul's celibate lifestyle, or with Thecla's teaching on celibacy — though one can presume that Paul practiced celibacy and Thecla promoted it. Their silence suggests that social standards were not offended by a man practicing celibacy and a woman teaching Christian converts to consider celibacy as an option to marriage. The fact that Thecla's choice of the celibate life was offensive indicates the prevailing notion of woman as man's possession. A woman's refusal to succumb to a suitor was an affront and outright threat to the patriarchal structure. However, if a man decided to remain single and celibate, he did not offend anyone in particular, but perhaps disappointed his parents by denying them grandchildren or risked looking odd. Conversely, if a woman taught celibacy as a lifestyle, few would have given much credence to her teaching. If a man did, the word carried weight and constituted a threat to the system that had denied women the freedom of choosing a life apart from marital sub-jugation and servitude. Furthermore, the distinct causes of Paul's and Thecla's suffering on account of celibacy could also point to an under-lying stereotype about how the sexes communicate, including how they communicate their faith: Women communicate with their body, while men communicate with their mind. Thus, one could assume that the refusal of a woman to lend her body for male sexual satisfaction and childbearing constituted a greater affront than her preaching.

Acts of Barnabas

The *Acts of Barnabas* describe the parting of the ways between Paul and Barnabas. Paul had problems with Barnabas, so Paul has John, also named Mark, travel with Barnabas. John describes their missionary activity in various Greek cities. In Amathus, John and Barnabas found "a great multitude of Greeks in the temple in the mountain, low women and men pouring libations" (495). A certain man, named Barjesus, had already been ministering to the Jews in the city, and "did not allow us to enter." But "a certain widow woman, eighty years old, being outside the city, and she also not worshipping the idols," received them in her home and gave them an hour's reprieve. The pair then left the city by shaking the dust off their feet "over against that temple." Only the eighty-year-old widow had offered them hospitality, symbolizing perhaps that she alone was open to hearing the Gospel message, possibly on account of her life of widowhood and celibacy.

Acts of Philip

The *Acts of Philip* is subtitled, "Of the Journeying of Philip the Apostle." The book recounts Philip's missionary activity under Emperor Trajan in the cities and regions of Lydia and Asia, with his sister Mariamme, Bartholomew, and Philip's disciples. When they were in the city of Ophioryma at the house of the Christian Stachys, many men and women came to hear them preach. Mariamme sat in the doorway of the house urging passersby to listen to the apostles' teaching and herself delivered a sermon urging the people to turn from the worship of the serpent, which the residents of the city practiced, and toward the living God. On account of their preaching, many were converted and came to belief in Christ. In the meantime, a woman named Nicanora, the wife of the proconsul, came to faith in Christ — though not as part of Philip's ministry — and was healed of various diseases. Hearing that Philip had come to town, she went to the house of Stachys and was greeted at the door by Mariamme, who addressed her in Hebrew. This address prompted Nicanora to admit that she was of Hebrew ancestry herself and to profess her faith before the Christians gathered at the house, where they subsequently prayed for her and where she was healed. Soon thereafter, Nicanora's husband appeared at the house, "raging like an unbroken horse." He laid hold of Nicanora, questioning her sudden cure, and threatened to punish her unless she told which physician had healed her. Nicanora replied: "O tyrant, cast out from thee this tyranny of thine... run away from the brutality of thy worthless disposition; flee from the wicked dragon and his lusts" (498); and she exhorted him to "make for thyself a life chaste and pure, that being in holiness thou mayst be able to know my Physician, and to get His name." Then she gave him an ultimatum. If he wanted her to continue living with him, "prepare thyself to live in chastity and self-restraint, and in fear of the true God." When "the gloomy tyrant her husband heard these words of hers," he grasped her by the hair, kicked her, and threatened to kill her, accusing her of committing "fornication with these foreign magicians." Then he had Philip, Bartholomew, and Mariamme seized and ordered the public executioners to "torture these deceivers that have deceived many women, and young men and girls." Following their torture, they are locked up in the temple of the viper, where the priests, along with a crowd of "seven thousand men," accused them of being "corrupters and seducers of men" because the three desolated the temple, killed the sacred serpents, and recommended to "live in chastity and piety, after believing in God" (499).

The proconsul's rage was kindled even further when the priests told him of the temple's desecration and the sacred serpents' death. "Why need you speak," he said, "when they have bewitched my own wife?" For he remembered he had observed his wife in prayer and how a sudden lightning had come upon her, so that he was blinded and was now "afraid of my wife, on account of her luminous Jesus." Then the proconsul had the three stripped of their clothes to "try to find their enchantments." Mariamme was stripped also "that all may see her, how she follows men; for she especially deceives all the women." Then the proconsul ordered that the whole city be summoned "that they may see indecency, that she travels about with these magicians, and no doubt commits adultery with them." But when the spectacle was to begin, a cloud of fire covered her and they fled.

Into this commotion stepped John,[3] who had arrived in the city and pretended to be one of its residents. He gained access to the place where Philip, who had been captured, was hanging head down from his ankles and where Bartholomew, also captured, was stretched out on the wall of the temple. At the sight of their torture, John delivered a sermon condemning the people's viper worship and the unjust punishment of "these men because they have told you that the serpent is your enemy" (500). The people recognized that he was not one of theirs and demanded that he be killed along with the three others. Philip became enraged by the people's blindness and wanted to "destroy them all," but was reproved by John, Bartholomew, and Mariamme, who reminded him of Jesus' suffering and his command not to return evil for evil and to exercise patience. But Philip would not hear of it and demanded their punishment from the Lord, after which a sudden earthquake shook the place and swallowed up the proconsul, along with the crowd and the priests of the viper, with only their voices coming up from below, pleading to Christ for mercy. The apostles were saved, along with "Stachys and all his house, and the wife of the proconsul, and fifty other women who had believed with her upon the

Lord, and a multitude besides, both of men and women, and a hundred virgins who had not been swallowed up because of their chastity, having been sealed with the seal of Christ" (500–501).

The Lord appeared to Philip and reprimanded him for wishing evil upon his enemies and bringing about their destruction, and punished him to a forty-day exclusion from paradise on account of his unforgiving spirit. Then, the Lord marked a cross in the air and allowed those that had been swallowed up into the abyss to climb back out, except for the proconsul and the viper. When the people just emerging from the abyss saw Philip, still hanging face down, they lamented their lawless action and came to faith in Christ. Philip recognized his wrongdoing before the Lord and the crowds, and, refusing to be taken down so he might die there, gave them his final instructions. "I command you," he said, that after his death there be built a church in this place, where the leopard and the goat come in together, that Nicanora provide for the believers until they die, and that they be buried by the gate of the church. Also, that they appoint Stachys bishop, lay peace upon his house and have "all the virgins who believe stand in that house each day, watching over the sick, walking two and two; but let them have no communication with young men, that Satan may not tempt them" (502). And following Philip's death, they did what Philip had commanded, and "all the city believed in the name of Jesus."

A second manuscript recounts the same story with a few variations. The theme of sexual abstinence between a married couple is pronounced, and women appear to be demanding it of their husbands once they are converted to Christ. Nicanora demands continence of her husband if he wishes to remain with her (508). Her husband accuses the apostles of having deceived "many souls of women," presumably in regard to sexual abstinence in marriage. The crowd in the city reports to the newcomer John that "they have even persuaded our wives to go away from us on the pretense of religion." Also, during the earthquake that swallows up the city's inhabitants, "the twenty-four wives who fled from their husbands" (509) are spared, in addition to those named in the first manuscript. In his concluding speech, Philip warns both men and women about sexual lust, saying that those who "commit fornication of their eyes, shall abound like the deluge" (510). Because of the temptation of the eyes, the apostle Peter reportedly "fled from every place in which a woman was" and still was embroiled in a scandal concerning his own daughter.[4] Virgins (who could be both male and female) are to protect their ears so that the hearing "be holy," and are encouraged to walk about in twos so as to remain mutually accountable and able to protect themselves from "the wiles of the enemy." Yet another manuscript[5] warns both men and women against a false appearance of celibacy. For "many women and men shall leave the work of marriage, and the women shall assume the name of virginity, but knowing nothing at all about it, and that it has a great and glorious seal. And there shall be many men in those days in word only, and not in its power; for they shall observe virginity in the members of their flesh, and commit fornication in their hearts" (510).

In conclusion, the *Acts of Philip* and its related manuscripts show Philip, Bartholomew, and Mariamme teaching sexual abstinence in marriage after conversion to Christ. Their teaching seemed to be particularly appealing to women, mainly for two reasons. First, it gave women permission to gain autonomy over their own bodies — at least in theory. And second, it constituted a powerful witness of their faith in Christ — possibly more powerful than a mere verbal profession of faith. If their husbands disagreed with the stipulation of discontinuing sexual relations, the women were prepared to leave. It is unlikely that many men were able or willing to follow their wives' stipulations. This inability or unwillingness on the part of men was especially advantageous to women who were in abusive marriages, such as Nicanora's. We hear of at least twenty-four other wives "who fled from their husbands" (509). Strengthened by their Christian faith, these women were now able to leave their husbands for just cause — not their husband's brutality and physical abuse, but the husband's inability "to live in chastity and self-restraint" (498). Thus, a woman's faith in Christ could liberate her from spousal abuse, including sexual abuse and rape. On the surface, men continued to be in control of their spouses by being given the option to choose between sexual relations or companionship with their wives. But their control went only as far as they could control their own sexual drive. The story portrays women as being better than men at exercising sexual self-control and choosing a life of celibacy.

Otherwise, the ultimatum given their husbands would have had no pungency and could not have produced the vehement protests and death threats to those promoting marital continence and the women demanding it.

With the formulation of behavioral regulations for celibates, such as avoiding the company of the opposite sex, the individual's call or charism to the celibate life moves in the background. Still, this charism as a spiritual gift emerges when the writer of the *Acts of Philip* distinguishes between those who have the charism and those who do not. The latter may practice celibacy, but know "nothing at all about it"; they do not have celibacy's "great and glorious seal"[6] and continue to "commit fornication in their hearts."

Acts and Martyrdom of the Holy Apostle Andrew

The *Acts and Martyrdom of the Holy Apostle Andrew* contains the account of Andrew's Christian witness to the proconsul Aegeates[7] in the city of Patras in the province of Achaia. The account had been sent to all the churches by the presbyters and deacons of the churches of Achaia as an eyewitness description of Andrew's martyrdom. Upon assuming office, Aegeates forced Christian believers to worship idols and Andrew confronted him. Following a lengthy dispute with Andrew, Aegeates had him imprisoned. The next day, following Andrew's refusal to make restitution to the gods for drawing the people unto another faith, the proconsul subjected him to torture. Again, Aegeates asked Andrew to repent. Again, Andrew refused, whereupon Aegeates had him fastened to the cross. Apparently, Andrew was not pierced with nails so that he would not die too soon and would endure protracted torment.[8] After four days, thanks to the protest of the crowd of twenty thousand "of the brethren" and fellow believers, Andrew was to be taken down from the cross. Among the believers appeared Maximilla, the proconsul's wife. But when the proconsul, along with the executioners, approached the cross to release Andrew, Andrew cried out to the Lord to be allowed to die there. As a result, no one was able to touch Andrew, "for their arms were benumbed," so that he died hanging on the cross. Following Andrew's death, Maximilla went up to the cross. And even though she was "the most powerful of the notable women," she took "no heed at all of those standing by," and took down Andrew's body with reverence (515). In the evening, "she prepared the body for the burial with costly spices, and laid it in her own tomb." Prior to Andrew's death, Maximilla "had been parted from Aegeates on account of his brutal disposition and lawless conduct." She had chosen for herself a "holy and quiet life; and having been united to the love of Christ," she spent it in the company of "the brethren." In an effort to win his wife back, Aegeates had promised to make her "mistress of his wealth," but she had turned him down. Because of Maximilla's rejection, Aegeates then prepared to bring charges against her and the other believers in Caesar's court. But before he could do so, he died.

Maximilla had left her husband because of "his brutal disposition and lawless conduct." Her faith in Christ provided her with an alternative to living in an abusive marriage. Now, she could choose between a life of terror and brutality at the side of her husband, or a life of peace and quiet and pious living in the company of her fellow believers; she chose the latter. Even the prospect of sharing her husband's wealth, previously denied her, did not change her mind, for shared wealth and power paled in comparison to the peace she experienced in fellowship with other believers. Despite her husband's stubborn attempt to lure her back to him, Maximilla was not tempted. She chose a celibate life in the community of other believers over her life of marriage and sexual intercourse. With her decision, celibacy was now associated with the surrender of worldly goods.

Acts of Peter and Andrew

In the *Acts of Peter and Andrew*, Andrew had left "the city of the man-eaters,"[9] and was carried to a mountain where Peter, Matthew, and Alexander awaited him. Peter asked Andrew about his mission work in the city of the man-eaters, and Andrew reported great bodily suffering and being dragged "through the streets three days, so that my blood stained the whole street" (526). Peter then admonished Andrew to "be a man in the Lord" and to rest for a little while. Soon, Jesus appeared to them in form of a little child, ordering them to go into the city of the barbarians and to preach there. Andrew was not allowed to rest but for an hour and was encouraged by the example of "Father Peter" to cast seed "into the ground in the field of the righteous," so that people "may come to the light." As a result of the apostles' preaching, many of the people came to faith in Christ, and the apostles' activity was accompanied by many miracles of healing and exorcism.

The miracles attracted a certain rich man named Onesiphorus, who came to the apostles inquiring whether he could perform the same type of miracle if only he believed in their God. Andrew replied that he too would do miracles if only "thou wilt forsake all that belongs to thee, and thy wife and thy children, as we also have done" (527). This answers filled Onesiphorus with such rage that he attacked Andrew, accusing him of being a sorcerer and demanding to know how anyone could order him to "abandon my wife, and my children, and my goods." And turning to Peter, hoping for a more reasonable answer, he said: "I see that thou art more sensible than he. Do thou then tell me to leave my wife, and my children, and my goods. What dost thou say?" Peter replied that it was easier for a camel to go through the eye of a needle than for a rich man to go into the kingdom of heaven. This answer enraged Onesiphorus even more, so that he now attacked Peter, demanding to be shown how a camel could go through the eye of needle. If he, Onesiphorus, could be shown, he would believe in God and he would see to it that the whole city did too. But if he could not be shown, he would make sure that Peter was severely punished. Peter prayed to the Lord, who then appeared in the form of a twelve-year-old boy, and gave the disciples encouragement. A needle and a camel were brought, and the camel walked through the needle and back again. Onesiphorus was not convinced and procured his own needle, camel, and a "polluted woman" to sit on the camel. As before, the eye of the needle opened, and the camel, with the woman atop, walked through it and back again. Moved by the miraculous sight, Onesiphorus was willing to believe in Jesus Christ. Moreover, he was willing to give all his possessions to the poor, which included "corn lands, vineyards, fields, twenty-seven pounds of gold, fifty pounds of silver, and many slaves" (527), if only "I also may do one miracle like you." Peter was grieved by this response and wanted to decline the request since he saw that Onesiphorus "had not received the seal in Christ." But the Lord encouraged Peter to give in to his demand. Onesiphorus came up, stood before the camel and the needle, and began to speak. His speech, however, is lost. The manuscript ends at that point.

Despite the manuscript's abrupt ending, the story still speaks to the subject of celibacy. It says that the apostles had taken literally the Lord's command to "abandon wife, children, and goods." Luke records Jesus as saying that "there is no one who has left house or wife or brothers or parents or children for the sake of the kingdom of God, who will not get back very much more in this age" (Luke 18:29b–30). It appears that the apostles had left their wives, children, and possessions. In regard to their wives, this departure could mean two things: either that the apostles had left their wives and lived in permanent celibacy; or, they had left their wives for the period of their missionary activity, so that geographic distance did not permit the apostles to have sexual relations with their wives, hence forced them into temporary sexual abstinence. The story seems to indicate the first possibility, in which the apostles had forsaken their wives and lived celibate lives. This radical form of discipleship is what troubled Onesiphorus so greatly. In fact, he interprets the apostles' sacrifice of wife, children, and goods to be the source of their miraculous healings and exorcisms. While Onesiphorus is enraged at the high cost, he fervently longs for the apostles' powers, hence goes so far as to surrender his possessions to the poor. In this way, he thinks he can meet the apostles' demand of total self-surrender at least halfway. But because he holds back, Onesiphorus does not receive the other half, namely, "the seal in Christ." The story may imply that unless one is willing to surrender one's possessions *and* one's wife (and children), Christ will not grant the believer the full range of spiritual gifts and powers. But the story is also a comfort to those who may have come to faith in Christ for all the wrong reasons. While Onesiphorus was motivated by a desire for power when he submitted to worshiping Christ, the Lord continued to be in charge and would "accomplish for him what he desires" (527).

Another aspect of the story relates to the apostles' having left their children. In the context of Luke, leaving one's children was not an act of escaping from parental responsibilities. Instead, it was an act of sacrifice for the sake of the kingdom. The believers now placed lower priority on the benefits of having children than before. The tie with one's own children and grandchildren was superseded by one's spiritual tie with other believers and believers-to-be. The hope of continuing the male lineage and living on through one's children was replaced by the Christian's hope of living on through one's children in the faith, those "who come up, and come to the light" (526). The story touches upon the theme of children,[10] particularly when Jesus appears to the apostles not as an adult but as a child. Twice Jesus appears to them, and twice he appears "in the form of a child" (526–27).[11] In these appearances, Jesus retains his sovereign role as the Lord Jesus Christ, who commands the disciples, salutes them, and then returns "into the heavens in glory" (526). At the same time, he symbolically shows that the disciples' own children of flesh and blood are of secondary importance to the "child" Jesus Christ. As this child, Jesus Christ is the only begotten son and offspring of God the Father. As this child, Jesus is the firstborn of all those who are yet to become sons and daughters of God. And as this child, he reminds believers of their call to reproduce by making disciples and "to go into the city of the barbarians, and preach in it" (526). During both appearances, Jesus speaks words of encouragement to his followers while sending them on his behalf to the lost and those yet to be born into the family of God.

Acts and Martyrdom of St. Matthew the Apostle

In the *Acts and Martyrdom of St. Matthew the Apostle,* Matthew is found resting and praying on a mountain when Jesus appeared to him "in the likeness of the infants who sing in paradise" (528). Matthew was worried about what to offer Jesus, and the Lord told him that "good discourse is better than a calf, and words of meekness better than every herb of the field. . . . " For, after all, the Lord was paradise incarnate and did not need other powers added unto him. "I am the power of the powers above," he said, "I the strength of those that restrain themselves, I the crown of the virgins, I the self-control of the once married, I the boast of the widowed, I the defence of the infants, I the foundation of the Church, I the kingdom of the bishops, I the glory of the presbyters, I the praise of the deacons. Be a man, and be strong, Matthew, in these words."

Then Matthew is sent to Myrna, the city of the man-eaters, to testify to the Lord and bring about the conversion of the city's residents. Upon entering the city, Matthew met Fulvana, the wife of the king, and his son Fulvanus and his wife, Erva, who "were possessed by an unclean spirit" (529). Matthew exorcised the demon, and the people were made whole and came to faith in Christ. While the king rejoiced at first over what Matthew had done for his wife and son and daughter-in-law, he eventually became jealous because "they were inseparable from Matthew." His jealousy turned into "rage and anger," fueled by the exorcised demon, so that the king attempted to kill Matthew, but failed. Meanwhile, the exorcised demon transformed himself into a soldier, saying: "I am the demon who dwelt in thy wife, and in thy son, and in thy daughter-in-law; and my name is Asmodaeus; and this Matthew drove me out of them. And now, behold, thy wife, and thy son, and thy daughter-in-law sing along with him church" (531). After the demon predicted that the king too would end up coming to faith in Christ, the king adjured him to depart without harming anyone. For the king had resolved to "take Matthew by craft, that he might kill him," which he did by piercing his hands and feet with iron nails and setting his body aflame. When taken to burial, Matthew was seen leaving his deathbed, walking before or after it and singing along with the multitudes, so that the king and the crowds "were struck with astonishment." In the course of the procession, the dead rose and demoniacs were made well by touching the bed. Once the procession reached the palace, Matthew rose up and went into heaven, "led by the hand by a beautiful boy" and "the child crowned Matthew" and then the two disappeared into heaven (532). But the king had an iron coffin made, placed Matthew's body in it, sealed it, and had it thrown in the deep part of the sea. And after the brethren had prayed, sung hymns, and had the bishop Plato make an offering, Matthew appeared to Plato, standing on the waters of the sea, accompanied by "the beautiful boy." The king happened to see this apparition from the upper part of his house, came to faith in Christ as a result, and ran to the bishop for repentance and confession and asked to be sealed in Christ. After the bishop had examined the king, he baptized him. Thereafter, Matthew appeared again and renamed the king Matthew.

In the story, Jesus appeared as a child, reminding Matthew to be strong and steadfast. Jesus is identified as the strength of those who abstain from sexual relations, including the widowed, those who were once married and now practice celibacy, and virgins. This means that those who live in celibacy cannot do so on their own, but are enabled only by the strength and "the power of the powers above" (528). When Jesus exhorts Matthew to be strong, he is in effect asking him to rely on the power of Christ within, to recognize his own lack of power so as to be freed for empowerment by Christ. By contrast, the story shows the king as a man in power who is unable to restrain himself. After Matthew had exorcised the demon from the king's wife, his son, and his daughter-in-law and healed them through the power of Christ, the king's family became inseparable from the apostle and the king was driven to rage, the result of his powerlessness to do anything about his family's affection for Matthew. In his fury, the only way to regain power over his family appears to be murdering Matthew. His rage disregards the fact that the king's family had been healed. Their healing is not good news but bad news to the king because it has contributed to their independence and their freely associating with the apostle. His rage drives the king to kill Matthew. But once the bloody deed is committed, the king recognizes the horror of his murderous deed. In this state of weakness, the king is able to repent, confess, and come to faith in Christ. By admitting to his own inability to rid himself of the guilt of his bloody deed, he opens himself up to the power of Christ. Thus, the story illustrates that the power of the powerful is not sufficient to free them from their anger, rage, and guilt. Only when brought low in recognizing that their powers have failed them can they accept "the power of the powers above" and be set free. Infants are powerless by nature on account of their dependency on adults. But adults need to learn to become powerless again and to make themselves powerless by giving up what would contribute to their power and independence. Regarding celibacy, this means that adults place themselves in a weak position by renouncing marriage, the prospect of children, and the economic and social advantages of having a family. By subjecting themselves to this weak position, they thus invite the power of Christ into their lives. In this way, Christ becomes "the strength of those that restrain themselves," "the crown of the virgins," "the self-control of the once married," and "the boast of the widowed."

Acts of the Holy Apostle Thomas

In the *Acts of the Holy Apostle Thomas,* the apostles were gathered in Jerusalem and casting lots to determine who was to evangelize which part of the world. India fell to Judas Thomas,[12] also called Didymus. But Thomas did not want to go and began arguing with the Lord, who had appeared to him. Meanwhile, a merchant from India named Abbanes came on the scene. This man had been commissioned by king Gundaphoros of India to buy a carpenter. The Lord, in the form of a man, offered up Thomas for sale and the merchant agreed to the deal, and "the apostle held his peace" (535). They set sail for India and stopped on their way in the city of Andrapolis. In that city, the streets resounded with flute-players, water organs, and trumpets, since the king was celebrating the upcoming marriage of his only daughter and had invited both rich and poor, bond and free, strangers and citizens to the festival. In fact, anyone in the city was expected to be at the feast, so that both Abbanes and Thomas went also, so "that we may not offend the king."

Thomas did not eat or drink anything to demonstrate that he had come to the place "for something greater than food or even drink . . . even that I might accomplish the will of the King" (536). While still at the table, a Hebrew girl playing the flute stopped at his side, and Thomas sang a song of a bride and groom at the wedding feast (536).

Prior to the song at the table, a wine-pourer had struck Thomas, who told the wine-pourer in Hebrew that "I shall soon see that hand that struck me dragged along by a dog." After the song was finished and the flute-girl had stopped playing, a dog brought a hand to the place of the banquet. It was the hand of the wine-pourer who had been killed by a lion outside at a well, and whose body had been torn to pieces. The flute-girl then testified that she had heard Thomas predict in Hebrew what would happen to the wine-pourer, saying, "This man is either God or God's apostle" (537). The king, concerned about his daughter, ordered Thomas to pray for her. When Thomas refused, the king took him to her against his will. In the company of the grooms-men, Thomas prayed for both the bride and the groom "that Thou mayst make what happens and befalls them to be for their good." After everyone, including Thomas, had left, the groom raised the curtain to the bridal chamber "that he might bring the bride to himself." But when he did, he saw Thomas still sitting there and talking to the bride. But what appeared to be Thomas was the Lord, who identified him-self to the groom as Thomas's brother. Then "the Lord sat down on the bed" and ordered the bride and groom to sit down on the seats. And he told them to keep in mind "what my brother said to you, and to whom he commended you; and this know, that if you refrain from this filthy intercourse, you become temples holy *and* pure, being released from afflictions and troubles, known and unknown, and you will not be involved in the cares of life, and of children, whose end is destruction; but if you get many children, for their sakes you become grasping and avaricious, plundering orphans, coveting the property of widows, and by doing this you subject yourselves to most grievous pun-ishments." The Lord then detailed the problems children could be to parents. "For many children become unprofitable, being harassed by demons, some openly and others secretly." And even if they were in good health, "they will be again good-for-nothing, doing unprofitable and abominable works: for they will be detected either in adultery, or in murder, or in theft, or in fornication, and by all these you will be afflicted." Instead, the Lord encouraged the couple to "preserve your souls pure to God," for as a result "there will be born to you living chil-dren, whom these hurtful things do not touch; and you will be without care, spending an untroubled life, free from grief and care, looking for-ward to receive that marriage incorruptible and true; and you will be in it companions of the bridegroom, going in along with Him into that bridal-chamber full of immortality and light."

The couple yielded to the Lord's instructions, and instead of giving themselves over to "filthy lust," they "gave themselves over into His keeping." When the king and "the mother" of the bride arrived the next morning, they found the bride and groom sitting opposite each other. Because the bride's face was uncovered, the father asked whether it was "because of thy great love to thy husband." But his daughter replied that "I am in great love, and I pray to my Lord to continue to me the love which I have experienced this night, and I shall beg for myself this [H]usband whom I have experienced today" (538). She was uncovered because "the work of shame and bashfulness has been removed far from me" and "because I hold of no account this husband, and these nuptials that have passed away from before mine eyes, since I have been joined in a different marriage; and because I have had no intercourse with a temporary husband, whose end is with lewdness and bitterness of soul, since I have been united to a true Husband."

The groom then continued with a prayer of gratitude, saying: "I thank Thee, Lord, who hast been proclaimed by the stranger and found by us; who hast put corruption far from me, and hast sown life in me; who hast delivered me from this disease, hard to heal, and hard to cure, and abiding for ever, and established in me sound health; who hast shown Thyself to me, and hast revealed to me all that concerns me, in which I am." The king tore his garments and sent servants to get Thomas "the sorcerer, who has come for evil into this city." But they only found the flute-girl, who was crying because Thomas had left without taking her with him. Once she heard about the young people's story, she rejoiced and went to them and stayed at the palace "until they had instructed the king also." But Thomas sailed off to the cities of India, where the other "brethren" eventually joined him.

The story extols the virtue of surrendering bodily pleasures in favor of matters of the spirit and God. This is illustrated by Thomas sitting at the wedding banquet, but not partaking of the food and drink. He had not come to satisfy his bodily pleasures, but his spiritual ones, conversing about God and the spirit with the guests, sharing with them the message of Jesus Christ he had been sent to proclaim to the people of India.

While at the feast, Thomas sings a song about an eternal, heavenly wedding banquet. The bride and her attendants have fastened their eyes on the bridegroom that "through the sight of him they may be enlightened." And the guests, including the couple, feast on "ambrosial food" and "wine which brings to them no thirst." In this metaphor of the wedding feast, the body and the spirit are set in contrast. Feasting on the heavenly food and drink steeps the people into "everlasting joy" and "exultation." By implication, feasting on regular food does not.

The song indicates that the couple's joys do not result from the anticipated sexual pleasures connected with the marriage. In fact, they are able to resist the "desire of the flesh" because they have their eyes focused on the Lord. Joy comes from focusing on the Lord, not on sexual gratification. This principle is reiterated when the Lord appears to the bride and the groom in the bridal chamber and reminds the couple of "what my brother said to you" in song. The couple is to "refrain from this filthy intercourse" so as to "become temples holy *and* pure." Thus, sexual abstinence in marriage is viewed as laying the groundwork for leading a holy life.

Both in Thomas's song and Jesus' appearance to the young couple, body and spirit are set in contrast. The body longs for the gratification of the senses, such as regular food and drink and sexual pleasure. The spirit longs for the gratification of the spiritual urges, such as drawing close to "the father of trust" and "the mother of wisdom." The body's desires are considered inferior, the spirit's desires superior. Both desires cannot be met without compromise. Spiritual matters are related to God, bodily matters are not. Therefore, spiritual matters are of greater importance than physical matters, and the former are to be sought after, while the latter are to be kept in check. The gratification of bodily, including sexual, desires is viewed as an obstacle to one's spiritual development. Thus, a married couple is encouraged to abstain from sexual intercourse because their abstinence will enhance their spiritual quest and development. Furthermore, sexual abstinence functions as a form of birth control and spares the couple the troubles and time involved in caring for children. On account of their children, parents may become greedy and "grasping," hence be sidetracked from their service of the Lord. Even when children are grown, parents continue to carry their children's burdens and suffer from their children's misdeeds. The childless couple, by contrast, is able to focus on making disciples and having "born to you living children" in the faith. By focusing on the

Lord as the "bridegroom," the couple will live in a "bridal-chamber full of immortality and light."

The *Acts of the Holy Apostle Thomas* continue in a separate story that describes Thomas reaching the cities of India and building a palace in the heavens.[13] Thomas's companion, Abbanes, made contact with the king Gundaphoros and introduced Thomas as the carpenter who would build the king a palace. The king gave Thomas detailed instructions on the type of palace he wanted built, left him with provisions for the building, and then departed. But instead of building the palace, Thomas took the money and dispensed it to the poor and afflicted, saying: "The king knows how to obtain royal recompense, and it is necessary for the poor to have repose for the present" (539). When the king inquired about the building progress, Thomas replied that the palace was built and that only the roof remained to be done. Again the king sent provisions, this time in form of gold and silver, and Thomas, as before, dispensed them to the poor and orphans and widows. When the king returned to visit the construction, he found out from his friends that Thomas had built nothing, but had dispensed the king's money to the poor, teaching about "one new God," healing the diseased, and driving out demons. The friends suspected that Thomas was a magician, yet were amazed at his compassion, gentleness, and fidelity in his dealings with the poor and his curing people without taking money from them. The king called for Abbanes and Thomas. When asked by the king where the palace was, Thomas replied that the king could not see it while he was alive, but would "when thou hast departed this life" (539). Enraged by the answer, the king had both Abbanes and Thomas thrown in prison and decided to have both of them killed that night by flaying and fire.

The same night, the king's brother Gad fell ill, blaming Abbanes and Thomas for his illness and demanding their death in retribution. After the king assured Gad that he would kill the two men, Gad died and found himself in heaven. In the company of angels, he espied the edifice that Thomas had built for his brother. Gad liked the palace so much that he wanted to live in the underground chambers, but the angels told him he can't because he did not own it. Gad asked the angels to be brought back to life so he could purchase the palace from his brother, since his brother had no idea what it looked like. Gad was brought back to life, to the consternation of his brother and the multitudes, and proposed to his brother to purchase the palace in heaven. The king did not understand, but when Gad informed him that it was the palace built by Thomas, he "understood about the eternal benefits that were conferred upon him and destined for him" (540). The king released the apostle and Abbanes and asked Thomas's forgiveness "that I may be worthy to be an inhabitant of that house for which indeed I have laboured nothing." Gad, supplicating before God, asked to "become worthy of this ministry and service" and "those things which were shown me by the angels." Subsequently, Thomas anointed both the king and Gad that "through the oil they might receive the seal" in Christ. But the Lord was revealed to the two men only in voice but not in body, so that the apostle prayed once again, addressing the power of the Most High as "compassionate mother," as the one in "charge of the male child," as "mother of the seven houses that there may be rest for thee in the eighth." In response to Thomas's prayer, they were sealed, and "they rejoiced and exulted," so that "many others also believed, and were added, and came to the refuge of the Savior" (541).

Thomas then proclaimed to these new believers, both men and women, boys and girls, bondsmen and free to "withhold yourselves from fornication, and covetousness, and the service of the belly; for under these three heads all wickedness comes" (541). For "fornication maims the mind, and darkens the eyes of the soul, and becomes a hindrance of the due regulation of the body," changing the person "into feebleness, and throwing the whole body into disease." Such "insatiableness puts the soul into fear and shame, arising from the things of the body." In like manner, "the service of the belly throws the soul into cares and troubles and griefs." Since faith in Christ had set them free from these desires, "you are without care, and without grief, and without fear."

Three stories follow in which Thomas deals with the evil of sexual desire. In the first story, "About the Dragon and the Young Man," Thomas discovered the body of a young man by the road. After praying for the young man, a great dragon came out of his den, saying: "I shall say before thee for what cause I have put him to death, since thou art here in order to reprove my works" (542). The dragon reported that he had fallen in love with a beautiful young woman, but the dragon saw her kissing a young man who "also had intercourse with her, and did with her other shameful things." So the dragon killed the young man for his actions, and "especially as he had dared to do this on the Lord's day." When asked by Thomas to identify himself, the dragon said that, among other things, he is "he who cast down the angels from above, and bound them down by the desires of women, that earth-born children might be produced from them, and that I might work my will in them" (542). In response, Thomas reproved the dragon, commanding him to "be ashamed and altogether put to death; for the end of thy destruction is at hand" (543). Before the dragon was swallowed up in a great abyss, Thomas ordered him to draw the poison out of the body of the young man, so that he was brought back to life.

The young man asked the apostle for forgiveness of his sin and acknowledged his conversion in Jesus Christ. He recognized that "I am without care and reproach" and "I am at rest" (543). For he had "been released from him who exasperated me to do these things" and "have found that kinsman of mine who is like the light." The young man entreated Thomas to "make me again to behold and see Him, now become hidden from me, that I may also hear His voice." For perceiving God's voice is "not of the nature of this bodily organ." And Thomas exhorted him to "take no heed for your life, what ye shall eat, or what ye shall drink; nor for your body, what ye shall put on: because the life is more than food, and the body than clothing" (544). While Thomas spoke, a great multitude came "to the assembly of Christ" and wished "to believe Jesus" as well.

The second story, "About the Demon that Dwelt in the Woman," finds Thomas going to the parents of the young man who was brought back to life. On his way, "an exceedingly beautiful" woman implored the apostle to help her find relief from the torment of her adversary, "who has assailed me for now a period of five years" (545). For she recognized that the apostle proclaimed "the new God" who "heals the bodies of those that are punished by the enemy" (544). The woman then recounted how "one like a man troubled and disturbed" had approached her, saying: "Thou and I shall be in one love, and we shall have intercourse with each other, as a man is coupled with his wife" (545). The woman had replied that she did not even consent to having intercourse with her betrothed, to the point of "entreating him not to marry me." How could she allow herself to have intercourse with someone else "as it were in adultery"? But her objections did not deter the man, who "came that night, and made me share in his filthy commerce." For the next five years the woman fled from the man by day, but "he came at night and abused me." Her only hope was that Thomas's prayer would "drive away from me the demon that torments me, that I also may become free, and may be brought to my former nature."

Thomas addressed the demon by such names as "irrepressible wickedness," "shamelessness of the enemy," and "offspring of the crafty and insatiable one." The demon then appeared and pleaded for mercy from Thomas, asking, "Why doest thou wish to use tyranny against us, and especially thou who teachest others not to use tyranny?" But recognizing Thomas as a "servant of Jesus Christ," he reluctantly released the woman, his "most lovely yoke-fellow, whom I found long ago and was at rest." The demon would now "go to some place where the fame of this man has not been heard," but would return to the woman as soon as she departed from Thomas and his teachings of Christ. For "when he has gone away, thou shalt be as thou wast before he made his appearance, and him indeed wilt thou forget, and to me there will again be opportunity and boldness." Thomas prayed for those standing by that "they may be purified from their former deeds, and may put off the old man with his deeds, and put on the new now declared to them by me" (546). The woman begged Thomas to give her "the seal, that that foe may not come back upon me again." Many others were sealed along with her. And the woman and all those "who had received the seal" were given the bread of the Eucharist by Thomas which "shall be to thee for remission of sins, and the ransom of everlasting transgressions."

The third story, "About the Young Man Who Killed the Maiden," begins with Thomas celebrating the Eucharist. Only those who had previously received the seal in Christ partook of the bread. Among the believers was a young man unable to receive the Eucharist because "his two hands immediately withered, so that he could no longer bring them to his mouth" (546). Approached by Thomas, the man confessed to having murdered his lover. Upon receiving the seal in Christ, the man had insisted on sexual abstinence with her, but she had refused "to live with me in chaste and pure intercourse." The apostle then decried this "maddening intercourse" and "the unrestrained lust" leading into "shamelessness," and he ordered the man to wash his hands in the waters that Thomas had blessed, and they were restored.

Then Thomas and the young man went to the inn where he had killed the woman. Thomas ordered the body of the woman to be set in the courtyard, and with laying on of hands prayed for the woman to be brought back to life. Then he "sealed the young man" and ordered him to take her hand and to pray for her as well. When the man did, imploring the Lord to "come to my help" and professing faith in Christ, the young woman sprang up. Immediately, she acknowledged to Thomas that it had been Christ, "that other who is with thee," who had spared her and brought her back to life and was now asking her to "be made perfect" through Thomas's teachings. Then she told of "that fearful and grievous place" from which she had just escaped. A man in filthy clothing had received her and shown her many chasms that emanated "a great stench and most hateful odour" (547). The man made her bend into each chasm, so that she could see there wheels of fire and souls hung upon these wheels that were dashing against each other. The man explained that these souls were from the woman's own nation and were being punished for a certain number of days, until others were brought in to replace them, for having "exchanged the intercourse of man and wife" (548). In another chasm, the woman saw "infants heaped upon each other, and struggling and lying upon each other," who were the punished souls' infants that had been "placed here for a testimony against them." In still another chasm, full of mud and worms, were found "the souls of women that left their own husbands, and went and committed adultery with others, and who have been brought to this torment." In yet another, souls were hung either by their tongue, hair, hands, or feet. The souls hung up by their tongue were those who had uttered "false and disgraceful words"; those hung up by their hair "are those that are shameless"; those hung by the hands were those who had stolen or had never given anything to the poor nor assisted the afflicted; and those hung up by the feet were those "who lightly and eagerly ran in wicked ways, and disorderly wickedness, not looking after the sick, and not aiding those departing this life."

Thomas then addressed the crowd, saying that since they had heard what the woman described, they had better "turn to this God whom I proclaim, and refrain from your former works and deeds which you have done without knowledge" so as not to end up like those she saw in death. He exhorted them to place their faith in "our Lord Jesus Christ, and He will forgive you the sins done by you heretofore, and will purify you from all the bodily desires that abide in the earth, and will heal you from the faults that follow after you, and go along with you, and are found before you."

As a result of Thomas's speech, the people believed and presented their souls to the living God and Christ Jesus. They also brought much money for the service of the widows. The people carried to Thomas those who were sick or tormented by unclean spirits, and they were healed. In gratitude, the people gave thanks to God. Thomas praised God, interceding on their behalf to be perfected by God. They had left their homes for the Lord's sake and become strangers; they had "abandoned our possessions, that we may have Thee for a possession that shall not be taken away"; they had left those "related to us by ties of kindred, in order that we may be united in relationship to Thee"; they had "left our fathers and mothers, and those that nourished us, that we may behold Thy Father, and be satisfied with His divine nourishment"; and they had left their "bodily yoke-fellows, and our earthly fruit, in order that we may share in that intercourse which is lasting and true, and bring forth true fruits, whose nature is from above, the enjoyment of which no one can take away from us" (549).

The metaphor of the palace in the second part of the *Acts of the Holy Apostle Thomas* serves to illustrate two realities: the reality of this life, and that of the next. The reality of the next life matters more because it is eternal, not temporary. The quality of the afterlife is proportionate to one's compassion and generosity toward the poor and needy in this life. But the degree of compassion one is able to demonstrate depends on the amount of troubles one has to deal with; the fewer personal troubles, the more time one has to devote to good works. In these stories, personal troubles come from "fornication, and covetousness, and the service of the belly," from satisfying one's sexual desires outside marriage, greed for possessions, and self-indulgence. They constitute a distraction from service to God. By faith in Jesus Christ, Thomas tells us, we are able to refrain from the urge to satisfy the desires of the body.

Believers will receive help in overcoming "the three heads" from which "all wickedness comes" by the power of the Most High. This power can be identified with the Holy Spirit, who is personified as "perfect compassion." The imagery describing the power of the Holy Spirit is predominantly female. The Holy Spirit is compared with a compassionate mother, one who tends to the male child, one who already indwells seven houses but seeks to make her dwelling in one more house — or in one more believer. Like a compassionate mother, the Holy Spirit will "purify their reins and hearts" and allow believers to be steeped in God's love and care, so that they can resist the temptations of the body and heart. The Holy Spirit will instill in them intelligence, thought, purpose, reflection, and reasoning, so as to help them resist these bodily and selfish urges, while enveloping them in her motherly care and concern.

The story about the dragon and the young man illustrates the dangers of fornication, or intercourse outside marriage, dangers that lurk not within them, but in the dark recesses beyond those who engage in illicit sexual intercourse. Both man and, indirectly, woman are punished for their misdeed. But the power of Jesus Christ is able to slay the dragon, forgive the man, and bring release from "him who exasperated me to do these things." In fact, the power of Christ unfolding in the believer allows for a new view of reality, one in which the concerns of the body move into the background, and which offers a state of carefree living and rest.

The dragon lives outside the person's body and is allowed to reign only when invited. The invitation comes with the act of engaging in illicit sexual intercourse. The dragon cannot reign against the will of the person. In the believer, this will is informed and enforced by the power of Jesus Christ. Once the believer has repented, forgiveness comes and the dragon is expelled. Thus, the person is viewed as inherently good and clean and equipped to withstand sexual immorality. Moreover, the believer is equipped to withstand "the desires of women" and the resulting birth of "earth-born children." While such language appears to blame women for men's weakness in reining in their sexual urges, it also serves to identify the audience, which appears to be men, not women — in particular, single men who are tempted to engage in sexual intercourse outside marriage. This could mean either that women had fewer difficulties in maintaining a celibate lifestyle, or that they had little or no say in initiating sexual intercourse.

The story about the demon dwelling within a woman describes a woman who has neither the freedom to refuse him, nor the power to keep him at bay. The sexual act on her part is the result of the same force, which wields its power both inside and outside of her. The woman is completely under the demon's spell; she has no control over her body, despite her desire to live a celibate life. Only through the power of Jesus Christ is the woman delivered from her internal and external oppressor. But the demon threatens to return and take possession of her again. She appears to have no power over her body, except by keeping her mind focused on Christ. Unlike the previous story, in which the young man is free to engage or disengage from sex, the woman has no choice. Her only protection is a wholehearted and all-encompassing devotion to Christ. Moreover, her fear of the demon's return — that is, her victimization as an object of sexual abuse, and her free will being relegated to utter passivity — drive her to seek protection. Not for reasons of spiritual edification or religious conviction, but for personal protection and in self-defense does she ask Thomas to be sealed in Christ by the laying on of hands. To Thomas, faith in Christ serves different functions for men and women. While for men it is a way of controlling their own moral behavior in matters of sexual conduct, for women it is a way of preserving personal safety and ensuring survival amidst the pervasive powers that reign both without and within. For men controlling their sexual behavior is an option; for women it is a necessity for safety and survival. For men sexual misconduct happens only when their own behavior prompts and invites an evil outside force, i.e., the dragon. For women sexual misconduct can happen anytime, even and especially against their will. The imminent threat to a woman's safety and will by external forces makes women more likely to seek refuge and protection through their connectedness with and faith in Christ.

In the third story, the young man, enraged by his own failure to renounce sexual intercourse and be faithful to his commitment to Christ, kills his lover. The significant difference between the two is that the man is a Christian and the woman is not. The man had been sealed in Christ, hence received the power to stem his sexual impulse to engage in intercourse; the woman had not. The dead woman was allowed to view the torment of those who had committed grievous sins. She saw the punishment for those who had had intercourse and for the off-spring of their sexual immorality. Based on the context and in light of the previous two stories, which are concerned with the sin of "fornication," it appears that these men and women were unmarried and were being punished for having had intercourse outside marriage.

Thomas's emphasis is on the believers' ability to refrain from acting upon "bodily desires that abide in the earth," that encompass sexuality, speech, property, and family ties. By Christ's power, these desires can be transformed from concern for self to concern for others. Speech can be transformed from "false and disgraceful words" to words that proclaim the truth and the word of God and leads others into recognizing Christ as Lord. The craving for property can be transformed into surrendering one's property for "the service of the widows" and the poor, the afflicted, and the sick. The craving for family ties can be transformed into the craving to "behold Thy Father, and be satisfied with His divine nourishment." And the craving for a mate and children can be transformed into "that intercourse which is lasting and true" and, instead of producing children in the flesh, can "bring forth true fruits, whose nature is from above" and whose "enjoyment" "no one can take away." Failure to allow for the transformation of bodily desires into those promoting Christ's reign is interpreted not as an inability, but as disobedience, a severe affront that robs others of hearing the message of Christ and enjoying its ultimately liberating and healing effects.

All three of Thomas's stories address single young people who engage in sexual intercourse. Sexual intercourse is blamed for the troubles that befall young people and they are discouraged from engaging in it. By implication, young people are urged to refrain from sexual activity as a whole because it might stimulate the desire to enter into marriage and have children. The assumption is that people marry because of sexual desire, but, to Thomas, being married and having children interfere with the cultivation of a spiritual marriage with Christ and the producing of children in the Lord. The message of Thomas and his fellow believers is to remain single, abstain from sexual activity, and practice celibacy.

Consummation of Thomas the Apostle

The *Consummation of Thomas the Apostle* describes Thomas's martyrdom at the hands of Misdeus, king of India. Juzanes, the king's son, Tertia, his mother, along with Mygdonia, the wife of the king's friend, Charisius, and Markia, had become believers (550). The group was very distressed over Thomas's imprisonment, and bribed the prison guard with "much money" to gain entrance to him. Only the women returned the next night and were allowed to "communicate in the Eucharist," were "confirmed" by him in the faith, and then commended to the Lord. Following Thomas's death and burial, "Misdeus and Charisius greatly afflicted Tertia and Mygdonia, but did not persuade them to abandon their opinions" (551). Thomas appeared to Tertia and Mygdonia, encouraging them not to forget the former things, "for the holy and sanctifying Jesus Himself will aid you." After that Misdeus and Charisius let up on their wives and "granted them their own will" (552).

The *Consummation* does not overtly address the topic of sexuality and celibacy, but it shows the appeal of the Christian message to women and the ensuing division between these women and their husbands. Tertia and Mygdonia maintain their "opinions" and profess their faith in Christ, even when their husbands, Misdeus and Charisius, threaten and abuse them in order to force the women into renouncing it. The violence that these women endure at the hands of their husbands is a direct result of their newfound independence in Christ. In this way, the Christian faith liberated these women into an identity separate from their marital status, and may have led to the couples' separation. The women found refuge in the community of faith, which served as their shelter and place of mutual support. The faith community freed these women from having to grant sexual favors to their husbands and allowed them to gain sexual independence through a life of sexual abstinence and celibacy.

Martyrdom of the Holy and Glorious Apostle Bartholomew

The *Martyrdom of the Holy and Glorious Apostle Bartholomew* describes Bartholomew's missionary activity in India, where he had taken up quarters in the temple of Astaruth. As the people came to the temple to pray for healing, Bartholomew was able to proclaim his God and to exorcise demons, including one that had possessed the daughter of King Polymius. In gratitude, the king loaded "camels with gold and silver, precious stones, pearls, and clothing" (554) to take to Bartholomew, but could not find him and returned to his palace. The next morning, Bartholomew appeared to the king in his bedchamber and told him that "these gifts those persons long for who seek earthly things; but I seek nothing earthly, nothing carnal." Instead, he longed to teach the king about his God and the Son of God, who "was born as a man out of a virgin's womb." Bartholomew paralleled Jesus' birth to Adam's — Jesus was born of a virgin and Adam was born of the virgin earth, which had neither been polluted by the blood of man nor opened for the burial of anyone. The virgin Mary "did not know man, so she, preserving her virginity, vowed a vow to the Lord God." She was "the first among women" to do so, saying, "I offer to Thee, O Lord, my virginity" that "she might remain a virgin through the love of God, pure and undefiled" and give birth to the Son of God by "the power of the Most High [that] shall overshadow thee." After the Son of God had been born of her and had been baptized, he was tempted by the devil during his forty-day fast, but resisted, saying, "Not on bread alone shall man live, but by every word of God." In this way, "the devil, who through eating had conquered the first man, was conquered through the fasting of the second man; and as he through want of self-restraint had conquered the first man, the son of the virgin earth, so we shall conquer through the fasting of the second Adam, the Son of the Virgin Mary." While the devil had power over the first Adam, he was "thrice conquered by Christ, the Son of the Virgin Mary" (555) when three times Jesus resisted the devil's temptation.

Bartholomew explained to the king that the devil continued to reign, especially in the temple. Here, "the devil himself by his own art causes the men to be sick, and again to be healed, in order that they may the more believe in the idols." In a demonstration before the king, Bartholomew confronted the devil living in the temple, drove him into an idol, and out into a desert place, so that the "same hour all the idols that were in that place were broken to pieces" (556). As a result, "the king, and also the queen, with their two sons, and with all his people, and with all the multitude of the city, and every city round about, and country, and whatever land his kingdom ruled over, were saved, and believed, and were baptized in the name of the Father, and the Son, and Holy Spirit." But when the king had "laid aside his diadem, and followed Bartholomew," the king's brother Astreges captured Bartholomew. In a contest over whose God was the true one, Astreges's idols were all broken in pieces, so that Astreges had Bartholomew beaten with rods, scourged, and then beheaded.

The powers of the devil are contrasted in this story with the superior powers of Christ. The devil was able to overpower humans because they would not restrain their carnal appetite, but he was unable to overpower Jesus because he would restrain it. Adam ate of the forbidden fruit, while Jesus did not. Adam satisfied his bodily pleasures by eating the fruit, Jesus refrained from satisfying his bodily pleasures by giving priority to the word of God. Adam lost out to the devil at the first temptation, Jesus prevailed over the devil on three occasions of temptation. Because Jesus was able to resist the devil, believers are empowered to do the same. They are no longer helpless victims exposed to the seductions of the body, but can control themselves through the power of Christ that dwells in them. This story marks the only instance in the Apocryphal Acts in which virginity is linked with Mary, the mother of Jesus. Mary is portrayed as the first woman to have offered up her virginity to God. Through her act of prayerful self-surrender and her abstention from sexual intercourse, God is able to bring forth his Son, Jesus Christ. Her virginity parallels that of the earth prior to the Fall, linking virginity to sinlessness, holiness, and sanctity. Believers are to lead a sinless and holy life, and are encouraged to follow Mary's example. When women and men emulate Mary by preserving their virginity and practicing a life of celibacy, they can become that holy womb that gives birth to sons and daughters of God through "the Son of the Virgin Mary."

Acts of the Holy Apostle and Evangelist John the Theologian

The *Acts of the Holy Apostle and Evangelist John the Theologian* constitutes the last book in the collection, and concerns John's exile and departure. It records the destruction of the temple in Jerusalem by Vespasian, who was succeeded as emperor of Rome by his son Domitian. Domitian had received a letter sent to him by Jews complaining about "a new and strange nation, neither agreeing with other nations nor consenting to the religious observances of the Jews" and "proclaiming a man as God, all assembling together under a strange name, that of Christians" (560). This letter prompted Domitian to issue a decree to "put to death all who confessed themselves to be Christians." Soon Domitian heard about a Hebrew in Ephesus named John, who was teaching that the Roman Empire "would quickly be rooted out, and that the kingdom of the Romans would be given over to another." He had John captured and brought to him for questioning. John confirmed to Domitian his teaching of a new king "through whom every earthly power and dominion shall be brought to nothing" (561). But the king became convinced of John's innocence and the benefits of his religion: he had seen John drink a poisonous potion and not be affected by it, and he had seen John bring back to life a prisoner who had drunk the same potion, and a servant woman of the court who had been struck dead by an evil spirit. So as not to violate his own decree, the king ordered John banished to the island of Patmos.

After Domitian's death, Nerva succeeded to the kingdom and, after a year, appointed Trajan, who in turn "recalled all who had been banished" (562). John returned to Ephesus, reminding the believers there "of what the Lord had said to them, and what duty he had assigned to each." After he made Polycarp bishop over the church, John cele-brated the Eucharist with the believers and had a trench dug for his resting place. He prays to the Lord, imploring him to "receive also the soul of Thy John, which has been certainly deemed worthy by Thee, Thou who hast preserved me also till the present hour pure to Thy-self, and free from intercourse with women" (563). John then recounts three times when he was tempted to marry. "When I wished in my youth to marry," the Lord appeared to him, saying, "I am in need of thee, John." A second time, the Lord strengthened him in his "bodily weakness" beforehand, and "when a third time I wished to marry, didst say to me at the third hour, in the sea, John, if thou wert not mine, I would let thee marry." In this way, the Lord "opened up the sight of my mind" and called "even the gazing upon a woman hateful" so as to "deliver me from temporary show, and preserve me for that which endureth for ever." Because of the Lord's presence, John was allowed to separate "from the filthy madness of the flesh," cutting out "its open actions," and afflicting and banishing "him who rebelled in me." After John finished praying, he sent the believers away. In the morning, they found only John's sandals and a fountain welling up beside them.

This account contains an intimate glimpse into the apostle and evan-gelist's struggle with celibacy. The Lord's presence allows John to see beyond the temporal to the eternal and far-reaching aspect of his ser-vice, so that John can banish his temptation. It is not John himself, but Christ within him, that equips him to resist the sexual desires of his bodily nature.

Conclusion

This chapter has examined the books of the Apocryphal Acts of the Apostles as gathered in the Ante-Nicene Fathers of Volume 8. Of the thirteen books in the volume, ten explicitly address celibacy or sexual abstinence in marriage, and another, the *Consummation of Thomas the Apostle*, mentions the physical abuse of women believers by their hus-bands on account of the women's faith in Christ. The *Acts of Andrew and Matthias* and the *Acts of the Holy Apostle Thaddaeus* make no reference to either celibacy or sexual abstinence. Ten books encourage Christian believers to live a life of celibacy or, if they are married, to refrain from sexual intercourse so as to better serve Christ. Four of these books encourage women who have come to faith in Christ to leave their abusive husbands;[14] four exhort young men and women to choose a life of celibacy over against marriage;[15] and three highlight the troubles associated with having children and encourage believers to "adopt" Christ as their child and to bring forth spiritual offspring.[16]

A recurring theme in these writings is the encouragement of believers to surrender possessions and kinships for the kingdom's sake. Two passages from the Gospel of Luke appear to inform this theme: Luke 18:29b–30, as we have seen, in which Jesus tells the disciples that "there is no one who has left house or wife or brothers or parents or children, for the sake of the kingdom of God, who will not get back very much more in this age, and in the age to come"; and Luke 14:26, where Jesus says in blunt language that "whoever comes to me and does not hate father and mother, wife and children, brothers and sisters, yes, and even life itself, cannot be my disciple."

Another theme contrasts the desires of the body to the desires of the spirit, the temporal against the eternal, the selfish versus the self-giving. This theme is characterized by Matthew 6:25, where Jesus exhorts his disciples not to be concerned about one's body, what to eat and drink and wear since life is "more than food, and the body more than clothing." Instead, believers are to consider "the upper world, about God and angels, about ambrosial food, about garments that last and become not old, about those things which eye hath not seen, nor ear heard" (544).[17] A related theme is the interdependency of body and spirit — what the person does with his or her body in this world will have an effect upon life in the next.

The writings portray those who practice the celibate life as heroes and heroines. There are many virgins, both male and female, widows, wives who have left their husbands, and celibate men and women who remain on the sidelines, others who figure prominently in the stories. Among the prominent figures are the apostles themselves, Thecla, and Mary, the mother of Jesus. Some of them are not only celibate but have deliberately preserved their virginity. In this virginal state, they have been able to give birth to Christ, either literally or through their proclamation, ministry, and missionary activity or through both. The correlation between celibacy and "birthing Christ" could explain why the writings contain numerous appearances of Christ as a child or young boy, who as such is still awaiting to be born in the heart of the nonbeliever. It should be noted that Jesus' own celibacy is never mentioned; he functions as a role model in this regard only in relation to his ability to resist the devil's temptation in the wilderness to place the carnal above the spiritual.

The ability to live a life of celibacy frequently is granted after the believer has received the seal in Christ, either by baptism (Thecla) or the laying on of hands or the anointing with oil. This seal is usually administered by the apostle or bishop. It appears to unleash the spiritual gift or charism of celibacy and serves as a protection from sexual temptation, while celibacy still requires cooperation and obedience on the believer's part. Much like faith, celibacy presupposes both the grace gift from God and willingness on the part of the believer (Matt. 19:11–12). Celibacy never stands on its own, but is intimately linked with Christ and an ongoing, deepening conversion experience.

Celibacy is recommended for the kind of quality of life it affords those who practice it. They will be free of cares and out of this freedom they can single-mindedly devote themselves to serving Christ and the poor and needy. At the same time, in a turn of irony, celibates are more likely to suffer on account of their faith by being persecuted, tortured, and killed. While their life may be spiritually peaceful and untroubled and unattached, they invite the troubles that come with following Christ when telling the truth, and confronting the injustices and abuses committed by those in positions of power.

Celibacy is of particular significance to women. It frees them from the pain of childbirth and the social and economic responsibilities of childrearing, along with the protracted caregiving that mothers assume throughout the adult child's life. Moreover, women are offered an alternative to the role of wife. They can refuse to conform to the patriarchal family system and its oppressive structures by remaining single. As single believers they have the opportunity to join the community of faith that then serves as their socializing and stabilizing force. They may move in with a widow convert, as Thecla does, or a group of widows; or they may live with local Christian converts, or choose to stay with their parents. Communal living offers an option to life with a husband. Women who have come to faith in Christ can choose between the economic advantages that marriage affords while compromising their faith convictions or live in relatively modest circumstances with like-minded believers while growing in faith and engaging their spiritual gifts. The option of celibacy as a liberating lifestyle is particularly evident in the case of women, such as Nicanora and Maximilla, who are in abusive marriages. Women believers are shown as demanding sexual abstinence of their husbands on account of their faith and to further their spiritual union with Christ. This demand may also serve to ward off other physical and verbal abuse by the husband and protect the woman's body as well as her integrity. If the husband is unwilling to abide by the woman's demand, she is resolved to leave, with the faith community receiving her into a safe haven and shelter from abuse. A woman's renunciation of sexual relations with her husband is shown in these books to offer her safety of body, dignity, and protection. Although the writings reflect that the offices of bishop and deacon are reserved for males, celibate women can enjoy a greater freedom in the exercise of their gifts than they might have in the context of marriage, unless the husband is a believer as well. Their fulfillment derives not from their social, domestic, maternal, and sexual responsibilities of marriage, but from their social and spiritual obligations to the faith community and their service and ministry to the community at large.

Through their life of celibacy as members of the faith community, women need not dress and adorn their bodies and groom their hair so as to attract suitors or to please their mates. They need not fret over their physical appearance and sexual appeal. Because of their celibacy, women can now relate to men in a new way. Men are no longer regarded as potential sexual partners or candidates for marriage, but can be seen as friend, brother, and co-worker in Christ. This new perspective lays the groundwork for women to interact with men without shame or secondary motives. Moreover, they are free to acknowledge and own their sexual desires and longings without being compelled to act on them. A woman's self-restraint in sexual matters in the here and now becomes a venue for greater autonomy and independence at a later point. This independence is requisite to a woman's exercise of her spiritual gifts, her freedom to minister in various distinct geographical locations, and the unfolding of her ministry and service to Christ.

Chapter 4

Early Theological Perspectives on Celibacy: The Church Fathers

Narrative and Reality

The Apocryphal Acts of the Apostles were written in the second and third centuries. Although these narratives may not detail the social-historical realities of life in the early church, the social concerns and conflicts underlying these stories were real. J. L. Fischer, in exploring the ways in which folk story reflects the historical situation of its tellers and audience, concludes that the folk story tends to concentrate on difficult social transitions and relationships that have become a subject of considerable conflict in that society.[1] In reviewing the particular nature of these so-called folk stories and legends and contrasting them with myths, Virginia Burrus says that the Apocryphal Acts of the Apostles were written by women for women and are witnesses of their own personal experiences in the Greco-Roman world. Some of these women found their roles as women and wives limiting and unsatisfying, and came into conflict with the social and political institutions that enforced their roles. Some of these women were inspired by Christian teaching to renounce marriage, not as a form of self-denial but as a venue to freedom. Some may have lived together in Christian communities. As a whole, they felt themselves united with Christ in a liberating relationship which surpassed and excluded their previous familial and marital relationships.[2]

Stevan L. Davies concurs that the Apocryphal Acts are the work of women, particularly celibate women, who lived in Christian communities. These communities were served not by the formal male hierarchy of the church and "virgin" men, but by women themselves. He believes the Apocryphal Acts stemmed from a period of transition, in which the charismatic leadership of the apostles and that of women was waning, and leadership was becoming more institutionalized and patriarchal. As the opportunities for female leadership in the whole church declined, female-directed communities came into being, with many of their leaders from the wealthier ranks of the Greco-Roman world.[3] Peter Brown would agree with both Burrus and Davies on the social conditions surrounding the writings of the Apocryphal Acts, but disagrees on their authorship. The Apocryphal Acts were likely to have been written by men, he says, because the stories "reflect the manner in which Christian males of that period partook in the deeply ingrained tendency of all men in the ancient world, to use women 'to think with.' " In other words, men then told these stories of celibate women to verbalize their own nagging concerns with the stance that the church should take to the world.[4] This world was represented by a Roman government, for example, which penalized the unmarried and childless for the first three centuries of the Christian era, as well as widows or divorced women who failed to remarry within two years. By A.D. 200, however, the Church had been actively encouraging both women and men to practice sexual abstinence both within and apart from marriage and had begun attaching less merit to motherhood.[5] Along with increasing numbers of men and women remaining single and celibate, the order of widows had sprung up in various Christian communities. These widows, along with some widowers,[6] included not only the old, poor, and needy who were left without family ties or a source of income following the death of their spouse, but many younger, educated, and wealthy members, who may have joined the order with the prospect of spending the rest of their lives in the service of the church.

The ideas about use of the body among Christians stood in clear contrast not only to the Roman government, but also to Judaism and its high praise of marriage. While the rabbis were aware of the radical asceticism of more recent movements in Judaism, they firmly maintained that the continuity and survival of Israel rested upon marriage. They felt it was better that all people abstained from sexual intercourse for some time than for some people to abstain all the time.[7] What the Christian faith proposed appeared to them as crass, drastic, and disruptive of the social and religious order. According to Brown, prominent Christian men and women began using "their bodies to mock continuity through the drastic gesture of perpetual chastity," thereby announcing the imminent approach of a "new creation."[8] The new view of the body also stood in contrast to Gnosticism. In his study on the early church, Henry Chadwick says that the common theme underlying the various sects of Gnosticism is their negative view of creation as something entirely alien to God and goodness. This view took on one of two forms in ethical practice: either that the sect demanded an ascetic life with rules for the mortification of the flesh and a prohibition of marriage; or that they disregarded the natural order altogether and freely gorged their senses and bodily appetites in orgies of immorality.[9] In his study on primitive Christianity, Rudolf Bultmann traces the influence of the Old Testament, Jewish, Hellenistic, and Gnostic ideas upon early Christian thought. He admits that the practical behavior of the church and its members resembled that of Gnosticism in that it rested upon a sense of superiority over the world, in an awareness that "neither death, nor life, nor angels, nor principalities, nor powers . . . shall be able to separate us from the love of God, which is in Jesus Christ" (Rom. 8:38–39). This absolute independence from the world, however, did not produce the individualistic, licentious type of mysticism of the Gnostics, but remained grounded in community and the body of Christ. While Paul, for example, allowed for marriage as a "necessary evil" and regarded celibacy as a special charism, he opposed the legalistic asceticism advocated by Gnosticism in favor of "a dialectic of participation and inward detachment," which fully embraced and participated in life.[10] Gnostics described the unworldly, higher self as a negating of the body and creation, while early Christians regarded this new inner being in Christ as the ability to love and participate in the fullness of creation without being ruled by it.

From an early period in some circles, and universally by around A.D. 300, the ideal of celibacy in Christianity among both men and women enjoyed a moral and cultural supremacy that remained unchanged until the Reformation.[11] While this ideal of celibacy was advocated by the Apostle Paul and promoted and advanced in the narratives about the heroes and heroines of the Apocryphal Acts, it emerges in doctrinal form in connection with the Scriptures of the Old and New Testaments through the teachers of the early church, the Church Fathers.

The sheer volume and breadth of the Church Fathers' writings on virginity, chastity, celibacy, widowhood, and marriage is impressive and suggests that the practice of continence among Christians, within and apart from marriage, had become more than the fancy of a few. We will examine the Church Fathers' arguments and usage of the Scriptures in promoting celibacy, particularly among women; the arguments they employed to justify marriage and having children; their views on celibacy as a gift from God given only to a few; and the advantages of the celibate life in relation to faithful discipleship in Christ.

Several underlying assumptions informed how the Church Fathers interpreted the Scriptures and need to be kept in mind when examining their commentary on the Scriptures regarding celibacy. Sandra M. Schneiders sums up the assumptions of the patristic and medieval periods in her discussion on Scripture and spirituality. First, the early church assumed that the Scriptures were inspired by God and pregnant with divine revelation, so that the interpreter required divine assistance in grasping their meaning. Only the believer, working from within the Christian community, could rightly interpret the biblical texts. This view led Origen, for example, the early church's greatest biblical scholar, to insist that the students at his catechetical school in Alexandria lead a quasi-monastic life that would strengthen the purity of their consciences and the intensity of their prayer life. Second, Jesus himself was the hermeneutical principle, both as the fulfillment of the Old Testament and by his own interpretation of the Scriptures during his lifetime. Third, biblical interpretation was not only dependent upon the faithful prayer and contemplation of the exegete, but also required scholarly integrity and an obligation to the tradition of the church. Throughout the work of study and exposition of Scripture, the task of the exegete was not to sever the New Testament from the Old, but to show the continuity between the two, with the New figuring as the fulfillment of the Old.[12]

The exploration of the Church Fathers' views on celibacy will concentrate on a selection of moral writings from the Church Fathers of the early church (Tertullian, Origen, and Methodius) from the East, following the initial, tentative Eastern Church's separation from the Roman Church in A.D. 382[13] (Gregory of Nyssa and John Chrysostom), and from the West, or the Latin Church (Ambrose, Jerome, and Augustine, the latter being the foremost leading theologian of the West and the major influence on subsequent Protestant thought). The time period examined spans from the second to the early fifth centuries.

The Early Church Fathers

Tertullian (160–220)

One of the most gifted orators of his age, Tertullian lived in Carthage, on the northern coast of Africa. Since his father was a Roman official, he was probably a Roman rather than a native. Trained in philosophy, literature, history, logic, and psychology, and fluent in both Greek and Latin, Tertullian was believed to have practiced law in his early years. As the first major theologian to write in Latin, he later published apologetic, polemical, and ascetic works. The Christian community Tertullian addressed in Carthage differed little from that of Rome. It was composed predominantly of married persons, while the leaders were elderly widows and widowers because they had experience of life.[14]

Tertullian's thought was heavily influenced by the teachings of Montanus, which arose in the 150s and 160s and soon evolved into one of the first grassroots movements in the history of the church. Montanus's teachings involved dramatic manifestations of Christian prophecy,[15] though the African wing of the movement — in contrast to the Phrygian original — emphasized apostolic succession, along with a less prominent role for women in church leadership. According to Montanus, only Christians perpetually open to the breath of the Spirit could lead lives in accordance with God's commands in Christ. Choosing a life of celibacy then provided the believer with greater freedom in exercising the gifts of the Spirit.

Tertullian wrote three treatises on the subject of celibacy and marriage. In "To His Wife,"[16] Tertullian advises his wife and "dearest companion in the service of the Lord" to renounce marriage after he died "exercising all the self-control of which you are capable," for she would do so for her own benefit (10). After all, "Adam was the only husband Eve had and Eve was his only wife" (11).[17] While the patriarchs practiced polygamy and kept concubines, their times had passed. Tertullian opposes those who "among other perversions of doctrine" taught that married couples separate and discontinue sexual intercourse. Marriage was conceded by Paul on the principle "that marry we may because marry we must." But Tertullian thought it quite enough to have succumbed once to the various reasons for marrying, such as "for the flesh or for the world or for the sake of posterity" and to "have satisfied all such wants as these in a single marriage," for the "servant of God is above all such supposed necessities" (17). Those who are widowed ought to be grateful for the liberty offered to them. Many abstained by mutual consent from the use of marriage and made themselves eunuchs because of their desire for the kingdom of heaven. Since they were able to practice continence in marriage, how much easier it should be for them when marriage ended. Those who were unable to restrain themselves while married would now be able to do so in bereavement and "make the most of a situation which removes what necessity imposed" (20).

If Tertullian's wife should decide to remarry, she was to remarry only in the Lord. Marrying another believer "is well within our power, and so failure here means that our guilt is the greater" (24). Christians who enter into marriage with pagans commit a "sin of fornication and are to be cut off completely from communion with the brethren" (27). But the unconverted person who married a pagan and later was converted to Christ was to preserve his or her marriage intact, though it would be difficult, particularly for the wife, whose husband might threaten to expose her to a judge in exchange for extorting property from her (31). Those living in such a mixed marriage would become saints, and they were given the hope of gain that through their conduct their spouse might be brought to faith as well. But people ought to marry in the Lord, if they marry at all, for they then are "as brother and sister, both servants of the same Master" and can "perform their daily exercises of piety without hindrance" and "need not be furtive about making the sign of the cross" (35). A Christian woman of wealth need not hesitate to consider as a husband a believer below her rank and means, for "she will receive a dowry ampler than her own from the goodness of one who is rich in God" (34).

The letter "On Chastity" is addressed to a man, a widower concerned with his loneliness following the death of his wife. The widower is told to "hold colloquy with the faith that is in him," but he also stands in need of counsel and advice since "the urgency of the flesh influences our thinking and usually opposes faith before the bar of conscience" (42). Tertullian offers him this advice, namely, not to remarry, arguing that the will of God is for us to be sanctified and made perfect as God is perfect. According to Tertullian, there are three degrees of perfection, all related to sexual activity. The first is to live a life of virginity from the time of one's birth; the second is to live a life of virginity from the time of one's second birth, that is, one's baptism, either by the mutual agreement of husband and wife to practice continence in marriage or by the determination of the widow or widower not to remarry; the third degree is that of monogamy, which is practiced when, after the dissolution of a first marriage, one renounces all use of sex from that time on. The first degree is one of blessedness, the second one of self-control, the third that of resignation to God's will. According to Tertullian, we practice this resignation when we do not yearn after what is taken away from us, but regard it as taken away by the Lord (42–43). Drawing on Paul, Tertullian affirms that widows and single people should marry if they cannot practice continence, since it is better to marry than to burn. But this is said in the sense that "it is better to have one eye than none." Even priests are allowed to marry only but once, and it "would be folly to imagine that lay people may do what priests may not. For are not we lay people also priests?" (53).

Tertullian likens a second marriage to fornication since both have in common the acting upon "the mere sight of a beautiful body richly adorned" in satisfying one's lust (56). It should be enough to have slipped from the level of immaculate virginity to a lower level by getting married, without slipping lower and lower "to a third stage and a fourth and perhaps to others even farther down" (57). Instead, people ought to renounce the things of the flesh in order to produce fruits of the spirit. For, in line with Paul, and according to the holy prophetess Prisca, "continence effects harmony of soul, and the pure see visions" (59).

Tertullian lists the reasons men think they need to get married. "We pretend that we need assistance in taking care of the house, controlling the domestics, keeping an eye on coffers and keys," he says, as if in the houses of married men all these things ran smoothly. People marry and procreate hoping for heirs or pretending to act out of consideration for the commonwealth, fearing "that our cities will decline, along with the falling birthrate." All these reasons are pretenses "to conceal our insatiable lust after the pleasures of the flesh," for "no man in his right senses would ever care to have children" otherwise (61). Even among pagans the practice of celibacy, perpetual virginity, or perpetual widowhood had been gaining acclaim. "We know about the Vestal Virgins, the virgins of Juno in a city of Achaea, those of Apollo of Delphi, or Minerva and Diana," or those who live a celibate life, such as the priests of that famous Egyptian bull, and those women who, of their own accord, leave their husbands and grow old in the service of the African Ceres. Since the devil "has found out a chastity also with which to work perdition," how much more guilty then is a Christian "if he refuses to embrace a chastity which effects salvation" (63).

The third treatise, "On Monogamy," is once more a defense of marrying only once and against remarriage. Tertullian places his doctrine on marriage between the "heretics who repudiate marriage" and the "sensualists [who] encourage it," between "heretical eunuchs on the one hand and your own extremists on the other" (70). He defines his own position as that of spiritualism, "because of the spiritual charisms which acknowledgedly are ours." These charisms help Christians see "that continence is as worthy of veneration as freedom to marry is worthy of respect, since both are according to the will of the Creator." The function of the Holy Spirit, the Paraclete, is to help believers realize the validity of both continence and marriage; it also shows this teaching's continuity with the Old Testament and clarifies the new revelation and "light burden" of continence that has become possible in Jesus Christ.

Another treatise, "On the Veiling of Virgins,"[18] was written as early as 204 in response to a group of young women who had decided to remain unmarried. Because of their decision, their fellow believers encouraged them to stand in the church at Carthage with their heads unveiled and their faces uncovered. By renouncing their sexual activity, they sought to symbolically express that they were now beyond the sexual shame on which the traditional veiling was based. Standing unveiled among the believers was to declare the redemption brought by Christ. This unveiling is paralleled in the *Apocryphal Acts of Thomas*, when the bride who had been visited by the Lord at night and converted to celibacy is found unveiled before her groom in the bridal chambers and replies to her astonished father, the king, "I am no longer covered, since the mirror of shame has been taken away from me."[19] Tertullian urged these celibate women to "put on the panoply of modesty" and to veil their head again for the sake of their sons, brothers, and fathers. By wearing the full garb of woman, they preserve their standing as virgin, while exhibiting their status as being wedded to Christ "to God alone" (37).

Origen (185–254)

Origen was one of the most prolific writers in the history of the church, leaving almost six thousand works of commentary, correspondence, treatises, and sermons. Following the martyrdom of his father in about 200, Origen settled in Alexandria, Egypt, and, at age eighteen, became the head of the catechetical school in Alexandria, as well as the church's spiritual guide and teacher of young Christians and recent converts. The school not only trained catechumens but provided open lectures on Christian doctrine and the exposition of Scripture. In 234, Origen was exiled and transferred his school to Caesarea, where he taught and preached regularly as a priest, following his ordination to the priesthood in 230. Origen is the only early church father believed to have taken literally Jesus' statement concerning those who make themselves "eunuchs for the kingdom of heaven" (Matt. 19:12). At the age of twenty, he is said to have gone to a doctor to have himself castrated, possibly to avoid slanderous rumors about the intimacy he enjoyed with women who were his spiritual charges. While this form of self-castration was not uncommon in his time, it merely made a man infertile and was no guarantee of chastity. Still, thus "exiled from either gender," it deprived him of the standard credential of a philosopher of his time — the flowing beard.[20] With Origen's teachings and commentary on the Scriptures, celibacy was no longer relegated to a postmarital matter for the middle-aged, but became popular among the young in Alexandria.

In his Commentary on the Gospel of Matthew (246–48),[21] Origen addresses marriage, divorce, and celibacy. In commenting on Matthew 19, he sees marriage as a man and woman being joined together by God. They are no more "twain, but one flesh." Paul knew this, saying "that marriage according to the Word of God was a 'gift,' like as holy celibacy was a gift." For while Paul hoped that "all men were like myself," namely, celibate, he would grant that "each man hath his own gift from God, one after this manner, and another after that." Origen warns against those who want to put asunder what God has joined by "falling away from the sound faith." For these people not only forbid "to commit fornication, but to marry," and by doing so dissolve "even those who had been before joined together by the providence of God" (506).

Origen explains when a bill of divorce is justified, and links the example by allegory to Christ, the husband, and to the synagogue, the wife. "He who is the Christ may have taken the synagogue to wife and cohabited with her, but it may be that afterwards she found not favour in His sight," because in her was found "an unseemly thing." This unseemly thing was that the Jews cried about Jesus, "Crucify Him, crucify Him." After the destruction of Jerusalem by which Christ was avenged, "I think, the husband wrote out a bill of divorcement to his former wife, and gave it into her hands, and sent her away from his own house" (508). But Christ has the power to change the law until a time of reformation since he is the Lord of the sabbath, and not its slave (509). The same principle of divorce may apply also to the soul, the wife, and the angel set over her as ruler and partner in conversation, her husband. Both soul and angel dwell in unity with each other as long as the soul is "worthy of the guardianship of a divine angel." But sometimes, after a long journey, "a cause may arise in the soul why she does not find favor in the eyes of the angel who is her lord and ruler." This cause is an "unseemly thing," so that a bill of divorce is written. In turn, the soul may be joined to another angel, again not finding favor in his sight because of another unseemly thing, so that this time she may even be hated by him, and again divorced. Origen concludes that "we must therefore take heed lest there be found in us any unseemly thing, and we should not find favour in the eyes of our husband Christ, or of the angel who has been set over us" (509).

Origen questions the practice of appointing to church authority only a man once-married without allowing room for digressing from Paul's command. After all, it seems possible that a man, who had been unfortunate in two marriages, and had lost his second wife while yet young, might have lived for the rest of his years in the greatest self-control and chastity. Instead, we "lay hold of the man who has been once married as our ruler" and "sometimes may not have been disciplined in chastity and temperance" (510).

In exploring the possible "unseemly thing" found in a woman that might cause a man to grant her a bill of divorce, Origen concedes that the husband might have contributed to it. For example, the husband might cause his wife to commit adultery by "allowing her to do what she wishes beyond what is fitting, and stooping to friendship with what men she wishes" (511); or by withholding himself sexually from her "when he does not satisfy her desires," for he then makes her oftentimes an adulteress, "even though he does so under the appearance of greater gravity and self-control." In light of the difficulties apparently involved in marriage, Jesus' disciples conclude that it is easier to take "refuge in celibacy" than to be married. But the Lord replies "that absolute chastity is a gift given by God, and not merely the fruit of training, but given by God with prayer" for "all men cannot receive the saying, but they to whom it is given" (512). However, this does not give people who wish "to remain pure in celibacy, but were mastered by their desires" an excuse for failing. Origen says that while it may be true that some have received the gift of celibacy, others who have not are free to ask for it. If these latter summon the will to ask, obeying and believing Christ who says, "Ask and it shall be given you," and do not doubt it, they will receive the gift, for "every one that asketh receiveth." The person asking of the gift of celibacy "must do everything in his power that he may pray 'with the spirit' and pray also 'with the understanding' and pray 'without ceasing.'" Matthew 19:11 then becomes "a stimulus to us to ask worthily of receiving," and God "will give the good gift, perfect purity in celibacy and chastity, to those who ask Him with the whole soul, and with faith, and in prayers without ceasing."

In commenting on Jesus' brothers and sisters (Matt. 13:55–56), Origen is cautious. "Some say," he says, "that the brethren of Jesus were sons of Joseph by a former wife, whom he married before Mary" (424). They do so because they "wish to preserve the honour of Mary in virginity to the end." They hold this view "so that that body of hers...might not know intercourse with a man after the Holy Ghost came into her and the power from on high overshadowed her." Origen does not seem concerned about maintaining the perpetual virginity of Mary.[22] What he is concerned with is affirming that Mary was a virgin when she gave birth to Jesus. "I think it in harmony with reason that Jesus was the first-fruit among men of the purity which consists in chastity." Mary may have had other children after Jesus, but Jesus was her first child and "the first-fruit of virginity." By her virginity, Mary was the first to model the type of sexual conduct that gives birth to Christ.[23] In the same way, Christians practicing celibacy give birth to Christ.

Origen expands on this process of giving birth in his exegesis on the Gospel of John (written before 231). In his beginning remarks in the Commentary of John,[24] Origen refers to the book of Revelation and the 144,000 who were not "defiled with women, for they were virgins (297)" as the twelve thousand first-fruits of each tribe of Israel. They are the levites and priests, not of Aaron's lineage, but of the order of Melchisedek, the high-priest who is Christ. Believers also are regarded as levites and priests by having "no possessions but tithes and first-fruits" (298) issuing from their study of Scripture. Most people devote most of their time "to the things of this life, and dedicate to God only a few special acts, thus... [having] but few transactions with the [high-]priest [Christ]." But those devoting themselves to the divine word entirely can be considered levites and priests. Following "the bodily separation we have undergone from each other," the believers' first-fruits will be the study of the Gospel. In another commentary on 1 Corinthians, of which only a fragment survives,[25] Origen explains the role of the body in service to God in Christ. "Do not think that just as the belly is made for food and food for the belly, that in the same way the body is made for intercourse. If you wish to understand the Apostle's train of reasoning, for what reason the body was made, then listen: it was made that it should be a temple to the Lord; that the soul, being holy and blessed, should act in it as if it were a priest serving before the Holy Spirit that dwells in you."[26] For the Christian believer then, the primary role of the body is not the enjoyment of physical pleasures — such as food, drink, and intercourse. The body's immediate physical pleasures are not an end in themselves, but are superseded by the pleasures of serving Christ with it. In this new role of the body as a temple, sexual abstinence and celibacy can create an environment conducive to the body's allowing the soul to serve in a priestly function. Rather than separating the body and the soul, Origen keeps them interconnected. Moreover, he does not relegate the body, along with its desires, to a subdued existence, but elevates it to the level of temple where the body allows the soul to give birth to the "first-fruits" offered in service to God.

Methodius (260–312)

Methodius was a Christian teacher, apologist, and premier critic of Origen. Writing in Olympus in Lycia, on the Aegean coast of southwest Turkey, he later became bishop both of Olympus and Patara. Following his move to the episcopal See of Tyre in Phoenicia, he suffered martyrdom at Chacis in Greece. While little else is known about Methodius's life, his writings constitute the largest body of Greek Christian works from his time.[27] Apart from works on the resurrection and creation, Methodius is best known for his dialogue in praise of celibacy, entitled "The Banquet of the Ten Virgins" or "Concerning Chastity."[28] Because of the work's similarity to Plato's, it was also called "The Symposium." But instead of portraying a gathering of sexually active men, Methodius's "Banquet" features a study circle of ten women celebrating their sexual abstinence and arguing the reasons for their resolve to live a celibate life. While Methodius, the male teacher, remains a discreet presence as Euboulios, the role of Socrates as teacher of philosophy falls to Thecla, the heroine of the *Apocryphal Acts of Paul and Thecla*.[29]

The Symposium opens with a dialogue in which Euboulios, a man, inquires of Gregorion, a woman, about "the meeting of Marcella and Theopatra, and of the other virgins who were present at the banquet, and of the nature of their discourses on the subject of chastity" (309). Gregorion relates what had been told to her by one of the virgins. According to Theopatra, the ten virgins had been invited by Arete, "the daughter of Philosophia," to a garden with an eastern atmosphere resembling "a second paradise." Following a "very rough, steep, and arduous path," the ten guests were greeted by a beautiful woman clothed in a white, shining robe, kissing them like a mother her daughters and saying that her prayers had been answered. For "you have come with toil and pain to me who am earnestly longing to conduct you to the pasture of immortality." She had seen them coming "by a way abounding with many frightful reptiles" and "often stepping aside, and I was fearing lest you should turn back and slip over the precipice." But they had arrived safely, "thanks to the Bridegroom to whom I have espoused you, my children" (310). After Arete had welcomed her guests, she invited each to "pronounce a discourse in praise of virginity," beginning with Marcella, the eldest and highest in rank.

Marcella declares that virginity is the best and noblest manner of life, the root of immortality, and its flower and first-fruits. It is the reason that the Lord promises entrance into the kingdom to those who have made themselves eunuchs. Celibacy is considered "a very rare thing, and difficult of attainment, and in proportion to its supreme excellence and magnificence is the greatness of its dangers" (310). Many have longed for it, but "have gone aside out of the way, from having conceived no worthy idea of the *virginal* manner of life." For it is not enough simply to keep the body pure, but one also needs to "care for the souls of men as being the divinities of their bodies, and adorn them with righteousness" (311). Virginity as a way of life is said to have gradually evolved over time. First people had to populate the earth; then they were taught to abandon the intermarriage of brothers and sisters and marry wives from other families; then, that they should no longer have many wives, then that they should not be adulterers, and then again that they should go on to continence, and from continence to virginity, so that from there they might "sail fearlessly into the peaceful haven of immortality" (312). Jesus was the first to have taught this doctrine, "since He alone, coming down to us, taught man to draw near to God," and was thus "saluted as first and chief of virgins." Only a few can aspire to the true practice of virginity, which is illustrated by the book of Revelation, where the Lamb, as the chief virgin, is in the company of only 144,000 virgins, "while the multitude of the other saints is innumerable" (313).

Theophila argues that Christ's preference for virginity, by virtue of his having become the chief virgin, does not preempt marriage and the birth of children. Because "after He had brought in virginity, the Word did not altogether abolish the generation of children." The ordinance of the Creator still prevails to "increase and multiply," so that "we must not be offended" at this ordinance, "from which, moreover, we ourselves have our being." If God continues to create human beings, "shall we not be guilty of audacity if we think of the generation of children as something offensive, which the Almighty Himself is not ashamed to make use of in working with His undefiled hands." Since we concede "to men the power of forming men," it would be "absurd to forbid marriage unions" (314). There are definitely some who cannot attain virginity, but all can be encouraged "to meditate and to keep the mind upon the transformation of the body to the likeness of angels," who neither marry nor are given in marriage. The church then can be compared to "a flower-covered and variegated meadow, adorned and crowned not only with the flowers of virginity, but also with those of child-bearing and of continence" (316).

In her discourse on Paul's teachings, Thaleia refers to Christ and the church as the new union of the first man and woman. The church consists of the souls who are betrothed and given in marriage to Christ. In it are found those who embrace the truth more clearly, because they have been delivered "from the evils of the flesh"; they have received the pure and genuine seed of Christ's doctrine, so that they are empowered to cooperate with Christ and can help "in preaching for the salvation of others" (320). The church also contains others who are still imperfect and beginning their lessons; they have been born into salvation and are being shaped, as by mothers, by those who are more perfect, "until they are brought forth and regenerated unto the greatness and beauty of virtue." These latter, having made progress and having become a church, "assist in labouring for the birth and nurture of other children, accomplishing in the receptacle of the soul, as in a womb, the blameless will of God." Paul serves as an example, first born and suckled by the preaching of Ananias and the renewal in baptism. But when Paul had grown to a man, being molded to spiritual perfection, he was made the help-mate and bride of the Word. By his receiving and conceiving the seeds of life, he becomes a church and a mother, "labouring in birth of those who, through him, believed in the Lord, until Christ was formed and born in them also" (320). For Paul says, "My little children, of whom I travail in birth again until Christ be formed in you" (Gal. 4:19) and again, "In Christ Jesus I have begotten you through the Gospel" (1 Cor. 4:15).

Theopatra explores the role of virginity as a help in withstanding the passions of the senses. These passions fall upon the soul that is like a vessel, otherwise "easily guided," but now tossed about by "the sudden bursts of the waves of folly which rush into them" (323). Virginity serves as a steadying force that "by it we might tie our bodies fast, like ships, and have a calm, coming to an anchorage without damage." Moreover, virginity is "an ally to those who are contending for and longing after Zion" (324).

According to Thallousa, those committing themselves to virginity are fulfilling "a great vow," given they are "willing to offer themselves of their free-will" (325). Of all vows, "chastity is the vow above all vows," because it not only keeps "the flesh untouched by intercourse, but also unspotted by other kinds of unseemliness" (326).

Thecla argues that being born into Christ produces qualities thought of as masculine. For as the church gives birth to those who are baptized, it produces "a masculine people, who should come back from the passions and weakness of women to the unity of the Lord, and grow strong in manly virtue" (337). Those in whom Christ is spiritually born "receive the features, and the image, and the manliness of Christ, the likeness of the form of the Word being stamped upon them." The church "swells and travails in birth until Christ is formed in us, so that each of the saints, by partaking of Christ, has been born a Christ" and those who "were baptized into Christ had been made Christs by communication of the Spirit." She says furthermore that doing good or evil is not a result of destiny and the stars, but of one's own free will and choosing. For there are two motions in us, "the lust of the flesh and that of the soul, differing from each other, whence they have received two names, that of virtue and that of vice" (343).

In a closing discourse, Arete, the hostess, emphasizes the main point of the discussion. Many may think they cultivate and honor chastity, but actually only few really practice it. For the practice of chastity is not limited to the body, but extends to the mind and soul. Many are prideful in their practice, thus "cleansing the outside of the cup and platter, that is the flesh and body, but injuring the heart by conceit and ambition" (351). In fact, someone practicing chastity alone apart from other virtues is inferior to those practicing "charity, mercy, and humanity." For it would be ridiculous to keep "the organs of generation pure, but not the tongue; or to preserve the tongue, but neither the eyesight, the ears, nor the hands; or lastly, to preserve these pure, but not the mind, defiling it with pride and anger."

The banquet ends with Thecla leading the choir of virgins in a responsorial hymn of thanksgiving. The hymn is set to the parable of the ten virgins and praises certain biblical characters for their virtues of martyrdom and sexual renunciation: These characters are Abel, who prefigures Jesus' martyrdom; Joseph, who repels the sexual advances of Potiphar's wife; Jephthah's daughter, who as a virgin is "slaughtered" and offered up like a lamb; Judith, a widow, who cunningly employs the sexual interest of Holofernes, commander of the Assyrian army, to cut off his head and thus deliver her people;[30] Susanna, a married woman, who would rather die than have sexual intercourse with the two judges who pressure her to do so;[31] John the Baptist, who was "led to slaughter" because of his sexual abstinence (17; 352);[32] and the Virgin Mary, who was suspected of premarital intercourse on account of Jesus' birth. While Thecla cantors the twenty-four-verse hymn, the choir responds with, "I keep myself pure for Thee, O Bridegroom, and holding a lighted torch I go to meet Thee." Two themes stand out in the hymn. First, the virgins have left family and home for the sake of Christ. Thecla sings, "Leaving marriage and the beds of mortals and my golden home for Thee, O King, I have come in undefiled robes, in order that I might enter with Thee Thy happy bridal chamber" (3; 351–52) and "I forget my own country, O Lord, through desire of Thy grace. I forget, also, the company of virgins, my fellows, the desire even of mother and of kindred, for Thou, O Christ, art all things to me" (5; 352). Second, the hymn praises martyrdom for the sake of preserving one's virginity from violent male aggressors. Thecla again sings, "it is far better for me to die than to betray my nuptials to you, O mad for women, and so to suffer the eternal justice of God in fiery vengeance. Save me now, O Christ, from these evils" (16; 352).

The Symposium concludes by returning to Gregorion and Euboulios, who are discussing whose expression of chastity is to be held in greater esteem: those who have hardly been tried, or those who have had to fight the fiercest battle in maintaining it. They eventually agree that "to be prepared against the entrance of the gales of the Evil Spirit, and not to be cast away or overcome, but to refer all to Christ, and strongly to contend against pleasures" earns greater praise than living "a virgin life calmly and with ease" (355).

The Eastern Church Fathers

Gregory of Nyssa (335–395)

Gregory was born into a wealthy Christian family in Pontus. The father, a rhetorician, died at a young age; the ten children were raised by their grandmother Macrina and their mother Emmelia, both committed Christians. Gregory's sister Macrina, also a Christian, shared in the care of the children's education. After the death of Macrina's fiancé, she devoted herself to a religious life and, eventually, established a female convent with her mother on the family property in Pontus, at a place called Annesi. Due to Macrina's influence, whose devotion Gregory later chronicled in his "Life of Macrina" (A.D. 379), her brother Basil also gave up the worldly life and became a hermit,[33] then founded a monastery in the vicinity of Pontus. His friend from his student days in Athens, Gregory Nazianzen, joined him there, and so did Gregory, who wrote his A.D. 368 treatise "On Virginity" during

that time. Following Basil's election to bishop of Caesarea in Cappadocia in A.D. 370, Basil appointed Gregory bishop of Nyssa, a small town
in Cappadocia. Despite persecutions and trials in his episcopate, Gregory gained acclaim by his writings and oratory, especially in defense
of the subject of the Trinity and the resurrection, so that the explana-
tory clauses added to the Nicene Creed are later attributed to him.
As the East replaced the primacy of Rome and Alexandria with other
sees, especially Constantinople, following the second ecumenical council, Constantinople I, in A.D. 382, Gregory became one of the leading
fathers of the Eastern Church.

Gregory's treatise "On Virginity"[34] advances a philosophy of the
golden mean. The purpose is to "create in its readers a passion for
the life according to excellence," which begins with virginity, though
they need to be "favoured and helped by the grace of God" in doing so
(343). The ultimate test of virginity's excellence, however, transcends
rational argument. For words cannot sufficiently convince, since "nature's greatnesses have their own way of striking with admiration" and
it is best "to evince our admiration of it by our lives rather than by our
words" (344).

The excellence of a life of virginity is visible in the Trinity. The
Father is incorrupt in "passionless generation," the Son excels with
"moral innocence," and the Holy Spirit is pure. Thus, virginity as incorrupt, passionless, and pure is inherent in the entire "supramundane
existence" (344). This means that while virginity remains in heaven
with the father of spirits, it also "keeps wings for man's desires to rise
to heavenly things," and represents the locus of mediation and union
between the human and the divine (345).

Gregory considers those blessed who are still young enough to choose
a life of virginity from the very start. They have not "debarred themselves from it by engagements of the secular life, as we have, whom
a gulf now divides from glorious virginity." Instead, those who have
had sexual intercourse, including himself,[35] had "to learn the good by
after-regrets" (345). Gregory gives a detailed account of the manifold
difficulties involved in married life and having children. If yet more
convincing is needed, he says, readers should listen to married women
who actually know it. "How they congratulate those who have chosen

from the first the virgin life," and did not have to learn the hard way, finding that virginity is fortified against all these ills and has "no orphan state, no widowhood to mourn" and always lives in "the presence of the undying Bridegroom" (347).

Being married lends itself to covering up the sin of pride. A man mad after notoriety, for example, makes his family responsible for his sin. He is driven to bring honor to his family name, and wants to leave historic records of himself in form of children. Such striving prevents him from seeing that all that is prized by the living "exists only in the conception of the unreflecting, and is in itself nothing" (349). There is no such reality as low birth or high birth, or glory, or ancient renown, or present elevation, or power over others, or subjection. Even wealth and poverty are no different as to the pleasures they can produce, for life goes on to the end at the same speed and either class has "the same power of choice to live well or ill." The person who thinks in spiritual terms will be able to travel the path neither softened by the pleasures nor beaten down by the hardships. But "the grosser mind looks down" and "bends its energies to bodily pleasures as surely as the sheep stoop to their pasture." Alienated from the life of God, this mind recognizes only the gratification of the body and "invents all the evil in this life of ours," including avarice, passions unchecked, unbounded luxury, lust of power, and pride. Ultimately, all vices result from one cherished passion. Once the passion is identified for the deceptive and fleeting satisfaction it brings, one can renounce attachment and get as far away as possible from the company of this emotional and sensual world.

Virginity is a help in beautifying the lines of one's character, since it directs the gaze toward the source of all beauty. Virginity is "the practical method in the science of the Divine life" to help people assimilate themselves with spiritual natures (351). In the course of its practice, the soul will transfer its affection from material objects to the intellectual contemplation of immaterial beauty. Virginity's aim is to create in the soul a complete forgetfulness of natural emotions.

As role models of virginity, Gregory cites Elijah and John the Baptist. In his opinion, they would not have reached their spiritual heights had they been married. They serve as object lessons on how not to become entangled in the aims of this world's effort, of which marriage is one and "the primal root of all striving after vanities" (352).

Gregory does not depreciate marriage as an institution since it is not outside the realm of God's blessing. But the married are cautioned to remember that all virtue is found in moderation, and that any declension to either side is a vice. In fact, he says, the person "who grasps the middle point between doing too little and doing too much has hit the distinction between vice and virtue" (352). While the pursuit of heavenly things should be a person's primary interest, "if he can use the advantages of marriage with sobriety and moderation, he need not despise this way of serving the state" (353). A good example of this choice is Isaac, who married when he was past his prime so that his marriage was not a deed of passion. He cohabited with Rebecca until the birth of his one set of children, and then, "closing the channels of the senses, lived wholly for the Unseen." In one's pursuit of heavenly things, habit is a powerful advocate. For habit will "not fail to produce, even in the most fretful, a feeling of pleasure through the very effort of their perseverance" (354). This pleasure is of such beauty that it cannot be expressed in words. It can only be admired by "our power of aesthetic feeling," since the senses are unequipped to grasp it.

People tend to stop short of seeking the supreme beauty in others. They look at someone and think they know him, but they often ignore the qualities of that person's soul. Unable to "perform this feat of mental analysis," they then give up their search for true beauty, sliding into "mere sensuality" or inclining their desires to a "dead metallic coin" or limiting their imagination of the beautiful "to worldly honours, fame, and power." In fact, the most debased "make their gluttony the test of what is good." But those who turn from their passionate longings toward what is seemly will find beauty and good (355). True virginity and the "real zeal for chastity" strive to attain "the power thereby of seeing God" (357).

Supreme beauty and divine good are not far removed from us, but are found within. The parable of the lost coin, or drachma, illustrates this point. The widowed soul reaps no benefit from the presence of the other virtues, or drachmas. Like the soul who searches for this one lost virtue in her home, we need to look within ourselves to find it. The coin may be hidden beneath the dirt of our fleshly impurities, which can be swept away by "carefulness of life." When the soul finds the lost coin, she calls in the other virtues or powers, such as reasoning and appetite, affections of grief and anger, to share in her delight. As a result, all other powers become transformed and look toward the beautiful and the good, doing everything for the glory of God, instead of serving as instruments of sin (358).

Virginity forms a barrier to death. The "virgin mother," for example, is joyful because she conceives "deathless children" by the operation of the Spirit. Those practicing virginity no longer propagate children who in turn become subject to death, but spiritual children who are marked by life and immortality. In the continent body, then, "the long unbroken career of decay and death, which has intervened between the first man and the lives of virginity which have been led, is interrupted" (359). The strength of death is broken and annulled, for death no longer finds "the places upon which he may fix his sting" (360).

Abstaining from marriage is only one aspect of virginity. Virginity is a "transcendent aim" that involves a turning away from any act that might be enslaving. People seeking to attain this aim need to be true to themselves in every respect, and to manifest this purity equally in every relation of life (364). Such purity includes modesty in food and drink and securing "for the body a continuous tranquillity," whereby need, not pleasure, becomes the measure and limit of our indulgence (367).

In conclusion, Gregory recommends a mentor who will teach by example and practice. For any theory divorced from living examples is like an "unbreathing statue." No one can be thoroughly instructed in the practice of virginity unless "he puts himself into the hands of one who has himself led it in perfection" (368). Since most embrace virginity while still young and unformed in understanding, they should "search out a fitting guide and master of this way" (369). Thereby the saintliness can be transmitted from the one who has achieved it to those who come within his or her circle. These mentors were no different from others in their earlier instincts and desires, but they listened to the call of temperance. If people desire to draw close to God, they "should become crucified with Christ, a holy priest standing before God, a pure offering in all chastity," thus preparing themselves by their holiness for God's coming (371).

John Chrysostom (347–407)

John was raised at Antioch by his widowed mother, Anthusa. After training for the bar and an education in the pagan classics, he turned to the study of the Bible. John spent four of his formative years as a monk on the mountains outside Antioch under the tutelage of an ascetic named Syrus. For another two years, he lived a solitary life in a cave. Ill-health, brought on by the rigorous regimen, made him return to Antioch, where he had previously served as a lector. Upon his return, he was ordained a deacon in A.D. 381, and, five years later, a priest. His oratory and preaching skills kept his congregation spell-bound and earned him the name Chrysostom or "Golden Mouth," for his "tongue was more fluent than the cataracts of the Nile."[36]

In 398 he was taken to Constantinople and consecrated bishop. His episcopate was troubled by controversies, which led to his exile in 404. John Chrysostom produced more treatises on asceticism and marriage than any other Greek-writing church father.[37] His thematic emphasis reflects the concerns of his time. By the late fourth century, celibacy was considered the most exalted way of life for Christians. Virginity and widowhood were no longer only conditions that would preserve energies for the Lord's service, but they were "professions" for which a solemn pledge was taken.[38] John's writings on celibacy and marriage need to be understood in light of this. Of particular interest are his homily on 1 Corinthians 7, which is a summary of his treatise "On Virginity," and the treatise "Against Remarriage."

John's homily on 1 Corinthians 7, Homily 19,[39] was preached in Antioch to an audience of committed celibates, male and female virgins, the widowed, and married couples. The sermon is a systematic exposition of chapter 7 of Paul's first letter to the church in Corinth. John places the chapter in the context of the letter. After discussing factionalism, incest, and greed, Paul "gives his audience a rest from such vulgarities and inserts some advice and exhortation concerning marriage and virginity" (25). One of the issues related to marriage is conjugal rights. Paul's advice is not just directed to clergy and priests, but to "everyone in general" (26). What are conjugal rights? John asks. First, "it means that the wife has no power over her own body, but she is her husband's slave — and also his ruler." The wife who refuses her husband offends God. "So, wife, if you want to abstain, even for a little while, get your husband's permission first," he says. In parallel fashion, John addresses the husbands. "As for you, husband, if a prostitute tries to seduce you, tell her, 'My body is not my own, but my wife's.'" While husbands have greater authority than wives in other matters, fidelity is the exception and both "husband and wife are equally responsible for the honor of their marriage bed" (27).

Abstinence in marriage can produce great evils. Conjugal rights are "a debt to be paid," so that if one abstains without the other's consent, "it is an act of fraud" and "theft." John particularly exhorts the women, because withholding themselves from their husbands "is what many wives do," thus committing "a sin which outweighs the righteousness of their abstinence." By doing so, they become "responsible for their husband's licentiousness and the broken homes that result." What good is that to the love and harmony of the household, when the husband forced into continence "frets and complains, loses his temper, and constantly fights with his wife?" he asks. Obviously, no good at all (27).

John expects self-control in the exercise of sexual abstinence. Such self-control is not considered a gift, but is up to the individual. But Paul does not force a person into abstinence who cannot attain it, instead recommends the person marry. It is a concession on Paul's part not to impose his own preferred state of continence on everybody, but to offer that "if you suffer with violent, burning passion, then relieve your pain and sweat through marriage, before you utterly collapse" (29). In his treatise "On Virginity" (OV),[40] John elaborates on the point by insisting that the decision for celibacy must be a completely free one (OV 115). But once a widow, for example, makes the decision for celibacy and has been enrolled in the church's ranks of widows, there can be no going back without her breaking a solemn promise to God (OV 58). John compares the decision to live a celibate life to an athlete's decision to enter a contest: the athlete freely chooses to participate, but once he has done so, there is no more choice, for "the law of the contest" prevails (OV 56). The same holds true for virgins. If someone has vowed to remain a virgin, she would be sinning if she married. Moreover, if a widow incurs condemnation for violating her pledge and seeking second marriage, "the judgment for virgins would be even greater" (40).

John opposes women leaving their husbands, and teaches that despite a desire for separation due to "abstinence, pettiness, or other motives," the wife should still remain with her husband. Even if they do not have sexual relations, "at least she won't take another man to be her husband" (30). What if the husband is rash, contemptuous, irascible, or treats her like a slave? John interprets Paul as saying that the wife is to bear such abuse patiently. Either "train him," or endure nobly "this unproclaimed war." If she is unable to control him, the wife must either "master the violence of her passion" and become single, or else "flatter her overbearing lord, and submit herself to whatever he wishes, whether he strikes her or bathes her in abuse or exposes her to the contempt of the household or the like" (OV 60). But if the wife chooses to remain single, she must practice "unprofitable self-control" — unprofitable because it arises not from the desire for holiness but out of anger for her husband.

Having an unbelieving spouse is no grounds for divorce. A wife, for example, does not engage in an impure act when having intercourse with her unbelieving husband. The purity of her faith is stronger than the impurity of his unbelief (31). There is also hope that the husband will be converted by his wife's influence. Such marriages should be left in peace (32). If the husband is "not contentious," it could very well be worthwhile to stay with him, for no teacher is as effective as "a persuasive wife" (33). To John, only fornication is sufficient grounds for divorce, for thereby the innocent marriage partner will become impure by intercourse with the unfaithful partner. A husband would not be criticized "for throwing a wife who had become a prostitute out his house" (31).

John discusses the nature of enslavement. Even slaves can be free if they do not transgress God's law. Thus Joseph was free, though he was in the services of Pharaoh. Joseph's brothers, on the other hand, were free men, but they were enslaved by their false pretenses to their father. In like manner, Potiphar's wife who pursued Joseph was enslaved to her lust. The same holds true for Cain, who was enslaved by "Lady Jealousy," who ordered him to kill his brother, Abel, lie to God, and grieve his father. Even in slavery of the body, Christians are free in their conscience before God in Christ. Not to become enslaved means not to listen to people "who order you to do disgusting things" or to one's own "wild impulses" (39).

One of the reasons Paul recommended celibacy was that "the time has grown very short" (v. 29). Rather than suggesting that Paul expected the imminent return of Christ and was hoping that celibacy might usher in Christ's second coming, John sees Paul urging Christians to make the best use of their knowledge of Christ during their brief earthly existence. In light of the brevity of life, they were to focus on developing their spiritual character — and celibacy served as a helpful tool. John is puzzled why Paul never mentions the rewards celibacy might offer in heaven. "The apostle has not even briefly mentioned these rewards," he says. "From start to finish he only calls to mind the release from life's annoyances" (OV 77). John suspects that Paul did so for pedagogical reasons, since more carnal people, which the Corinthians were, "consider less significant what cannot be seen here and now" (OV 80). John also suggests that the motivation for celibacy has been significantly altered since the time of Paul. No longer viewed as a practical measure to expedite the coming of God's Kingdom, celibacy had attained a status that raises human beings to the ranks of angelic powers — who, according to Jesus, neither marry nor are given in marriage. It is easier to obtain the Kingdom of Heaven through virginity than through marriage (OV 67), but John admits that Paul is correct in saying that virginity repays even while it is being achieved "because it releases us from so much work and anxiety" (OV 81). Since Paul tells those who are married to live as if they were not, it makes little sense to get married at all.

John at last calls on the virgins to listen. Virginity encompasses more than sexual abstinence. A virgin is defined by detachment from worldly cares. If we want to live with our eyes focused on heaven and its splendor, we should abandon earthly things because, in reality, they are "childish playthings" (OV 109). For we have been united with a groom who not only demands all our affection from us, but also our life. While sex is not evil, it is yet again another affection and, hence, a hindrance to someone who desires to be devoted to prayer. Regardless then of whether we presently live in virginity or are in our first marriage or in our second, the important thing is to pursue self-control and holiness so as to be counted worthy in meeting Christ (42).

John addresses his treatise "Against Remarriage" (AR)[41] to younger widowed women. He puzzles over the reasons why women who have cursed "ten thousand times themselves, the marriage brokers and the day on which the bridal chamber was prepared," would want to marry again. Some, he says, choose to forget the past, some view marriage as deliverance from widowhood, some think widowhood disgraceful and choose the hardships of marriage for the sake of empty glory and excessive conceit, some are driven by sexual desires. While he wishes in no way to reproach these women and affirms that remarriage is in accordance with Paul's teachings, as long as it is "in the Lord," John feels that a woman who remarries demonstrates her "great love of the world and attachments to earthly things" (AR 131). Moreover, her second marriage is indicative of scarcely being able to "keep from sex" and of "a soul weak and carnal, one tied to the earth" (AR 131–32).

Since John regards the epistle of 1 Timothy as Paul's work, he places it in the context of 1 Corinthians 7. In this epistle, Paul advises younger widows to remarry. He says this not because he believes remarriage is better than celibacy, but a necessity for those who lack self-control. Paul does not address those who wish to keep their widowhood, only those who would prefer to remarry or who intend to "secretly prostitute and dishonor" themselves (AR 134–35).

John says that to contend that a woman will only gain worries and complete ruin in business affairs without a husband is an excuse to hide one's weakness (AR 136–37). Women are perfectly capable of managing their own affairs. Women are "better suited" than men in household matters, rather than in accruing and collecting wealth away from home; in fact, many women have managed households much more ably than their husbands and raised their orphaned children. It may be true that a widow will have greater difficulty in asserting her authority with slaves, managers, and stewards who may act boldly once the husband is gone. But though widows may gain the reputation of audaciousness because of their sharp reproof of the domestics, it is preferable to one of lewdness, dissoluteness, and faithlessness on account of remarriage (AR 139). John also points out that men's love for virgins is more "frenzied and impetuous by far." What is true of clothes, houses, and belongings is also true of a wife: "we are not disposed in the same way toward what has been used by another" than toward what is new (AR 141).

It is likely that those widowed at a young age enjoy more honor and gifts than those widowed in old age. This is so because one has outdistanced the other in chastity by many laps. While right actions may appear unpleasant on account of the initial hardships, the future advantages and wages will be great. John appeals to the widows to detach from the earth, aspire to the life found in heaven since they have been married to Christ, and to do "everything in such a way as becomes women who possess such a bridegroom" (AR 149).

The Latin Fathers of the West

Ambrose (339–397)

Ambrose was born at Trier in the Rhineland into a wealthy Roman family of Christian background. At the time of Ambrose's birth, his father was governor of the Gauls, in an area that extended over Spain, Britain, and Gaul. After his father's death, his mother, his elder brother Satyrus, and Ambrose attended St. Peter's in Rome, where Marcellina, his elder sister, received the veil of a consecrated virgin from Pope Liberius. In 370, following the study of law, Ambrose was appointed governor of Emilia-Liguria, the province of northern Italy whose capital is Milan, which was, at the time, the residence of Roman emperors. When the bishop of Milan died four years later, Ambrose, who was only a catechumen at the time, was elected bishop by public acclamation. Within a week, he was baptized, ordained, and consecrated bishop. Ambrose served both as pastor of the metropolitan church and adviser to the imperial family on matters of church and state. Ambrose's philosophical background and knowledge of Greek gave him a unique advantage, but he did not use his wide reading to develop a contemplative theology; rather to promote the social and political role of the Catholic Church in Roman society and to advance his own austere spirituality. According to Peter Brown, Ambrose's system of thinking can be characterized as "a series of potent antitheses" — Christian and pagan, Catholic and heretic, Bible truth and secular guesswork, and mind and body.[42] Among Ambrose's favorite topics was the exhortation to celibacy, particularly of women, so that mothers used to forbid their daughters to hear him. The three books of "Concerning Virgins" are addressed to his sister Marcellina in A.D. 377, with the treatise of "Concerning Widows" following shortly after.

Ambrose makes the birthday of St. Agnes, a virgin and martyr at age twelve, the occasion for writing "Concerning Virgins."[43] While girls her age are usually unable to bear even the angry looks of their parents, she was "fearless under the cruel hands of the executioners, she was unmoved by the heavy weight of the creaking chains, offering her whole body to the sword of the raging soldier, as yet ignorant of death, but ready for it" (364). Agnes's example shows that virginity is not praiseworthy because it is found in martyrs, but because virginity makes for martyrs (365). Both Elijah and Miriam are precursors of this type of life. With the Lord's arrival, joining together the Godhead and flesh without "any confusion or mixture," virginity could spread throughout the whole world for it was now "implanted in human bodies" (364).

Ambrose denies any virtue inherent in the practice of celibacy among nonbelievers, such as the vestal virgins, the Phrygians, or the Pythagoreans. Their celibacy was set for only a certain length of time, so that at first "chastity is enforced by law," but then "authority given for lust" (366). They teach that their virgins are not to persevere, that in fact they are unable to do so. What sort of religion is that, he asks, which turns modest maidens into immodest old women? Moreover, virginity cannot be commanded or legislated, but it must be "wished for, for things which are above us are matters for prayer," not mastery (367). With that, heaven became "the native country" of virginity (366).

The advantages of virginity are greater than those of marriage. The married woman is enslaved to her husband and offspring, trying to please them; while "studying to please others, she displeases herself."

There is little left that is her own, so that all she has to love is her own perceptions (367). In fact, women wishing to be married are "more wretched" than condemned criminals, since the latter "desire to be set free," but "you to be bound" (372). In contrast, virgins do not know such torments and enslavements. Instead of ornaments, they wear "holy modesty" and "sweet chastity." Their beauty is not of the mortal body but of the immortal soul. But God "loves even in less beautiful bodies the more beautiful souls." Ambrose exhorts parents to train their daughters to virginity, so that she who was borne for so long in her mother's womb might not "pass under the power of another" (368). While not wishing to degrade marriage — for those who do so "declare that they ought not to have been born" (369) — he wants to clarify that virginity, as "the gift of a few only," is the more excellent way. In closing the first book, Ambrose encourages those seeking to commit to a life of virginity to scale mounting parental opposition. Parents may refuse a dowry, but Christ is a "wealthy Spouse." They ought to regard the anxious entreaties of their parents as their "first battles," and conquer their affections first. For "if you conquer your home, you conquer the world" (373).

In book 2 of his treatise "Concerning Virgins," Ambrose gives glowing descriptions of female models of virginity, such as the Virgin Mary, Thecla, and a virgin at Antioch. In sketching Mary, Ambrose superimposes behavior expected of consecrated virgins of his time, while claiming support from Scripture. Mary was "humble in heart, grave in speech, prudent in mind, sparing of words, studious in reading." She did not cause pain to her parents even by a look, disagree with her neighbors, despise the lowly, avoid the needy, or go to gatherings of men that might make her blush. There was nothing gloomy in her eyes, nothing forward in her speech, nothing unseemly in her demeanor; no silly movement, no unrestrained step, no petulant voice. She was sparing with food, careful with sleep, and diligent with reading, so that even "when her body was sleeping her soul was awake." This is how the Evangelist describes her in his Gospel, says Ambrose, this is how the angel found her, and this is why the Holy Spirit chose her (374–75). Her example serves as an inspiration to us all. And "what a procession shall that be" in heaven, when Mary, whom Ambrose calls Miriam, taking her timbrel, shall stir up the choirs of virgins, singing to the Lord because they have "passed through the sea of this world without suffering from the waves of this world" (376).

In the same way that Mary instructs in the discipline of life, Thecla teaches the discipline of death and martyrdom. Ambrose considers Thecla married, but because she avoided "nuptial intercourse" and had been "condemned through her husband's rage," says Ambrose, she "changed even the disposition of wild beasts by their reverence for virginity." This goes to show, he says, that "virginity has in itself so much that is admirable, that even lions admire it" (376).

The last example he raises is a virgin at Antioch who, because of her refusal to sacrifice to idols, is thrown into a brothel as punishment. Before losing her virginity, she chances upon a soldier hiding there from his pursuers and exchanges clothes with him. Both are eventually captured and killed, but she dies a virgin (378–79).

In book 3, Ambrose sums up the charge Bishop Liberius gave to Marcellina at her consecration as a virgin. The behavior expected of a virgin is similar to that which Ambrose had attributed to the Virgin Mary. Visits with parents and those of the same age should be kept to a minimum, for modesty is worn away by social exchange, so boldness breaks forth, "laughter creeps in, and bashfulness is lessened." Since women are to keep silent in the church, how much more so virgins to whom silence commends itself as modesty (382). Moreover, virginity is to be "first marked by the voice," so that modesty closes the mouth, religion removes weakness, and habit instructs nature. The telltale mark of a virgin ought to be gravity, along with "a modest approach, a sober gait, a bashful countenance." In fact, the virgin who cannot be identified at first glance ought to be pitied (383). To these exhortations, Ambrose adds his own. One ought to wipe off "the filth of earthly vices" and thus "purify our utmost souls from every defilement of the flesh" (384). There ought to be "the joy of the mind" that is "not excited by unrestrained feasts, or nuptial concerts," for "modesty is not safe" there, "and temptation may be suspected where excessive dancing accompanies festivities" (385). Drawing on the dance of Salome who demanded of the king the head of John the Baptist, Ambrose exhorts mothers to teach their daughters religion instead of dancing. In closing, Ambrose responds to his sister who had asked whether suicide was permissible when virginity was threatened. He says that it is, since the act of suicide is actually "an instance of martyrdom," and "God is not offended by a remedy against evil" and "faith permits the act" (386). In support, he mentions St. Pelagia, who died at age fifteen to preserve her virginity from her persecutors, and who was followed in death and martyrdom by her mother and sisters, who chose to drown themselves in the river rather than succumb (387).

The treatise "Concerning Widows"[44] is written to balance Ambrose's discussion of virgins and to advise against remarriage. Quoting the apostle Paul, Ambrose lists the character traits of a Christian widow: she is to show piety, practice hospitality and humble service, serve in ministries of mercy, help out generously, and do good works (393). Widows, as much as virgins and married women, have a counterpart in the Church. For the Church is all at once a virgin, married, and a widow; she is a widow in that she has lost her husband in the suffering of Christ's body, she is married on the day of judgment when she will receive the Son of Man again, and she is a virgin in that she keeps herself pure for the bridegroom to come. Ambrose lists several examples of honorable widows in Scripture, such as Anna, the widow with the mite in the Gospel of Luke, Naomi, Judith — and even Deborah, the only woman judge of Israel, who to him is a widow and whose son is Barak.

Ambrose offers many reasons why widows should choose to remain unmarried, even when they are still of childbearing age. The example of Deborah shows that women can be strong, despite "the weakness of their sex," leaving them no excuse for marrying again. Grief for the husband, regular work, care of the house, and anxiety for children are all good remedies against the "wantonness" of the soul. Mourning attire, constant weeping, and grief "impressed on the sad brow in deep wrinkles" will restrain "wanton eyes," check one's lust, and turn away "forward looks" (399). The sorrows of a widow serve as "a good guardian of chastity." In fact, "enjoyment is more perilous for widows than difficulties." Still, widows will not go without support, for, like Peter's mother-in-law, they have the nearness of Peter and the affinity of Andrew, his brother, "that they may pray for you," so "your lusts give way." Widows ought to treat their bodies as dying daily "that by dying you may live again." Above all, they are to "avoid pleasures, that you, too, being sick, may be healed" (400). While some things may be permissible in the abstract, they are not permissible "on account of age." For it is unseemly "to have children younger than one's grandchildren" (401).

Christ heals Peter's mother-in-law; likewise, widows ought to pray for their own healing, so that they may see more clearly through their lust. For "the Creator of all teaches us that we ought to be mindful of our own nature, and to discern the vileness of our body" (401). Prayer sees to it that "desire is put to flight" and "lust departs." As a result, "you who were afflicted by an intense disease of the body will begin to minister to Christ." While weak and languid at first "under the fever of various desires," the will eventually rises up to become strong. For no one "who is sick with his own sins, and far from being whole, can minister the remedies of the healing of immortality" (402).

Ambrose advises that widowhood "not be shunned as a penalty, but to be esteemed as a reward." For God "incited virtue by rewards, instead of binding weakness by chains." This reward consists in becoming "holy in body and spirit." It is a reward "far above the toil, grace beyond need, and the wages above the work" (405). This reward will come when the luxuriance of earthly life is "checked off" as with a knife, and the way for a more "blessed fruitfulness" in Christ (406) is prepared by continence.

Jerome (342–420)

Jerome was born at Stridon in Dalmatia and completed his classical education in Rome, where he was baptized about 365. On a visit to Gaul he was introduced to monasticism and, for some years, associated with a group of ascetically minded clergy at Aquileia in Istria, near his home. In 372, he left for the East, settling with the hermits of the desert near Antioch, where he began to study Hebrew. From 379 to 381, Jerome studied at Constantinople during the episcopate of Gregory Nazianzen. Following his return to Rome, Jerome served as secretary to Damasus, bishop of Rome from 382 to 384. Under Damasus the Roman Church abandoned Greek for the Latin vernacular in worship. Furthermore, Damasus commissioned Jerome to revise the

Latin Psalter and the New Testament, which would later prompt him to produce the Vulgate Bible, a translation of the Bible from the original languages into Latin. At the time, many of the leading families of Rome were converting to Christianity and became attracted to the new monastic movement and committed themselves to a life of celibacy. Jerome served as their spiritual guide, particularly to the widow Paula and her daughters Blaesilla and Eustochium.

With Damasus's death in 384, the aristocratic-monastic party fell out of favor in Rome, so that Jerome, along with several friends, went again to the East. After visiting the monks of Egypt and the shrines of Palestine, he settled as head of a monastery at Bethlehem in 386, while Paula presided over a neighboring convent. Jerome's extensive correspondence with Christians in Rome and monks and nuns in both East and West offers vivid pictures of life at the time, in part inspired by the Greek historian Eusebius, whose *Chronicles* Jerome had translated into Latin while in Constantinople. In several letters, Jerome urges a life of celibacy.

One of Jerome's best-known letters is Letter 22,[45] addressed to Eustochium, Paula's daughter (Blaesilla had died in 385, allegedly as a result of unwise austerities in her monastic life), and was written in Rome in 384. He lays down the motives for a life of virginity and the rules by which to regulate one's daily conduct. The purpose of his letter is not to praise virginity, but to preserve it. He tells Eustochium that to know that it is a good thing is not enough; it must be guarded "with jealous care" (31). She should practice virginity as a reminder that she is "fleeing from Sodom." Not pride, but fear is to mark her monastic vows, for she walks "laden with gold" which "you must keep out of the robber's way" (23). While God can do all things, "he cannot raise up a virgin when once she has fallen" (24). Therefore, virgins ought "never let suggestions of evil grow," but "slay the enemy while he is small," dashing them against the rock which is Christ. Jerome relates his personal experience of fasting in the desert with a mind brimming with "bevies of girls," "burning with desire," and the fires of lust "bubbling up before me when my flesh was as good as dead" (25). He knows that if such temptations arise among men in the austerity of fasting, how much more will they "with a girl whose surroundings are those of luxury and ease." Thus, he advises abstinence from "wine and dainties," for "a rumbling and empty stomach" is indispensable for preserving one's chastity. Based on Job's observation about Behemoth (40:16), Jerome also warns against the devil's strength, which is in the loins and in the navel, which, to Jerome, represent the reproductive organs of the two sexes. In his assaults on men, then, the devil operates in the loins; in his assaults on women, in the navel and a woman's desire for children (26).

Virgins ought to shun the company of married women and widows who wish to be married again. For married women pride and "plume themselves" because their husbands are in high positions. And many widows do not welcome the opportunity for continence when it has come, and dress up their "plump bodies" in billowing red cloaks and fill up their houses with flatterers, including clergy, who turn circles around them and at night become the object of these widows' unchaste dreams (28).

Jerome affirms his support of marriage. He does not wish to detract from marriage when setting virginity above it. In fact, married women "may congratulate themselves that they come next to virgins" and those who desire to replenish the earth may do so if they like. But virgins are higher up in rank than the married and belong not on earth, but in heaven, since the command to increase and multiply was given after the Fall and "after the nakedness and the fig-leaves," representing sexual passion (29). Jerome also praises marriage because it produces virgins, and exhorts mothers to nurture their daughter's virginity, and not compel her to do as they did and marry and bear children. "Are you angry with her," he asks, "because she chooses to be a king's wife and not a soldier's?" He tells mothers that a virgin daughter confers on the mother a high privilege, namely, that of making her "the mother-in-law of God" (30).

The life of virginity was foreshadowed by the prophets. In the time of the patriarchs and matriarchs, such as Abraham, Leah, Jacob, and Rachel, only those who could boast of children were considered happy. But gradually "the crop grew up and then the reaper was sent forth with his sickle" and the prophets emerged. Among those who lived a celibate life were Elijah, Elisha, Jeremiah, and "many of the sons of the prophets." In those days "the virtue of continence was found only in men," says Jerome, for Eve still continued to travail in children. But now that a virgin has conceived and has borne us a child, "the chain of the curse is broken." Death came through Eve, but life has come through Mary. The gift of virginity has been bestowed "most richly upon women, seeing that it has had its beginning from a woman" (30). Through Mary, the Son of God was able to set foot upon the earth where he formed for himself a new household that would serve him on earth in the same way as the angels do in heaven.

In their dress and demeanor, virgins ought to avoid excess. But they need not dress in "mean attire" and "sombre dress," sit in too low a place at a gathering, or "mimic the tottering gait of one who is faint" from fasting. They also need not assume the appearance of men, or cut off their hair to "look like eunuchs," or clothe themselves "in goat's hair, and, putting on hoods, think to become children again by making themselves look like so many owls" (34).

Virgins also ought to stay away from certain men. You see these men "loaded with chains and wearing their hair long like women," not to speak of their beards "like those of goats," black cloaks, and bare feet braving the cold. Some men seek the presbyterate and the diaconate to be able to see women with less restraint and think of nothing else but their own dress, using perfumes freely, curling their hair, having fingers glistening with rings, and walking on tiptoe across a damp road, not to splash their feet; their single object is to know the names, houses, and characters of women. But since they do not act as clergymen, but bridegrooms, they are to be avoided at all cost (34).

Moreover, virgins are to guard against covetousness. While they have surrendered their property by their monastic vows, they need to surrender thoughts of their own comforts as well. You may see women cramming their wardrobes with dresses, says Jerome, changing their gowns daily, dying parchments purple, while Christ lies at the door naked and dying. Moreover, they "sound a trumpet" when they help the needy to gain personal acclaim. Such selfish concern chokes the faith and disavows the fact that God will provide, as he does for the birds of the air and the lilies of the field (Matt. 6:25–26) (37).

Jerome concludes his letter with a final admonition: It is better to endure the current life of simplicity and celibacy than to waver and become "slaves forever" (40). So whenever "this life's idle show tries to charm you" and "you see in the world some vain pomp," the virgin must focus "on the reward of your present toil," namely, entry into paradise. There, Mary will meet her, accompanied by virgin choirs; Miriam, with timbrel in hand chanting with the choirs; Thecla, flying with joy to embrace her; Christ, the spouse to welcome her; and the companies of the chaste, with Sarah leading the wedded and Anna the widows, coming to meet her (41). This paradisical vision then should strengthen the virgin to persevere in her chosen life on earth.

In 383, a year prior to the letter to Eustochium, Jerome had written a treatise on "The Perpetual Virginity of Blessed Mary."[46] The treatise, also titled "Against Helvidius," was written to disprove Helvidius's position that Mary had other children besides Jesus. Jerome maintains three opposing positions: first, that Joseph was only putatively, not actually, the husband of Mary; second, that the "brethren" of the Lord were his cousins, not his brothers of flesh and blood; and third, that virginity is better than the married state. As part of the argument, Jerome says that not only did Mary maintain her virginity, but Joseph did as well. Because of Mary, Joseph "was a virgin, so that from a virgin wedlock a virgin son was born." Since he was considered a holy man, Joseph could not have committed fornication, nor is there any scriptural evidence that he had another wife; Jerome believes that he served as guardian to Mary and maintained his virginal state (344).

The state of virginity marks the beginning of a new rule. While people in the Old Testament who lived under the old rule were married, people living now are under the new rule in Christ, which supplants the command to "be fruitful and multiply," and offers the choice of remaining celibate and "cleaving to the Lord" instead. Under the new rule, the virgin is no longer called a woman, for "the distinction of sex is lost," and she is "defined as she that is holy in body and in spirit" (344).

In another treatise, "Against Jovinianus — Book I,"[47] written in 393, Jerome counters a claim by Jovinianus that virgins, widows, and

married women are of equal merit in the eyes of God (348).[48] Jerome
retorts with an exposition of Paul's letter, 1 Corinthians 7, selections
from various books of the Old and New Testaments, and the praises
of virginity and of marrying only once derived from the pagan world.
Jerome draws on Peter, as well as Paul, "because in both cases the spirit
is the same." Peter says that "prayers are hindered by the performance
of marriage duty" (1 Pet. 3:2–3). He challenges husbands to imitate
their wives in continence, for by doing so they give honor to their
wives. According to Jerome, Peter lays down the law for husbands and
wives, condemns outward ornament, and praises continence, "which
is the ornament of the inner man." He is saying that "since your outer
man is corrupt, and you have ceased to possess the blessing of incorruption characteristic of virgins, at least imitate the incorruption of
the spirit by subsequent abstinence" (351). The couple may begin the
practice "with short periods of release from the marriage bond," where
they give themselves to prayer. Once they have "tasted the sweets of
chastity," says Jerome, they may desire the perpetual possession of what
delighted them temporarily (355).

Christ loves virgins more than others because they give what is not
commanded of them. It indicates greater grace to offer what one is not
forced to give than to render what is exacted. Christ is more pleased
with those who have made themselves eunuchs "not of necessity, but
of free choice" (355), so that they cannot be placed on the same level
with those who have not. For it is a mark of great faith and virtue "to
offer oneself a whole burnt-offering" and to be holy both in body and
in spirit (356). He that cannot bridle "his virgin, that is, his flesh,"
may marry; but he who has the power of self-control "to keep his own
virgin, shall do well." Since one is something good, the other something
better, there cannot be the same reward (358).

Jerome concludes by saying that no one needs to be afraid that all
will become virgins because virginity is a hard matter "and therefore
rare." Many begin, few persevere, so that the reward is great for those
who do (373). The "great and precious" reward consists in becoming
partakers of the divine nature by having escaped from the corruption
of lust (377).

Augustine (354–430)

Augustine was born at Tagaste, in northern Africa. His father, a Roman official, was a pagan and converted to Christianity only when Augustine was already a bishop; his mother, Monica, was a devout Christian and raised her son accordingly. In 370, Augustine went to Carthage to study rhetoric intending to become a lawyer, but devoted himself to literary pursuits instead. The following year, he took a mistress with whom he lived for thirteen years and with whom he had a son, Adeodatus, born in 372. A year later, Augustine embraced Manichaeism, to which he adhered for nine years. Manichaeism's body-soul dualism seemed to him to explain theological and biblical difficulties and excused moral lapses among those who were merely hearers, as he was — as distinct from the elect, who had to practice celibacy. For the next decade, Augustine taught rhetoric at Tagaste, Carthage, Rome, and eventually Milan, where he accepted a chair in rhetoric in 384. Hoping that Augustine might become a Christian, his mother arranged for a wife from a wealthy Milanese Christian family and sent away his mistress while Augustine was with his father. But since the girl Monica chose was two years short of marriageable age and Augustine could not do without sexual intercourse, he found himself another mistress. Under the influence of the Neoplatonist writings of Plotinus and the sermons of Ambrose extolling celibacy and virginity, Augustine called off the alliance, experienced a conversion in 386, and was baptized the following year. His mother died during their return to Tagaste in northern Africa, where he later founded a monastery; his son died two years later. In 391, Augustine was ordained a priest at Hippo while living in a monastic community he had established. In 395, he became coadjutor with Bishop Valerius of Hippo, and was made bishop of Hippo the following year upon Valerius's death. In this role for the next forty years, Augustine assumed the leadership role in defining and defending Christian thought against the Manichaean, the Donatist,[49] and the Pelagian sects. His profuse writings — including about two hundred treatises, some three hundred letters, and nearly four hundred sermons — influenced Western philosophy, ethics, and Christian thought on the issue of celibacy and sexual conduct for the next one thousand years. They continue to be of major import to both Roman Catholic and Protestant traditions to this day.

Through his life, Augustine retained a vivid sense of the conflict between good and evil in the world and in the soul, which influenced his views on the human body and sexual intercourse. In the first nine of the thirteen chapters of his *Confessions* (A.D. 397),[50] Augustine describes in form of a narrative prayer the stages of his faith journey from adolescence to his conversion experience in Milan at age thirty-two. Of particular grief to him are his sexual experiences and cravings which began at age sixteen with "the mud of my fleshly desires and my erupting puberty" and kept his mind engulfed "in murky clouds" and a "whirlpool of sins" (62). He knew no proper restraint, such as friendship or the union of two minds, and was unable to distinguish between love and lust. Augustine deplores the fact that no one in his family arranged a marriage for him to give him tranquility of mind and the contentment of using his "sexuality to procreate children" the way the Lord had ordained (63).

Obsessed with sex, Augustine felt it was the result of a law that possessed his body. This law "held sway in my lower self" and dragged his mind along and held it captive against its will (194). Thus, "a craving for sexual gratification" fettered him "like a tight-drawn chain." His release was occasioned by a visitor named Ponticianus, who had come to his house on a business matter and shared with Augustine and his friend Alypius his knowledge of the life of the monk Antony of Egypt. Completely unfamiliar with monasticism, including the fact that a monastery existed right outside Milan under the auspices of Ambrose, Augustine heard how two men at Trier, upon meeting some monks and reading from *The Life of Antony,* had resolved to call off their marriages and committed themselves to a life of celibacy. Their fiancees followed suit (196–97). In the course of Ponticianus's story, Augustine was forced to recognize "how despicable I was, how misshapen and begrimed, filthy and festering." He recalled his own struggles. Praying for the gift of chastity, Augustine had told God, "Grant me chastity and self-control, but please not yet" for fear that he would be instantaneously healed of his "morbid lust," which he was more "anxious to satisfy than to snuff out" (198). Now he was ready to seek this freedom.

Augustine hears taunting voices plucking at his "garment of flesh," inquiring whether he will be able to live without "these things" as "forbidden to you, all your life long" (204–5). But the voices begin to subside when he catches a vision of "the chaste, dignified figure of Continence," which is "calm and cheerful," though modest, with a "pure and honorable charm," stretching out her kindly hands to welcome and embrace him, "hands filled with a wealth of heartening examples." In the company of Continence are a "multitude of boys and girls," "a great concourse of youth and persons of every age, venerable widows and women grown old in their virginity." On account of them, Augustine realizes that Continence is "by no means sterile, but the fruitful mother of children conceived in joy from you, her Bridegroom." Augustine sees her smiling at him with a challenge, as if to say, "Can you not do what these men have done, these women? Could any of them achieve it by their own strength, without the Lord their God? He it was, the Lord their God, who granted me to them." Then Continence encourages him to close his ears "against those unclean parts of you which belong to the earth and let them be put to death" (205).

Recalling how Antony had been converted by reading a single Gospel passage, Augustine then fetches the book containing the Apostle Paul's letters. Opening it, his eyes fall on Romans 13:13–14, which says: "Not in dissipation and drunkenness, nor in debauchery and lewdness, nor in arguing and jealousy; but put on the Lord Jesus Christ, and make no provision for the flesh or the gratification of your desires." Augustine had no need to read on, but received "the light of certainty" (207) to embark on a life of celibacy in service to God in Christ by "no longer seeking a wife or entertaining any worldly hope, for you had converted me to yourself" (208).

Upon his return to northern Africa and ordination to the priesthood, Augustine's views on the nature of sexual desire, celibacy, and continence were shaped by his work in the parish. His focus was on married couples, and in particular the husbands, rather than the orders of male and female celibates and widows in his congregation. In a sermon on John 6:55, Sermon 82,[51] Augustine exhorts both the baptized and catechumens to become worthy by their sexual conduct to receive the elements of the Eucharist. Married men who are baptized, for example, are to act as role models to catechumens by the way they "keep the fidelity of the marriage-bed" with their wives. Since husbands expect their wives to be chaste, they ought to walk themselves where they expect their wives to go. "Thou requirest strength from the weaker sex," he says, so be the true head of the household and "the first to conquer" the lust of the flesh. It is deplorable that in the practice of marital continence, men are weaker than women, and more easily subdued by the "enemy" in their "struggle," "war," and "combat." Moreover, men are deceived into thinking that having sex makes them look more like men, when the opposite is the case (505).

In turning to unmarried men who wish to marry, Augustine exhorts them to keep themselves virgins for their future wives. Since "thou lookest for one unpolluted, be unpolluted thyself." Doing so will actually bestow greater glory upon the man than the woman. After all, the woman is kept a virgin by many external laws, such as "the vigilance of parents," "the very modesty of the weaker sex," and her "fear of the laws" of society. What will keep men virgins until marriage is solely the fear of God, who "seeth thee," no matter whether the lamp is lighted or extinguished or whether "thou enterest into thy closet" or the confines of the heart. Finally, those who have taken celibate vows are to "chasten your bodies more strictly." Remaining within the confines of the permissible is not enough. Instead of simply refraining from sexual activity and unlawful involvements, they should "despise even a lawful look." In doing so, they emulate the angels in heaven and model the life of the resurrection while still on earth. In summary, everyone is to aspire to sexual continence, the unmarried to virginity, the married to "wedded chastity," and the widowed to "holy widowhood." Those who do not should not partake of the Eucharist and approach "that Bread" (505) until they have mended their ways (506).

In a sermon on the parable of the ten virgins of Matthew 25:1–13, Sermon 43,[52] Augustine says that all Christians are virgins and are to act accordingly. For all are members of the Church, who is the supreme Virgin and bride of Christ — not just women and men of holy orders, or the clergy. Since all are virgins by their calling, all are expected to use their five senses properly by abstaining from "unlawful seeing, unlawful hearing, unlawful smelling, unlawful tasting, and unlawful touching," and carry the lamps of their good works (402). Foolish virgins are those who practice abstinence and good works to please others. Appearing to do all the right things, they run out of oil as soon as the outward praises stop and are exposed before God for how empty they are inside. The wise, on the other hand, carry "the inner oil of conscience" and, on the last day, will find themselves in the "spiritual embrace" of the Bridegroom (405).

Augustine elaborates on what he means by "wedded chastity" (402) in his treatise on "The Good of Marriage."[53] The treatise was written in A.D. 401 as a rebuttal to Jovinianus who considered the married state equal to that of virginity or widowhood, so that many consecrated virgins were leaving the order to marry. Augustine construes marriage as a threefold good that involves the benefits of procreation, of fidelity, and of sacrament (48). The good of marriage as a sacrament, he says, is that marriage is "an association of fidelity that cannot be dissolved" (16), hence symbolizes the divine union of Jesus Christ with the church. This "marriage bond is not loosed except by the death of the spouse" (48), so that even when couples separate on account of sterility and remarry in hopes of having children, "they commit adultery" (31). It is better to die of hunger than eat food sacrificed to idols, in the same way that it is better to die childless than to seek progeny from an unlawful union (32). Augustine defines the other two goods by negative injunctions, stressing self-restraint and the denial of sexual pleasure. Fidelity means the absence of adultery and the "chastity of souls" lived out in faithful "companionship between the sexes" (12–13); such a great good is fidelity that "it ought to be preferred even to the health of the body" (13). Procreation, on the other hand, "makes something good out of the evil lust" of sexual desire. The only purpose of marriage is procreation, so that children might be born "properly and decently" (33). All other instances of marital intercourse serve passion instead of reason (24), by "satisfying [one's] concupiscence," hence are "a venial sin"(17).[54] To keep from sinning, Augustine recommends that Christians practice "wedded chastity" by abstaining from marital intercourse at all times, except for the purpose of procreation.

In another line of argument, Augustine seeks to demonstrate that celibacy and wedded chastity were practices by the leading figures of the Old Testament. To him, Abraham, for example, did not lack "this type of continence," but possessed it if "only in habit" (42). For while Abraham may have used marriage far differently than Christians do nowadays (43) because of "the difference in times," he still had intercourse only as "the duty of caring for others," not on account of its "unreasoning and wicked lust" (33). Likewise, "Sara possessed that virtue and did what was suited at that time" (44). Therefore, we cannot compare ourselves to the patriarchs and matriarchs of old and claim superiority in our practice of celibacy, but should recognize that with them we hold in common that we are spouses and parents "not for the sake of this world, but for the sake of Christ" (51).

For balance, Augustine the same year writes "Holy Virginity,"[55] in which he defends Mary's perpetual virginity,[56] and offers practical exhortations on the conduct of virgins. Foremost is a reminder to virgins to remain humble, not on account of "so great a blessing" to experience "the swelling of self-conceit" (184). The virgin may think "that it comes to her from herself that she is such," instead of recognizing that "this best gift comes from above, from the Father of lights" (195). Humility has to be genuine and free of comparison with married women. For while the virgin may not yet be a Thecla, the married woman may already be a Crispina (199).[57] Moreover, those "who neither possess nor profess" virginity may be able to excel at something the virgin does not (203).

Augustine reiterates the threefold good of marriage in the first book of his two-book treatise against Julianus[58] and the Pelagians,[59] titled "Marriage and Desire,"[60] written in 419. The treatise maintains that even though marriage produces infants born in original sin who stand in need of redemption through Christ, marriage is still good. The treatise's focus is the need of infants to be cleansed of original sin through baptism, but it also distinguishes the good of marriage from the evil of sexual desire. The word "desire" in the title of the treatise is often translated as "concupiscence," which to Augustine in this context meant sexual desire.[61] The treatise was written to Count Valerius, whom he commends for his "exemplary life" of wedded chastity (29), "this good of yours, a gift of God."[62] One makes bad use of marriage, says Augustine, "if one uses it like an animal," to receive the pleasure of sexual desire, instead of to procreate (30). The "evil of concupiscence" that avoids "being seen and seeks privacy out of a sense of shame" does not detract from the good of marriage (33). In fact, one can use this "evil" for good in two ways in the context of marriage: either by bridling it as it "boils with inordinate and unseemly impulses," or in the interest of procreation. The patriarchs used sexual desire both ways. They had many wives only so as to increase the number of offspring, not out of a desire "to add variety to their pleasure"; for the same reason no woman had many husbands — unless she was a prostitute, since this would not have produced more children, but only "more frequent pleasure" (34). To the patriarchs procreation was "an important duty," geared toward generating and preserving the people of God in whom Christ's coming had yet to be announced (37).

The good of marriage in regard to procreation, however, can be destroyed by the couple themselves. They do so when they have intercourse while interfering with the conception of a child "either by an evil intention or by an evil act." Such evil intentions or acts include the taking of drugs to produce sterility, and the destruction of the fetus — or later of the unborn, within the womb. This type of behavior does not constitute marriage but debauchery and "dark savagery" and identifies the wife as a "prostitute of her husband," and the husband as an "adulterer toward his wife" (39–40).

Concupiscence did not exist in paradise, but resulted from the Fall. Now that it is part of human existence, "one should not be subservient to it." One way is not to marry and to "practice abstinence," since we live in the "time for holding back from embraces" and already have "in all nations such a great abundance of children who need to be reborn spiritually"; but this is recommended only to those "to whom it is given" (Matt. 19:11). Another way is to marry, whereby "a lack of self-control is rescued by the good of marriage" (40). For the married, this concupiscence is "decreased daily" as they practice continence, but in those who give in, concupiscence will gain such strength that, despite old age and the fact that these "same parts of the body are less capable of being aroused for that activity," it continues "its fury more shamefully and more impudently" (46). Augustine ranks celibacy above marriage, but he establishes marriage as a good as long as the couple practices "wedded chastity," engaging in intercourse only for the sake of procreation and refraining from birth control. Thus, except for the act of procreation, all Christians are enjoined to practice celibacy by refusing to act upon their concupiscence, or sexual desire.

This overview of eight leading Church Fathers spans the beginning stages of theological debate on celibacy, and shows gradually evolving developments and key emphases. Earlier lines of argument in favor of celibacy move into the background, or are lost altogether and subsequently replaced by others. The practical rewards and benefits of celibacy in this world are postponed to ethereal benefits in the next. Likewise, the early focus on prophetic gifts released by the practice of the celibate life virtually disappears. In regard to women, a previously gained autonomy from social pressures of childbearing and marital submission is transformed into a subsequent subjugation to strict behavioral codes for professing virgins and widows. The next task will be to chronologically trace these theological developments up to Augustine. We will then have characterized the theological environment that spawned the Reformation and will be able to identify the theological views regarding celibacy that the early reformers of the sixteenth century so vigorously opposed.

Chapter 5

Theological Developments on Celibacy I: The Church Fathers and the Reformation

The Church Fathers: A Summary

By A.D. 200, celibacy had been established among Christians as the preferred ideal over marriage. Many, though still only a minority, renounced not only marriage but possessions, and lived a life of devotion to prayer and works of mercy. The practice of celibate living for both men and women had gained acclaim, especially among the more affluent members of the Christian faith. The order of widows had been well established and virgins consecrated themselves to perpetual virginity, while mostly living at home.[1] By the end of the third century, various communities of men and women, usually living in separate quarters, had sprung up in both East and West, largely owing to the difficulties involved in living a celibate life in the context of home and family. By the beginning of the fourth century, some of these communities — starting with those in the East and then spreading to the West — had organized themselves under a rule with special clothing and a common purse. Their gradual withdrawal into separate communities may have weakened the local congregations by reducing the number of devout leaders. But with their leaving, the focus began to shift to married couples in the church and the ideal of marital sexual abstinence, so that by the early fifth century, the doctrine of marital celibacy had been fully developed.

In the four hundred years of theological debate on celibacy, beginning with the second century, the key arguments changed and evolved. In their theological discussions on celibacy, the Church Fathers responded in large part to sociopolitical, religious, and theological developments in their respective parishes, provinces, and countries. While these developments may have shaped their arguments, their arguments in turn influenced subsequent trends in the history of the church's doctrine. The present discussion will chronicle the evolving doctrine of celibacy as formulated by the Church Fathers, beginning with a summary of how these early theologians used Scripture in promoting celibacy, particularly among women; how they justified marriage and having children; their views on celibacy as a gift from God given only to a few; and the advantages of celibacy for faithful Christian discipleship.

Arguments from Scripture on Celibacy

The Church Fathers concentrate on Paul's first letter to the Corinthians, chapter 7; less frequently on Matthew 19:12. Both men and women are said to gain from the practice, as they are no longer subject to the earthly and economic concerns involved in caring for a family and can dedicate themselves more fully to doing the Lord's work. Women have more to gain than men; they are no longer dependent upon the rule of potential husbands, are freed from the responsibilities of having to raise children, can preserve their body's beauty and autonomy, and gain ownership over their lives by their freedom in Christ. Men have as their role models Paul and the disciples, women have Mary. Mary becomes a particularly powerful model, since she is the first among those practicing celibacy to give birth to Christ. Thus, she models each Christian's responsibility of giving birth to Christ in others — a responsibility that will be helped along by sexual abstinence. Jesus' celibacy is mentioned only in the context of his resisting the bodily temptation for food and status in his encounter with the devil in the wilderness. The metaphor of Jesus as bridegroom is frequently employed to encourage particularly women to preserve their virginity as brides of Christ who, on the last day, will be wedded to their heavenly groom.

The injunction in Genesis to be fruitful and multiply is reinterpreted as meaning to multiply those who become spiritually reborn. Christians can offer the first-fruits of their celibacy in the form of study and devotion to Scripture, prayer, and acts of mercy toward the poor, thus deepening and increasing the faith of others by their life of sacrifice and self-surrender, much like the priests of old. Both men and women of the Old Testament are said to have practiced wedded chastity by offering up their bodies to produce children, through whom eventually Jesus would be born. Men were the first to commit to celibacy, as exemplified by some of the prophets, including John the Baptist. Only with Mary did the practice gain preponderance among women, eventually finding wider acclaim with them than men.

Arguments to Justify Marriage

An elevated regard for celibacy and virginity over marriage left the Church Fathers struggling to formulate valid reasons for marriage. The marital state came to be viewed as a blessed and providential gift from God, useful for procreation and raising children. It also prevented fornication by offering people a theologically acceptable way to satisfy their sexual drive. Unlike today, however, in early Christianity the good of marriage did not consist in a complementary partnership and union of mind that advances mutual spiritual growth and enhances service to the Lord. If anything, couples were thought to be hindered by the marital state and its inherent responsibilities and temptations. To preclude distraction, couples were encouraged to practice sexual abstinence, which would deepen their prayer time and commitment to Christ's body, the church. The sole good of marriage was in the propagation of the human race, in giving birth to children who in turn might devote themselves to a life of celibacy and virginity.

According to the Fathers, marriage allowed people to imitate their creator in the work of procreation. Marriage was considered good as long as sexual desires were satisfied in moderation. If the marriage ended in divorce or with the death of a spouse, remarriage was discouraged, regardless of whether the couple had children. The opportunity to be single, hence celibate, again, was viewed as a release from the bondage of worldly cares that marriage had imposed.

The Fathers felt that human nature inclined people to be more attracted to marriage than the single state. The reasons for this attraction varied, and could include the search for status and social acceptability, overcoming loneliness, and the desire to live on through one's offspring, but they invariably involved people's urge to act on their sexual drive. To remove the stain of sexual licentiousness and passion from marriage, the Fathers recommended that couples exercise moderation in the frequency of sexual intercourse and set aside periods of sexual abstinence, provided both partners agreed. The injunction to secure mutual agreement is directed particularly at women, who seem to have been more inclined to practice sexual abstinence than men and who may have used the practice of withholding their bodies from their husbands to wield control, communicate their faith, and bring about their husbands' conversion.

Still, the stigma of unbridled sexual desire attached to marriage bond remained. So, the Fathers eventually began encouraging couples to practice marital celibacy at all times, except when intending to have children. With that, engaging in sexual intercourse without wanting to procreate became a sin, though a pardonable one. Couples were to practice marital celibacy early on in their marriage, with old age enhancing the discipline of abstinence. This habit of "wedded chastity" was viewed as stimulating spiritual pursuit and decreasing the risk of adultery.

With the stain of sexual passion removed, marriage emerged as a threefold good. First, marriage becomes the only appropriate locus for the birth and raising of children; second, it is praised for the mark of fidelity that keeps the marriage bed undefiled and the partners loyal to each other; and third, it gains the status of a sacrament[2] through the marriage vow that binds the partners to each other for life. The word "sacrament," or *mysterion* in the Greek, had mainly been associated with baptism as a lifelong sacred sign of one's pledged fidelity to Christ. Now marriage is thought of along these same lines. Those who marry pledge their fidelity to Christ and to each other for life, just as the baptized pledge themselves to Christ for life.[3]

The marriage vow finds its counterpart in the consecration vow taken by virgins, widows, and members of monastic communities. By viewing the marriage vow as sacred, the status of marriage was significantly raised to a level it did not previously have within the church; the recognition marriage now is afforded by the church approximates that previously bestowed on it by the secular and political world of the

Greco-Roman empire. With marriage receiving the status of divine sacrament, however, the celibacy of consecrated virgins, widows, and members of monastic communities lost somewhat and, in later years, would never gain back the same recognition it once had during the first five centuries of the church.

Celibacy for the Few

The Fathers maintained that people have an innate tendency to give in to their sexual drive. This tendency, which was later called concupiscence, meant that only a minority of people would be willing or able to commit to the celibate life.

The Fathers distinguish between celibacy as a divine gift, or charism, and as a personal human endeavor. Drawing on Matthew 19:12, they agree that only those to whom this gift is given by God can practice celibacy. But no one is prevented from asking for this gift, and Scripture assures Christians that whosoever asks will receive. Thus the gift is not reserved for only a few, but may be granted to all if only they ask. The reason why more people do not ask for this gift is their attraction to worldly, material, and carnal pursuits.

Some people may be more disposed than others toward a life of sexual abstinence. This disposition is not necessarily based on personal effort and merit, but is given to them by God. God does so for the sake of variety, not to penalize some and reward others. Since God has given some a greater advantage over others in this regard, the former should not take personal pride in their efforts at self-restraint. The latter, however, who have difficulty resisting the temptations of the body and their sexual nature yet do so regardless, are to be admired all the more and will gain greater esteem in the eyes of God.

The practice of celibacy is shaped by habit. This habit is easier to develop the earlier on in life it begins. While initially the habit of celibacy may focus on the body by fostering temperance, it eventually extends to the mind and soul, beautifying the lines of one's character and one's whole inner being. The mind is continually trained to transfer its attraction from material objects to those of spiritual beauty and wisdom.

The pursuit of celibacy is greatly enhanced by the presence of role models. While both the Old and New Testaments offer male and female role models for an integrated life of celibacy, the best guide in life is a mentor — someone who has wrestled with bodily temptations, yet has resisted them and is able to sympathize with the novice and offer encouragement and guidance along the way.

Celibacy and Faithful Discipleship

The Gift of Prophecy

Initially, the life of celibacy was viewed as bringing to fruition certain spiritual gifts, or charisms, in the believer that would advance the overall ministry of the church. Among these gifts are prophecy, teaching, preaching, healing, exorcism, and church leadership. The early Church Fathers, especially Tertullian and Origen, most commonly refer to prophecy as the gift that results from the celibate life. Among men, the gift of prophecy was a by-product of the celibacy of Elijah, Elisha, Jeremiah, and John the Baptist. Among women, the gift of prophecy was given by celibacy to Miriam and Deborah, the judge, and to Anna, the widow, and the four virgin daughters of Philip the evangelist.[4] One of the most prominent celibate female prophets is Thecla, the heroine, described not in the sacred Scriptures, but in the apocryphal writings of the *Acts of Paul and Thecla*. Although the Church Fathers make frequent reference to Thecla, who had become a legendary figure and role model to many virgins and women practicing celibacy at the time, they ignore her influential role as apostolic leader,[5] similar to Paul's, and her gifts of teaching, healing, and exorcism as part of her ministry. Another celibate woman with prophetic gifts was Prisca,[6] who had established an influential Christian ministry of her own by the middle of the second century in Rome. In elaborating on spiritual gifts and prophecy in particular, Tertullian quotes Prisca as saying that celibacy produces "harmony of soul, and the pure see visions."

The Gift of Martyrdom

Later on, celibacy came to be regarded as producing martyrs, not prophets. The fruit of celibacy maturing in the believer is no longer the gift of prophecy, but the gift of martyrdom. It is a curious shift of emphasis; celibate believers no longer directly contribute to the current life and ministry of the church, as they had done through their gift of prophecy. Instead, they lend indirect benefit to the church and to Christianity at large by validating it and demonstrating that the church's teachings are so sacred and supreme that they are worth dying for. The Fathers argue that celibacy will empower Christians to die fearlessly for their faith and convictions. As examples of such fearless resolve in the face of death, the Fathers identify men and women who fit two criteria: they never married, and they had been killed, which include Abel, John the Baptist, and Thecla (who was never married and assumed to have been killed — contrary to the account of the *Apocryphal Acts*).

Moreover, the Fathers maintain that the truly celibate is willing to die rather than succumb to forced sexual intercourse. Examples of such heroism are invariably women and include Susanna and Thecla. Ambrose is tireless in recounting the stories of girls and women[7] willing to die to preserve their virginity that gives them the gift to endure and suffer martyrdom.

By the end of the third and beginning with the fourth centuries, faithful Christian discipleship is marked by martyrdom, by an unrelenting, courageous, and willing submission to the powers that threaten the life of the Christian. In contrast to the gift of prophecy, this type of discipleship is defined by an attitude of passivity and a nonviolent and frequently silent submission. Two reasons may account for this shift from active to passive, from prophecy to martyrdom: One, two severe persecutions of Christians occurred within a period of fifty years. The Christian persecution of 248 under Emperor Decian sought to restore stability to the crumbling Roman Empire by requiring its citizens, Origen[8] among them, to sacrifice to Roman gods; the second persecution occurred in 303 under Emperor Diocletian and began in the East in Nicomedia and spread outward into Africa. Many Christians suffered torture and death on account of their faith, and the church's way of honoring their sacrifice and retaining memory of them was to regard martyrdom as a supreme charism and gift. The second reason for the shift from active to passive may have been that the involvement of women in leadership positions in the church was by now frowned upon, and that the roles of ordained deacon and overseer, i.e., priest and bishop, had been reserved for men. The gifts of prophecy and leadership were considered unfit for women and needed substituting to fit the patriarchal view of women as the weaker sex, subject to male authority in the family and the church. Thus, women's spiritual gifts were made to correspond with passivity and submission. Women were considered praiseworthy in their Christian discipleship if they remained passive, nonviolent, and silent, thus enduring violence and abuse even unto death. In the case of virgins and widows, nonviolent resistance leading to death was not necessarily credited to their courage and faith, but to their celibate state. Celibate women were martyred not because they proclaimed their faith convictions in the face of persecution; instead, they were martyred because they were striving to preserve their virginity and the purity of their bodies.

Internalized and Postponed Rewards

In another development, the rewards of celibacy for both men and women move from the concrete to the abstract. Paul had alluded to the fact that the unmarried could give more undivided time to the work of the Lord, while the married had to be concerned with the things of this world. The benefits of the unmarried state then were immediate and concrete. As Origen suggested, the unmarried could deepen their life of prayer, study, knowledge, and interpretation of Scripture. They could also expand on their services of mercy to the poor, and could impart wisdom by teaching the young, tending to and healing the sick, and giving testimony of God's activity in their own lives, thereby leading nonbelievers to faith and bringing about their rebirth in Christ.

By the end of the third century, these concrete results of faithful Christian discipleship in celibacy change to the more abstract. Methodius praises virginity because it will lead to "the pasture of immortality." The process of the new creation and its transformative powers become internalized. Believers will see Christ being formed in them and be made "Christs" themselves. They can cooperate with Christ and help "in preaching for the salvation" of others, who in turn will assist still others in their spiritual rebirth. Thereby, celibacy facilitates the "receiving and conceiving" of the seeds of life.

By the middle of the fourth century, Gregory of Nyssa recommends celibacy as a method for leading a divine life, marked by moderation, the complete forgetfulness of natural emotions, and the progressive beautification of one's character. By enlisting the entire range of gifts, celibacy will transform the person, producing a life of greater stability, self-awareness, integrity, and calm. The immediate reward is "aesthetic" in nature, manifest only to the eyes of the soul. By practicing celibacy, believers strive to attain the power of "seeing God" and prepare themselves in holiness for the coming of God in Christ.

With the end of the fourth century, celibacy's rewards are largely postponed to the afterlife. To John Chrysostom, celibacy releases believers from enslavement to lust and worldly attachments and raises them to the angelic state. They are to focus on the "future advantages and wages," which will be great, and they will have, in contrast to the married, an easier time gaining entrance to the Kingdom of Heaven.

To Ambrose, the purpose of celibacy was to become holy in body and in spirit in this life in preparation for the next. Celibacy's rewards are "far above the toil" and its "wages above the work." Heaven is the "native country" of virginity, and reaching it will require battles and conquests. In writing to virgins and widows, Ambrose instructs them in the practice of a celibacy marked by self-denial, solitude, and silent acquiescence. The greater their gravity, sobriety, and modesty in demeanor, attire, and speech, the better their prospects of finding themselves in the company of Mary and her choirs of virgins on the last day.

To Jerome, celibacy and marital abstinence cultivate in believers "the inner man" and a life in the spirit. Celibates lose "the distinction of sex" in their pursuit of becoming ever more holy in body and in spirit. When tempted by luxuries and lust, virgins, for example, are to contemplate their future entry into paradise, where the company of Mary, Miriam, Thecla, Christ, Sarah, and Anna stands ready to welcome them. The immediate reward of celibacy consists in partaking in the divine nature and being freed from this world's corruption by lust. But the heavenly rewards will be even greater than the earthly ones, and will certainly exceed the rewards of those who do not practice the celibate life.

And to Augustine, the heavenly reward of celibacy is finding oneself in the "spiritual embrace" of the eternal bridegroom, Christ. Celibacy is to be practiced both by the unmarried and married believers, who will reduce the strength of concupiscence that resulted from the Fall and that continually seeks to enslave people. They will come to model the life of angels and of the resurrection here on earth while preparing for a life in heaven.

The shift in the fruits of celibacy from the more immediate gifts to a more internalized piety and to a postponed heavenly reward may be due to two factors. First, the Fathers identified the gift of prophecy from among the more immediate gifts resulting from celibacy. Other gifts and privileges were associated with prophecy, such as preaching, teaching, and a central leadership role in the local community of faith. Each community of faith, however, could only accommodate so many leaders exercising a prophetic preaching and teaching ministry. Since there were many more members within a congregation practicing celibacy than there were available "offices" of leadership, the gifts resulting from celibacy had to shift from what was associated with only a few to what could be associated with many. Prophecy, the gift of a few, was replaced as celibacy's reward by the gift of the many, an internalized piety, a refinement in character, and a preferred status in the heavenly realm.[9]

The second possible reason may have been that the gift of prophecy had become linked with apostolic leadership and authority, based on the ministry of the apostles, such as Peter and Paul, and their missionary and evangelistic activities. If the Church Fathers had continued to regard prophecy as the primary fruit of the celibate life, many celibate women of the time would have theoretically qualified for the prophetic office, hence leadership positions in the church. These leadership positions, however, had been firmly lodged in the hands of men by the end of the second century. The trend began when traveling missionaries, such as the apostles and early evangelists, came to appoint local, stationary clergy — overseers[10] and deacons, who were subject to general apostolic oversight.[11] The earliest guide on church offices, the *Didache* or *Teaching of the Apostles*, was presumably written between 70 and 110, and encourages congregations to appoint for themselves bishops and deacons that are to be "men of honor," thus corresponding in their male exclusivity with church orders written in the early to mid-third century.[12] When in the second century, the roles of bishop and priest became separate offices, bishops were believed to have taken over the prophetic and apostolic office of the traveling missionaries, apostles, and evangelists, while priests held the lower office of local teachers. With the role of prophet already filled by a male bishop and the association of prophecy with apostolic, hence male, leadership, women disqualified as agents of prophetic activity.

Other Developments

Infant Baptism

With the church's elevated regard for marriage and one of the goods of marriage pertaining to procreation, concern shifts to the spiritual future and destiny of children. Despite the redemption of both parents from sin through Jesus Christ, despite both parents' baptism, despite their practice of sexual abstinence except for the purpose of procreation, the child born from the union is believed to be tainted with original sin. Augustine puzzles over why this should be the case, but resolves nonetheless that it is so, and consequently formulates the doctrine that children need to be baptized soon after birth to be transferred from the power of darkness "into the kingdom of their Lord."

The adoption of infant baptism as a sacrament further devalued the vows of virgins, widows, and members of monastic communities. Infant baptism ran counter to the view that baptism was a seal of protection to preserve one's virginity and celibate practice. This view may have originated two hundred years earlier with the story of Thecla, who had requested baptism from Paul for the sake of protecting her virginity, but the baptism never took place; so when her life — hence her virginity — was threatened, she baptized herself. With that, many Christians of the second and third centuries came to associate the rite of baptism with the perpetual renunciation of sexual activity.[13] Moreover, these Christians believed that beginning with their baptism and on account of their sexual abstinence, they would receive the rewards that would grant them a jubilant welcome into the heavenly realm. Now, however, with the practice of baptizing infants, it appeared that these infants would receive the same or similar rewards that celibate adult believers had been hoping to attain by a lifelong and disciplined practice of sexual renunciation.

Freedom of Choice

The Church Fathers affirmed that commitment to the celibate life had to be a free choice. According to Tertullian, only the power of the Holy Spirit, the Paraclete, will reveal to the believer the "light burden" and freedom in Christ afforded by the practice of celibacy. No external authority, only personal conviction by the Spirit will prompt and guide believers toward celibacy. Origen issued a warning against those who wanted to prohibit marriage categorically. Their followers, he says, are yielding to "seducing spirits and doctrines of demons." According to Methodius, virginity is a gift from God and cannot be legislated. Some people may be drawn to it without the inner conviction and power to persevere because of the recognition it affords, but would be much better off to marry. To Gregory of Nyssa, choosing a life of virginity will not be prompted by rational argument and convincing, but by observing others in their practice. People will be drawn to this life because they recognize a beauty of character in those living it and come to admire them for it. To Ambrose, celibacy cannot be commanded but must be "wished for" in prayer; it is not a matter of mastery because it is a thing "above us." According to Jerome, choosing a life of celibacy is a mark of great faith and virtue. It is an act of "free choice," not necessity, and implies one's willingness to "offer oneself a whole burnt-offering" so as to grow in one's pursuit of holiness in both mind and spirit. Augustine holds that living the celibate life only comes at the invitation of Continence and requires the Lord's help. While many are attracted to this life for the sake of praise and honor, only those who bear the inner conviction of their conscience can be true to it.

Celibacy Requirement for Clergy in the Western Church

A sign of the church's high regard for celibacy was the development of the celibacy requirement for clergy in the Latin Church. This trend began in the third century, and by the end of the fourth, deacons, priests, and bishops of the Western Church were expected to practice celibacy as part of their ecclesiastical office. The earliest reference to clerical celibacy comes from Pope Siricius (d. 399), who succeeded Pope Damasus in 384, and sent a decretal to Bishop Himerius in Spain requiring married priests to refrain from cohabiting with their wives. Later the requirement is found in the canons of several Western synods, such as the Council of Carthage of 390.

Three views have emerged concerning the historical reasons for the requirement.[14] The first view, based on Siricius's argument,[15] holds that clergy were to abstain from sex so as to keep themselves ritually clean for the celebration of the Eucharist; when eventually the Eucharist was celebrated more frequently and then daily, the requirement of ritual purity became permanent in the form of the celibacy requisite. The second view is that the high regard for celibacy put pressure on the clergy to adopt the same standards that many members of their congregations and dioceses were embracing.[16] The third view incorporates the other two, but adds that by adopting celibacy for themselves, male clergy in the West were better able to preserve their authority and prerogatives over the growing group of female celibates in their churches, particularly consecrated virgins and widows, who were often well educated and came from wealthy and influential Roman families. This third view has been advanced by David G. Hunter, and is based on the way bishops at the time sought to bring these women under their influence, particularly in their selection and supervision. This exertion of episcopal power is exemplified by the veiling ceremony of consecrated virgins.[17] During the ceremony, the bishop presided, bestowed the veil, pronounced the benediction, and delivered the sermon of exhortation. One of these sermons is recounted by Ambrose to his sister Marcellina in "On Virginity," in which he reiterates the exhortations of Pope Liberius during her consecration and veiling ceremony in Rome. The control of the bishops over consecrated virgins included limiting their number, setting an age requirement,[18] and determining where and with whom they should live.[19] At the same time, these women were frequently held up as role models for priests, particularly by Jerome. Hunter maintains that bishops sought to bring these celibate women under their power, either because they felt threatened by their example of piety and spiritual integrity, or to expand their own episcopal authority.[20]

These women wielded their own *indirect* power by prompting through their devout life the new celibacy requirement for Western clergy. It is a development that may have given rise to resentment among the clergy and widened the gap between consecrated celibate women and celibate male clergy. While this gap appears in the early fifth century in the writings and preaching of Augustine, it would eventually lead to a distinction in congregational life between female and male celibacy, where male celibacy is afforded higher regard. This new division into male and female celibates is also noticeable in later centuries when the church begins to elevate certain celibate men and women to sainthood. For example, for the period from the sixth century through the eleventh century, approximately only one out of seven of those declared saints were female.[21] This preponderance of male saints is all the more surprising since many priests and even bishops in Western Europe had wives, despite the fact that beginning with the seventh century, the church sought to enforce clerical celibacy. The ninth Council of Toledo (655), for example, condemned the children of married ecclesiastics to slavery. Councils outside Spain found it necessary to repeat similar canons directed against clergy who married, continued marital sexual relations, or had women living with them, but often with only moderate success. It was not until 1049 that a crusade against married clergy ensued under the instigation of the hermit Peter Damiani. As a result, the Synod of Mainz (1049) forbade clerical marriage and imposed severe penalties for disobedience, including deposition from office; and the Council of Rome (1059) decreed that no one should attend mass said by a married priest.[22] Women religious might have been faithfully practicing the celibate life, but it was largely the few faithful among the male clergy who received ecclesiastical recognition and praise. The separate status of male and female celibates crystallizes with the Council of Trent in the sixteenth century and the adaptation of the seven sacraments of the Roman Catholic Church. Of these seven, five apply to members of the Church at large (with baptism open to potential members), while two are reserved for those who have made a vow of lifelong commitment to God in Christ: either the married in their marriage vows or the male clergy (who mostly came from monastic orders) in their ordination vows. By regarding both marriage and priestly ordination, or holy orders, as sacraments, the church thereby withheld sacramental recognition from consecrated celibate women.

Lowering the Status of Celibate Women

For four hundred years, beginning with the second century, the church had defined faithful Christian discipleship by various degrees of sexual abstinence. In this hierarchy, virgins ranked first, then came widows, and lastly married couples. The early establishment of a ceremony involving the veiling of virgins and of the order of widows seems to confirm that the majority of those found in the "top" two echelons were women. While there most certainly were men who had committed to a life of virginity and widowhood, the Church Fathers' writings on celibacy, virginity, and widowhood do not make specific mention of a ceremony designed for male virgins, nor a separate order of widowers. Celibate men then, in an effort to obtain community, either joined monastic orders or prepared themselves for ordination to church office under the auspices of a bishop. The Fathers of the Western Church illustrate this by their own lives, whereby Jerome — though ordained a priest — chose the first option, Ambrose the second, while Augustine chose both monkhood and priesthood. With many men who were committing to celibacy leaving the local congregation for monastic life, others remained either anonymous in their decision or noncommitted; or they held the publicly acclaimed ecclesiastic office of deacon, priest, or bishop. For example, it is the anonymously committed or the non-committed that Augustine addresses in the church at Hippo when exhorting men to practice sexual abstinence for their wives-to-be.[23] Moreover, many men, wanting to remain in public life, were unwilling to commit themselves to the Christian faith; while they may have been enrolled as catechumens, they demonstrated their noncommittal stance by irregular church attendance and the postponing of baptism.[24] This situation in local congregations left mainly the celibate male clergy, on the one hand, and consecrated virgins and widows, on the other, to contend with each other for supreme moral standing, ecclesiastical recognition, and heavenly rewards.

Both clerical celibacy and the raised status of marriage requiring "wedded chastity" eventually reshuffled the three-tier ranking of virginity, widowhood, and marriage. Now, not just those who had preserved their virginity, but every Christian was considered a virgin and needed to act accordingly since all were members of the church who was virgin and bride of Christ. Moreover, male (celibate) clergy, such as Augustine, began pointing out to their congregations that celibacy for men was much more difficult than for women. Since women were naturally constricted to conform to certain societal and parental expectations in matters of sexual conduct, men did not have this implicit advantage, which meant that male celibacy was much harder to attain and therefore more greatly esteemed by God. In addition, celibate single women were questioned about their motives for consecration, and were consistently reminded to remain humble and take no credit for their sexual abstinence, piety, and self-discipline.

The Reformation

Beginning with the sixth century, monastic communities were springing up throughout the West, modeled after their Eastern precursors of a hundred years earlier. With his Latin translation of the Egyptian monk's *Life of Antony*, Athanasius (296–373) had introduced the model of monastic life to the West. As bishop of Alexandria beginning in 328, Athanasius spend only twenty-eight of forty-five years in possession of his see, exiled five times for his Nicene orthodoxy against the Arians in the struggle between the Roman Empire and the church. His exile first at Treves (Trier) in 335, then at Rome (340) may have allowed him to bring monasticism to the West. As Jerome founded a monastery in Bethlehem yet kept in touch with the West, Ambrose supervised a monastery at Milan's outskirts, and Augustine at Hippo founded a monastery in Northern Africa, the monastic movement slowly developed. The earliest monastic communities were composed of men. Monasticism for women in the West began in or before 512, when Bishop Caesarius of Arles (serving as bishop from 502 until his death in 542) established a convent that was ruled by his sister Caesaria. Only consecrated virgins and widows were admitted to the convent; this was a lifetime commitment and involved renunciation of all claims to material wealth. While some convents accommodated as many as three hundred women, the vast majority were much smaller and were mostly housed on family property. By the seventh century, their numbers vastly increased as it became a status symbol for wealthy families to found their own convents, often representing no more than an extension of the household. With the growth of convents in the West, consecration ceremonies of virgins and widows within Western congregations became less frequent. Concurrently, the consecration of predominantly widows to the office of deaconess[25] — begun possibly in the late second century to assist in women's baptism and anointing and their subsequent instruction — dwindled with the decline of adult baptisms, until the office was declared unlawful by the Council of Orleans in 533 and eventually disappeared.

The first monasteries for men organized on a large scale operated under the Rule of Benedict, written between 530 and 540 in Monte Cassino, Italy, by Benedict of Nursia (480–543). The Rule suggests familiarity with the *Life of Antony* and the writings of Jerome and Augustine and required of its members the vows of celibacy, poverty, and obedience — later to be known as the three evangelical counsels of the consecrated life. Around 530, Benedict founded a convent for women with the help of his sister Scholastica,[26] who oversaw the convent's operation, so that by the end of the sixth century Benedictine monasteries dotted the continent with the number of nuns rivaling the number of monks.

By the seventh century, the spread of monasticism had left local congregations virtually emptied of unmarried Christians practicing committed celibacy. Men and women were leaving the cities to move to rural monasteries and cloistered communities. With the disappearance from congregational life of consecrated virgins and the order of widows, worshipers began to associate not women but men — represented by the male celibate clergy — with holy living and the practice of lifelong sexual abstinence. Hence, public regard and recognition shifted from female to male celibacy, and may have contributed to the subsequent decline of female monasticism and the position of celibate women beginning in the eighth century. While the convent was still the most viable option for women who felt called to a life of single-hearted devotion and service to the Lord, its public image suffered in two ways: first, the convent was coming to be regarded either as a repository for women considered burdensome by their relations[27] or as fulfilling a redemptive function[28] for the parents, who had often committed a girl long before her puberty;[29] and second, convents required of the parents or guardians a sizable dowry modeled after the marriage contract,[30] so that women entering the convent were perceived as chattel purchasing heavenly rewards, in part for themselves, but more so for their families. Despite a renewed upsurge in female monastic life in the twelfth and thirteenth centuries, the celibacy of males gained much wider recognition in the public eye than that of females. This difference in status is reflected in the fact that men far outnumbered women in monasticism. In the early thirteenth century in England,[31] for example, there were more than 600 Augustinian and Benedictine monasteries for men, but fewer than 150 women's houses. Approximately 14,000 men lived in monastic communities compared to only 3,000 women.

Two hundred years later, with the beginning of the age of Reformation, little had changed concerning the ratio of male and female monastics.[32] From the perspective of church members, celibacy as a supreme good was modeled through male representatives only, namely, the clergy, who had been largely recruited from within monastic orders. Male celibacy was viewed as honorable, female celibacy as degrading; males were motivated by free will, females by coercion and fear; males by the dignity and sanctity of the priesthood, females by private suffering to effect collective redemption; males by an honest endeavor to please God, females by a covert attempt to seek status in suffering or simply to avoid the pains of marriage and domestic life. Despite the male-female distinction, however, the negative perception of female celibacy in particular led to a negative perception of celibacy in general. Except in the context of ordained church office, the celibate life of both men and women had a bad reputation among the populace of

Western Europe, which called into question the celibacy requirement for clergy.

What the Church Fathers had hailed as the practice of a divine life, the progressive autonomy from worldly bonds, and the habit-shaped prayerful divesting of the chains of lust and concupiscence had now, one thousand years later, come to be perceived as a confining way of life, a *via dolorosa* in imitation of Christ's suffering filled with both self-imposed and other-inflicted punishment. Moreover, what had initially promoted greater equality[33] between the sexes and among economic classes by the practice of transcending the gendered body toward unity of the spirit and the surrender of one's property for communal benefit was now polarizing the sexes, separating the classes, and creating a gulf between a celibate clergy and their noncelibate congregations. In part, it is this situation replete with economic disparity, abuse of power and privilege, and religious superstition that necessitated the Reformation and prompted the drastic reforms initiated by its prime proponent in Germany, the Augustinian monk and priest Martin Luther.

Martin Luther (1483–1546)

Luther was born at Eisleben, the northern region of Germany, to devout Christian parents. Though their social rank was that of peasants, the father had moved from farming to mining, so that the family had a sufficient income from the half a dozen foundries they owned. Following studies at Mansfeld, Magdeburg, and Eisenach, Luther attended the University of Erfurt to become a lawyer and jurist. Shortly after receiving his master's degree in 1505, Luther was knocked to the ground by lightning and in terror over barely escaping death vowed henceforth to be obedient to God by taking monastic vows with the Augustinian Eremites at Erfurt the following year, despite the objections from his father. Selected to study for the priesthood, Luther was ordained a deacon in February of 1507 and a priest in April. In 1508, he began teaching moral philosophy at Wittenberg and Erfurt. In 1510, Luther went to Rome with a fellow monk to request that the stricter houses of their order not be compelled to admit the more lax houses into their jurisdiction. As a pilgrim, he visited the major Roman shrines but was appalled by the spiritual laxity he observed, especially among the clergy. Back at Wittenberg in 1511, his vicar and confessor, Johann Staupitz, named Luther to study for the doctorate in theology in preparation for assuming Staupitz's professorship in Bible. The following year, Luther was made subprior of his monastery and became a professor of theology.

Long plagued by spiritual distress, a sense of condemnation and guilt, and his inability to please a seemingly angry and wrathful God by good works and severe acts of self-deprivation, Luther found eventual relief. While preparing for his lectures on the Psalms in 1513 or 1514, he experienced what approximates a dramatic conversion experience when he interpreted the term "God's righteousness" to mean that God had imparted righteousness in people through Christ. With that insight, Luther identified the gospel as the message of God's work for people's benefit — for their being made righteous before God in Christ — rather than God's demand that people strive to become righteous for God's benefit. Salvation was not the result of monastic or clerical vows, good or self-sacrificial works, or acts of self-deprivation in suffering; it came by faith in the love and mercy of God in Christ. With the Christian being justified and made righteous before God in faith, good works followed. It was the thought that determined the direction of all of Luther's subsequent teaching, preaching, and reforming activity.

Luther's reform activity began when he gained the Wittenberg faculty approval of his theological views and he subsequently posted the Ninety-Five Theses on the University's castle door in 1517. They objected to the papal abuse of indulgences — financial contributions, that is, for the remission of the past, present, and future sins of the giver or those designated by the giver. A steady stream of writings[34] followed in the form of commentaries, sermons, theological treatises, tracts, catechisms for schools, hymnody, church postils[35] for pastors, a revision of the mass that included lay participation, and the first translation of the entire Bible from the original languages into the German vernacular. Among the issues Luther addressed were the abuse of papal spiritual authority, the exploitation of the superstition of the masses, the complex sacramental system, the role of good works and faith in God's act of salvation, the equality of Christians as a "priesthood of all believers," monastic vows, and the celibacy of the clergy.

From the abuse of papal authority, the practice of indulgences, and the disparity between clergy and laity within the congregation and the sociopolitical order of the day, Luther derived the need for his subsequent attack on the sacramental system. In his 1520 treatise of *The Babylonian Captivity,* Luther called into question both the sacraments as the exclusive channels of grace and the prerogatives of the clergy who administered them. By reducing the number of sacraments from seven to two — baptism and the Lord's Supper — with the argument that these alone had been directly instituted by Christ, Luther sought to weaken the power of the clergy. With the repudiation of the sacrament of Holy Orders, priests were no longer regarded as a separate, higher order of Christians, but became part of the priesthood of all believers commissioned for service in the congregation and hence relieved of their vow of celibacy. The same year, Luther wrote the *Address to the German Nobility,* meaning the ruling class in Germany, in which he demanded that clergy be held accountable and tried in civil court for ecclesiastical extortions and abuse of privileges. Moreover, Luther called for mendicant friars — most of them untrained in scriptural interpretation, pastoral care, and church doctrine — to be relieved of hearing confession and of preaching, to reduce the number of monastic orders, and to abolish clerical vows so as to permit clergy to marry and put an end to "unchaste chastity."

In 1521, while Luther was under a year-long protective, secret custody at the Wartburg Castle by order of Frederick the Wise,[36] three priests were married and subsequently arrested by Cardinal Albert of Mainz, while fifteen monks of Luther's own monastery in Wittenberg withdrew, which begged the question whether they should be forced to go back and, if not, were allowed to marry. Luther's immediate response[37] was that the vows of a monk were different from those of a priest since the former had taken them voluntarily, while the latter had them imposed. Prompted to search the Scriptures on the subject, Luther summed up his findings in his treatise *On Monastic Vows,* addressed to his father and sent to the faculty at Wittenberg. Luther felt that divine providence had prompted him to take monastic vows, so he was in a position to speak from personal experience. The monk's vow, Luther concluded in the treatise, is unfounded in Scripture and may obstruct charity and liberty. "Marriage is good, virginity is better, but liberty is best," he said, so that monastic vows rest on the false assumption that there is a special, superior calling or vocation that sets celibate monastics over against other noncelibate Christians. Not only did the treatise promote equal standing before God among all Christians on account of their baptismal vows, but it gave the practice of celibacy itself a bad name. According to the faculty member at Wittenberg Justus Jonas, professor of canon law and theology, Luther's treatise On Monastic Vows was the one work that emptied the cloisters and monasteries. While Luther had attacked the view that monastic vows could confer supreme status and divine favors, the validity of lifelong monastic vows in general was called into question. Luther's own order ruled that its members should be free to stay or leave as they pleased, so that by January 6, 1522, the Augustinian congregation at Wittenberg had disbanded.

In his exegesis of the New Testament, Luther connected the practice of celibacy with the theme of justification by faith, not works — a theme he had derived from the Old Testament[38] when preparing his lectures on the Psalms. Those practicing celibacy, he says, were never justified before God by their sexual abstinence; they were only justified by their faith, which might produce the practice. Luther illustrates this point in an exposition on the widow Anna in Luke 2:33–40 as part of the 1521 Church Postils for the Sunday after Christmas.[39] Anna did not become godly and devout because of her works of fasting and praying and going to church, and those who think so are "blockheads" and "apes and hypocrites." She was a godly prophetess first and foremost on account of her character (280). Moreover, she was without children or parents to take care of, for "otherwise she would not have served God but the devil by not departing from the temple and neglecting her duty of managing her household." If a married woman were to follow Anna's example and leave her husband and children, her home and parents "in order to go on a pilgrimage, to pray, fast and go to church," she would "tempt God, confound the matrimonial estate with the state of widowhood, desert her own calling and do works belonging to others." It would be "as much as walking on one's ears, putting a veil over one's feet and a boot on one's head, and turning all things upside down," for one must not neglect "the duties of your calling and station" in life (281) since God may be served in every calling. Only the "blind legalists" think that the deeds of a widow are more to be praised than the deeds of a married woman, when, in fact, only character counts and the faithfulness in which one's calling is carried out. Anna did so beautifully no matter her station in life, for she "was a godly maiden, a godly wife, and a godly widow, and in all these three estates she performed her respective duties" (282).

Luther then offers a "spiritual" allegorical interpretation of the story of Anna. The three stages of her life, virginity, marriage, and widowhood, represent life before the law and grace, life under the law, and life under grace, respectively. According to Luther, the Gospel writer says nothing of Anna's virginity because this signifies "the unfruitful life before either the law or grace has been in operation, and which is worthless before God" (291). The second stage, her married life of seven years, represents "the life of this body, because all time is measured by the seven days of the week (288)" or the life under the law of the saints of old and "the people of Israel under the law, in their outward conduct and temporal life" (289). The third stage represents her widowhood, where she "walked in the freedom of faith and the Spirit, fulfilling the law not only with outward works like a bond-servant, but rather in faith"; thus, widowhood signifies freedom from the law through faith in Christ. If a person wants to become a believer, he or she must first acknowledge and recognize the law, which kills and condemns, so as to be made ready through repentance to be lifted up to "the spiritual, inner man" by faith in Christ. The fact that Anna lived as a widow for eighty-four years signifies seven times twelve, with seven representing the temporal, bodily life and twelve, the number of apostles representing grace received in abundance through the Spirit. Through her fasting, Anna "continually disciplined her body, not because she desired to do a meritorious work, but in order to serve God and to subdue sin." Likewise in prayer, meaning not only oral prayer, "but also the hearing, proclaiming, contemplating and meditating on the Word of God, Anna offered up her soul unto God" (297). Her fasting and prayer stand in contrast to those who only fast "to please the saints or at special seasons," which is entirely "worthless"

(297); and those who only pray "as a duty obligatory upon them," believing they have done enough "when they are pious for themselves and pray only for themselves," instead of serving God "by petitioning him to relieve the general good of Christendom" (298). Luther looks at the five people brought together in the Luke passage, the infant Christ, his mother Mary, Joseph, Simeon, and Anna. In this small number of people, says Luther, "every station in life is represented, husband and wife, young and old, virgin and widow, the married and the unmarried." This goes to show that Christ "begins to gather around him people of every honorable station" in life so as not to be alone (299).

In 1523, Luther completed a commentary on 1 Corinthians 7. The commentary was dedicated to Hans von Löser, who was married the following year and at whose wedding Luther officiated.[40] In part, Luther felt the need to expand on the brief commentary his colleague Philip Melanchthon had written on the chapter the previous year, in which Melanchthon criticized Jerome as "superstitiously extolling celibacy" and said that "neither celibacy nor marriage is prescribed" and that "either one is to be chosen without sin."[41] Luther also wanted to respond to John Faber's 1521 treatise that, in addition to challenging Luther's disdain of papal authority and the jurisdiction of the church of Rome, outlined a detailed defense of priestly celibacy.[42]

The Commentary on 1 Corinthians 7 opens with a dedication,[43] in which Luther explains his reason for choosing to comment on this particular chapter of Paul's Epistle. "This very chapter, more than all the other writings of the entire Bible," says Luther, "has been twisted back and forth to condemn the married state" and "to give a strong appearance of sanctity to the dangerous and peculiar state of celibacy." At one point, he too had considered celibacy the normal "ordinary" way of the Christian life, but the "last three years have taught me how little chastity there is in this world outside marriage, both in convents and monasteries." By preaching about marriage, he wants "to tear the veil from the chastity which is of the devil," stem fornication, and prevent "our poor youth" from being "so pitiably and dangerously misled by falsely glorified chastity" (3).

In the Preface to the Commentary, Luther introduces his argument that marriage is better than "free fornication" in the guise of clerical chastity. People such as Johann Schmid of Constance (who later called himself Johann Faber) view the state of marriage as "a superfluous, presumptuous human thing that one could dispense with and do without," thus filling the world "with their foolish and blasphemous scribbling and screeching against the married state." They advise all men against it, while their actions demonstrate "that they cannot do without women" and run after them day and night (5). Faber dismisses marriage with the argument that "there is much effort and labor connected with it," as if, says Luther, "this ass must first teach us what every village peasant knows." The reason why God created women is not that they be "strangled or banished" or "for the purpose of fornication." Instead, God created woman "that she should and must be with man" (6). It is a "great sin" that as Christians we should have to first ponder "whether women ought to be married or not" as though wondering "whether we ought to eat and drink in this life" (7).

Luther's Commentary is a verse-by-verse exposition of the entire chapter, addressing first the mistaken notion that celibacy could be imposed from without. Some people, particularly those who "founded monasteries and nunneries," thought to preserve chastity by "many laws and regulations," such as "keeping the boys away from the girls and the girls from the boys." Celibacy, says Luther, "is a gift from heaven and must come from within" and "one has to have the heart" for it (10). Those who think that "the bitterer chastity is for some," the more precious it will be to God, or who force "outward chastity upon young people" without considering their inner will and desire for it, are "reprehensible murderers of souls." In fact, such outwardly imposed suffering is a "sinful suffering," and the only escape from this sin is to get rid of it "through marriage and in no other way" (11).

Luther disagrees with Jerome, who had given celibacy greater regard than marriage. "Before God," says Luther, "a married woman is better than a virgin," even though "the married woman has much labor and trouble here on earth, and the virgin much happiness, ease, and comfort" (11).

In general people avoid marriage, says Luther, because "no one likes to subject himself to such evil days." Many proverbs attest to this awareness, saying, for example, "Fool, take a wife, and that will end your joy," or "Marriage is brief joy and long disgust," or "It takes a brave man to take a wife." Even Moses was aware of this fact when decreeing that a newlywed man should not be drafted into the army or charged with an office for one year following marriage, as if he were saying, "The joy will last for a year; after that we shall see." But a de-vout Christian who lives by faith "can adapt himself to these evil days and not complain, cry out, and blaspheme God" when married. If then one cannot have "the happy days of celibacy, then one must accept the evil days of marriage, for it is better to suffer evil days without sin in marriage than happy days without marriage in sin and unchastity" (11–12).

Luther leaves it up to the Christian couple to determine what con-jugal rights are, as long as each partner recognizes "that no one rules over his own body" and things are done under "the law of love." While it may be well and good to be moderate in all things, "one should not set up absolute laws in these matters." On matters of temporary ab-stinence for increased devotion, it is better to "see prayer and fasting be relaxed" than to deny one's body to the marriage partner. What-ever other reasons there are for sexual abstinence, Luther leaves for married people to work out. For that there should be many reasons, including "anger and dissension," is to be expected "in a state created and instituted for evil and not for happy days" (14–15).

Paul wishes that all could have the gift of celibacy so as to be re-lieved of "the labor and cares of marriage" and be concerned only "with God and His Word." But since "this great gift" is not granted every-one, "marriage is just as much a gift of God" as celibacy. In regard to women, this means that "marriage and virginity are equal before Him" and nuns are no better than married women. Those who "glo-rify nuns" contrive "fictitious crowns for them and all kinds of virtues and honors." Thereby, they "produce vainglorious, unchristian, and even ungodly people who rely more on their station and work than on faith in Christ and God's grace." They call them "brides of Christ," when they are "brides of the devil, because they do not use chastity as it should be used," namely, "to make people here on earth freer and more capable to give attention to God's Word rather than to marriage" (16–17).

Marriage then is a "common gift," says Luther, while celibacy is "reserved for the few as a very special gift." Since this special gift is not "our doing, possession, or capacity," no one can either vow it or keep such a vow beforehand, unless God "has already given it to me or I am certain of His promise to give it to me" (17).

It is unjust and wrong to call marriage a "secular order" and certain others "religious orders." For doing so only judges by surface observations and characterizes only the outward function of the body. One can only call religious what describes the "inner life of faith in the heart, where the Spirit rules." Moreover, the life of members of religious orders is "just as outward, temporal, and carnal as those of married people," especially since the former "are most securely provided with all the necessities of the body" and most likely would not have entered the order otherwise. The "majority in the monastic and clerical orders," says Luther, are merely "on the lookout that their stomachs and bodies get their due," which leaves little room for looking to heaven and trusting that God will provide. How different that is in the case of marriage. For once "you take a wife," you experience the "first shock," having to wonder "how are you going to support yourself, your wife, and child." Since "this will go on for your whole life," marriage teaches and compels us "to trust in God's hand and grace, and in the same way it forces us to believe." Marriage by its very nature forces one to turn "to the most inward, highest spiritual state, to faith," while the religious orders are "by nature of a kind to tempt men to scatter themselves in temporal and outward things so that they have enough for their bodies" and do not "have to have faith and trust in God." This tendency makes religious orders "earthly, worldly, and heathenish" and marriage "a heavenly, spiritual, and godly order" (18–20).

Luther distinguishes between religious orders and the state of chastity. Religious orders, he says, are "good for nothing" and it were indeed better that there were none and that everyone were married. The state of celibacy is, according to the Apostle Paul, "a technique and service for God's Word and faith"; but the religious orders use their celibacy for "merit, credit, and glory before God and the world, and they place their reliance on it, which is against faith" (21).

Luther maintains that Paul was married once and then became a widower, or that his wife had consented "to live separately from him for the sake of the Gospel." He reaches this conclusion based on his reading of Scripture and a Jewish tradition "where everyone had to marry, and celibacy was not allowable unless by special permission and as an exception made by God" (22). On the basis of Philippians 4:3 in which Paul says, "And I ask you also, true yokefellow, help these women, for they have labored side by side with me in the Gospel," Luther maintains that "true yokefellow" could mean Paul's wife "because he does not mention her name and otherwise never uses the address" (22).[44]

Luther argues against clerical celibacy. In Scripture, married men became bishops and priests, including the apostles and Paul, who most likely was a widower and "still presumes to have the right to take a wife," according to 1 Corinthians 9:5, where he says: "Do we not have the right to be accompanied by a believing wife, as do the other apostles and the brothers of the Lord and Cephas?" It is "a shameful pretense," says Luther, "to confess marriage a godly thing and a holy sacrament and then not permit such a godly thing and holy sacrament to stand beside the holiness of priests." If married men were allowed to become priests, "there would not have been so much trouble" and "there would have been far fewer whoremongers" among the unmarried clergy (23–25).

For a Christian, the only appropriate context in which to give in to the "evil desires" of the human flesh is marriage. It is true that the Christian is both spirit and flesh and, "according to the spirit," has no need of marriage. But because of the flesh, which "rages, burns, and fructifies," "we do not cease to be God's creatures, you a woman and I a man," so that God has given marriage as "the proper medicine" for "this very disease" (26). There are indeed those who have the gift of celibacy. While they may suffer from the "heat of the flesh" and its "evil desires and are tempted," their suffering is "transitory." The majority of people, however, cannot bear this "heat" and "suffer so severely that they masturbate." Instead of wasting "precious time" with protracted carnal thoughts and attempts to subdue the flesh with "fasts or wakes," they ought to be married; this, says Luther, would have applied to Jerome,[45] as well as to many of the other fathers. It goes to show that "for every chaste person there should be more than a hundred thousand married people" (26–28). For it is better to live "an unhappy marriage than unhappy chastity," since the latter "is a sure loss," but "the former can be of use" (30).

Luther says that, according to Paul, the widowed are free to remarry, but the divorced are generally not. Divorce is allowed for Christians "when two people simply cannot get along together." In all other cases, however, "everyone is obligated to carry the burden of the other and not to separate from him." The exception to the law of remarriage following a divorce is for a divorced person who does not have the gift of celibacy and whose divorce was caused by the other's refusal to be reconciled, by adultery, and by hindering the partner's practice of the Christian faith (32–34). In this case, says Luther, remarriage after divorce is permissible — even if one had "ten or more" marriages that resulted in divorce that way; it is permissible, so that no one is "driven into the danger of unchastity" due to the "wantonness and wickedness of another" (36–37).

The Christian owes God nothing but to believe and confess, and to serve one's neighbor in love. This means that it is of no importance to God whether one marries or remains unmarried, becomes this or that, or eats this or that (45). Likewise, it makes no difference to God whether we are poor or rich, young or old, beautiful or ugly, learned or ignorant, layman or priest, because it is our faith that makes us equal and gives us "the same possessions, the same inheritance" before God. One could even say, says Luther, that "he who is called as a man is a woman before God. And she who was called as a woman is a man before God" (44). The making of spiritual regulations and "monasticizing" is all wrong when "these people bind themselves to outward things from which God has made them free." At the same time, "where these people should be bound, namely, in their relations" with and service to others, they are "of no use to anyone but themselves, thus working against love." With their regulations and airs of being above other Christians, they make a "hellish prison out of heavenly freedom" and "a hostile freedom out of loving service," so that instead of being "higher in heaven," they "shall sit in the deepest hell" (47).

The state of celibacy is a noble one and "highly to be respected on earth." It is "a very precious thing," full of "pure radiance," and "nothing that we do on earth is greater or more beautiful." "If it were not St. Paul," says Luther, "I should truly be vexed that he gives such miserly praise and small honor" to it. But celibacy is not commanded, hence is a free choice, and because it is not commanded, it has no specific rewards attached to it before God. Unfortunately, however, "our poisonous nature simply cannot tolerate that it should not preen itself before God in works." People conclude that virgins count for more both on earth and in heaven, and come up with such "nonsensical teachings of the devil" that give them "special little crowns[46] in heaven" and "makes them brides of Christ." While all "the poor misguided young people go wild" striving toward this little crown and wanting to fill heaven with virgins and brides of Christ, "the Christian faith is despised and forgotten and finally extinguished" when it alone can win the crown and make us brides of Christ (47–48). When the apostle Paul says that in light of the "present distress" it is better to remain unmarried, he means the threat of persecution for the Gospel's sake, the danger of losing one's goods and friends and life, or of facing exile or execution. It is the temporal blessing, says Luther, not the heavenly reward, that the state of celibacy confers, and even Jerome has "misinterpreted Paul" here (48–49). Those who have "made a trade out of their virginity" have good reason to be "very peeved" now, for they have preserved a "lost chastity" (50).

Celibacy is honorable in and of itself and affords greater temporal rewards than marriage. "I shall not try to relate the sorrows of married life," says Luther, since "I am told that I know nothing about it and have not experienced it." But the witness of the married in this world should be sufficient proof for it, apart from the witness of Scripture in Genesis 3:16–19 and 1 Peter 3:7. But it is important to note that though the troubles of marriage are "outward unpleasantness, strain, and boredom," they are "bodily" and not "spiritual," so that "nobody should despise" marriage as if it were displeasing to God (50–51). Since it is "a great and noble freedom to be unmarried," people should restrain their curiosity, "stay away from marriage, and not deliberately call forth such misfortunes unless forced by necessity" (52).

The temporal rewards of celibacy are its "utility in this life" (54), that is, one's ability to give undivided attention to the Lord's service. By being undivided in attending to the Word of God, "the unmarried person is of much use and comfort to many people, yes, to all of Christendom," which should be "great and noble" reason enough "to keep everyone from marrying who has the grace to remain single." By contrast are the monastics "who neither pray nor learn God's Word but torture themselves with the regulations of men and murmur and howl in the choir" without being of any divine service (53).

In conclusion, Luther says that "it is well not to marry unless it is necessary." The ability to remain single does not come by "command, vow, or intent" but "solely by the grace and the miraculous hand of God." Guardians, for example, may not "restrain an unmarried woman against her will" to remain unmarried. Since the celibate state cannot be effected from without, "they are nothing but abominable murderers of souls who put young people into monasteries and nunneries and keep them there by force" (54–55).

In 1523, the same year Luther wrote the Commentary on 1 Corinthians 7, some nuns in a neighboring village sought his advice on their plight.[47] Given the general social unrest arising from a papal, ecclesiastical, and monastic system steeped in superstition and power abuse, many monks and nuns had been leaving monasteries and convents. Luther took it upon himself to arrange for their escape from the cloister, though the abduction of nuns was a capital offense. At Easter, he had a respected burgher and merchant, Leonard Kopp of Torgau, bundle twelve nuns into his covered wagon.[48]

Three of them returned to their homes, while the other nine went to Wittenberg. Luther felt responsible for finding them homes, husbands, or positions of some sort. Two years later, one of the nuns, Katherine von Bora, who was twenty-six, was still awaiting marriage. When her prospective husband married someone else, Luther arranged for another candidate, whom Katherine would not accept. Instead she suggested, presumably in jest, Luther himself — an unlikely match since Luther, at forty-two, was way past the customary age of marriage. Luther related the comment to his parents. His father thought the proposal realistic, in the hope that Luther would pass on the family name. But the suggestion commended itself to Luther quite for another reason: Since he fully expected to be burned at the stake as a heretic within a year, he was hardly the person to start a family; but he reasoned that marriage to Katherine could give her status and be a testimony to his own convictions on clerical celibacy. In May, Luther told Katherine, "I believe in marriage, and I intend to get married before I die, even though it should be only a betrothal like Joseph's." In June 1525, they married in the presence of his parents, university faculty, and friends, with a banquet at the now vacated Augustinian cloister, where the couple would make their home.[49] Though Luther said later that "I would not exchange Katie for France or for Venice, because God has given her to me and other women have worse faults," he gave three reasons for his marriage: to please his father, to spite the pope and the Devil, and to seal his witness before martyrdom.[50]

In 1535, Luther once again lectured on Paul's Epistle to the Galatians,[51] as he had done in 1516, and published the lectures in form of a commentary. "Not that we want to teach something new," he wrote in his preface, but "there is a clear and present danger that the devil may take away from us the pure doctrine of faith and substitute for it the doctrines of works and of human traditions" (3). Ten years into his marriage, which appeared to have been a happy one, his view on marriage and celibacy remained interrelated with the doctrine of justification by faith. It is a "universal principle" that no one is justified by works of the Law, Luther says. "A monk shall not be justified by his order, a nun by her chastity, a citizen by his uprightness, a prince by his generosity." For the law of God is far greater than "the works chosen by self-righteous people," so that the only thing that justifies is faith (141). If people really looked "at this captive, the Son of God," and the "inestimable price" given for their sins, they would not attempt to bring their "cowl or tonsure or chastity or obedience or poverty." Instead, they would "curse, defile, spit upon, and damn them, and consign them to hell" (175–76).

It should strike horror into a person just to hear the term "monk" or "tonsure" or "cowl" or "monastic rule." People "adore these abominations and boast that they are the height of religion and sanctity," when they are "the filth of human righteousness and the doctrines of demons." By teaching that "monasticism is a new baptism," they "spit upon and recrucify Christ, the Son of God." With their rebukes, slanders, and insults, "they pierce Him through, so that He dies most miserably in them." And in his place, "they erect a beautiful bewitchment," so that people become so "demented" that they do not acknowledge Christ as the Justifier, Propitiator, and Savior but think of him as an "accuser, a judge, and a condemner, who must be placated by our works of merit" (199–200). Whoever enters a monastery with the idea that by the observance of the monastic rule he will be justified is entering "a den of robbers who recrucify Christ" (201).

When Paul contrasts the Spirit with the flesh (Gal. 3:3), says Luther, he does not mean by flesh "sexual lust, animal passions, or the sensual appetite"; instead, he means "the very righteousness and wisdom of the flesh and judgment of reason," that draws righteousness from "whatever is best and most outstanding in man." Our opponents are twisting this truth when they say "that now we have taken wives and are ended [up] with the flesh" — as if "celibacy or not having a wife were a spiritual life" (216–17).

At the time of the fathers such as Jerome, Ambrose, Augustine, and others, says Luther, the papacy still had a "sanctity and austerity" of life. The clergy rigorously observed celibacy, which "is a remarkable thing in the eyes of the world, a thing that makes a man an angel." But now the papacy has an evil reputation for simony, extravagance, pleasures, wealth, adultery, sodomy, and countless other sins. However, it is not even these abuses that need to be attacked as much as their false doctrine. We are fighting, says Luther, against the papacy's "fictitious saints, who think they lead an angelic life when they observe not only the commandments of God but also the counsels of Christ and works that are not required or works of supererogation." All these are "a waste of time and effort," unless they have grasped that "one thing" and that "good portion" that Mary had chosen, and that "cannot be taken away from them" (458–60).

John Calvin (1509–1564)

Calvin was born at Noyon in northern France into a Christian family. His father was a lawyer with the local Roman Catholic cathedral chapter, his mother the daughter of an innkeeper who died when Calvin was only five or six. His father remarried shortly thereafter. At age twelve, Calvin received a benefice from the bishop of Noyon, and another one in 1527, requiring him to enter the minor orders, wear a tonsure, and perform ecclesiastical duties. Following his studies of theology and philosophy at the College de Montaigu in Paris — the same school Erasmus attended — Calvin received his master of arts degree. On the advice of his father, then at odds with the cathedral chapter, Calvin decided not to enter the priesthood as planned but to continue studying law at Orleans. When in Paris, Calvin heard a sermon with a Lutheran sound by his friend, the new rector of the university, Nicholas Cop, which raised such furor that both Cop and Calvin were forced to flee. In 1534, Calvin wrote his first significant work,[52] "On the Sleep of the Soul," followed by the preface to a French New Testament. He completed work on the *Institutes of the Christian Religion* in 1535, which became an overnight success. Calvin's conversion had probably occurred in 1533, but he still thought of himself as a Christian humanist, not a reformer. During a detour to Geneva, he was implored by Guillaume Farel, the leader of the Reformation in the city, to stay and assist him in the work of reforming the church.[53] Calvin became one of the city's three pastors and in 1537 submitted articles for a new church organization. Forced to flee the city in 1537, along with Farel, Calvin stayed at Strasbourg, where in 1540 he married a widow and convert from Anabaptism, Idelette de Bure, who died nine years later.[54] In 1541, following his revision of the *Institutes* — which became three times longer than the original — and the first of his Bible commentaries (on Romans), Calvin returned to Geneva, where he emerged as the reformulator and leader of a new theology. In 1559, he established the Geneva Academy,[55] which offered religious education to the children of Geneva and trained pastors and students of theology by the hundreds from France, England, Scotland, and Holland, who, upon returning to their respective countries, would advance the Reformed faith there — often not without suffering persecution. Calvin's great achievement was to give the tenets of the Reformation (*sola gratia, sola fide, sola Scriptura*) a clear, systematic exposition and to incorporate them into the church's life and the civic setting of Geneva. He considered Luther his "most respected father," through whose ministry "the purity of the gospel" had been restored, but went beyond him in presenting more clearly the elements of a newly formed Protestant theology.

As a second-generation Protestant, Calvin was guided by Luther's doctrine of justification and his exposition on the law, baptism, and Christology, and by Calvin's friend and Luther's associate, Melanchthon. In his expositions on the Old and New Testaments, Calvin relied on Augustine, whom he cites continually on the doctrines of free will, grace, and predestination. His legal and humanist training, influenced by Duns Scotus and Erasmus, are evident in his biblical exegesis,[56] in his reshaping of church polity, in the internal structure of the Reformed church and its cooperative relationship to civic government, in his efforts at social justice and the relief of the poor, and in his emphasis on the unity of the church at large. Though best-known for the *Institutes*, Calvin left behind an extensive body of writing, *Corpus Reformatorum*, comprising fifty-nine volumes of his collected works. He wrote biblical commentaries on nearly every book of the Bible,[57] published sermons,[58] a harmony of Exodus-Deuteronomy, a harmony of the Gospels, tracts and treatises directed at theological opponents and the radical reformers, an extensive compendium of letters, and liturgical and catechetical works involving the versifying of French psalms, a confession of faith, and a catechism. In his writing, teaching, and preaching, Calvin was above all a humanist and a pastor, encouraging Christians to focus on the centrality of Christ in their practice of faith; and in their studies to return *ad fontes*, to the original sources, the Bible and the classical and patristic writings.

In 1543,[59] Calvin published his apologetic work on "The Necessity of Reforming the Church,"[60] addressed to Emperor Charles V.[61] The purpose of the treatise was to demonstrate "not whether the Church suffers from many and grievous diseases," but "whether the diseases are of a kind whose cure admits of no longer delay" (185). Calvin says that administering the cure cannot wait. To that end, he attempts to show that the particular remedies employed by the Reformers, especially Luther, "who held up a torch to light us into the way of salvation," were "apt and salutary" (185–86), so that now "all our controversies concerning doctrine relate either to the legitimate worship of God, or to the ground of salvation" (187). Calvin then contrasts the worship practices in the Catholic Church and the proliferation of superstitious beliefs attached to the sacraments with those in the Reformed churches and their doctrines, which he sees as conforming with the views of Augustine and the practices of the ancient church.

Calvin opposes the celibacy requirement for priests since not all may have "the gift of continence." It would have been so much better never to have instituted this law than to shut priests up "in a furnace of lust" and to "fetter consciences" whose freedom Christ vindicated by his own authority. While virginity may be worth extolling "to the skies," priests are exhibiting in deed that they are not complying by it and are using it as a license "to commit gross sin," while, at the same time, deeming "themselves better than others, for the simple reason that they have no wives" (212–13). Calvin denies that the priests' vows of perpetual celibacy are voluntary, instead views them as "forced," thus "leading miserable consciences into a deadly snare, in which they must perpetually writhe till they are strangled" (213).

It is true that the human custom of prohibiting priests to marry is ancient, as much as is the vow of perpetual continence taken by nuns and monks. But the will of God and "the clear declarations of the Holy Spirit" are manifested in Scripture, which says that "marriage is honourable in all" (Heb. 13:4) and has Paul speak of bishops as husbands (1 Tim. 3:2; Titus 1:6); therefore the will of God outweighs human custom. Moreover, the apostles themselves did not think it expedient that priests refrain from marriage, neither did Paphnutius at the Council of Nicaea who declared such a law as intolerable when it was brought up for discussion, even though he himself was a bachelor. At the Council of Gangra (Canon 4) a law is even pronounced against those who distinguish a married from an unmarried presbyter so as to absent themselves from worship, which indicates that back then existed more equality than in times to come. So it is true that while the ancients disallowed marriage for priests, we allow it. Moreover, the Catholic Church does not seem to be all that insistent on complying to ancient practice, for otherwise it would punish the licentiousness of its priests more severely. For example, the Council of Neo-Caesarea punished a priest convicted of adultery or fornication with deposition and excommunication. Today a priest who marries is deemed as committing "a capital crime," while one who commits a "hundred acts of libertinism" is fined only "a small sum of money" (214–15).

In his *Institutes,* first published in 1536 and finalized with his 1559 edition,[62] Calvin addresses clerical celibacy and vows in chapters 12 and 13 of book 4.[63] Chapter 12, where Calvin discusses the celibacy requirement for the clergy (paragraphs 22–28), is titled "The Discipline of the Church: Its Chief Use in Censures and Excommunications." In it he recounts how originally the bishops censured their clergy for various transgressions and were themselves subject to their priests' evaluation. So long as this severity was in force, says Calvin, the clergy expected from the people no more, and actually less, than they required of themselves (12.22). Now that fornication prevails among the clergy, they are "callous to all crimes" while relying on "their foul celibacy." The priestly celibacy requirement has both "deprived the church of good and fit pastors" and has brought in a "sink of iniquities," while casting many "into the abyss of despair." It is a "doctrine of demons" as foretold by Scripture (1 Tim. 4:1, 3), which says that in the last days there will be those who forbid marriage. The "papists" presume they are not meant and they distance themselves from other heretics who forbade marriage, such as Montanus,[64] the Tatianists,[65] and the Encratites[66] when they say that they approve of marriage for everyone else. That is like saying that a law is not unjust when only a part of the city is oppressed by it (12.23). They also say that a priest should be distinguished from the people by some mark, as if Christ had not already foreseen "in what ornaments priests ought to excel" (12.24). The argument of ritual purity does not hold up either, because today's pastors no longer play the same role as levitical priests, who were charged to reconcile the people to God before the Tabernacle as the heavenly judgment seat. The apostles prove that marriage is not unworthy of the holiness of any office, and Paul is a witness that they not only kept their wives but took them along with them (1 Cor. 9:5) (12.25). Likewise, Paphnutius prevailed at the Council of Nicaea (325), when he declared that marriage is honorable and that lawful cohabitation is chastity (12.26). Later, however, "the too superstitious admiration of celibacy became prevalent," accompanied by "unrestrained rhapsodic praises of virginity." The result was that the dignity of marriage was "so weakened and its holiness so obscured" that a man who did not refrain from it seemed to lack the willpower to "aspire to perfection." Consequently, canons developed that prohibited those who were already priests to marry and that would qualify only celibates or those practicing marital abstinence to be taken into priestly office. It is true that these regulations were approved of antiquity, but one should consider "the example of the earlier church of greater importance" than what was customary in antiquity. Furthermore, antiquity did not "impose" clerical celibacy but simply preferred a celibate to a married man, or asked those who married to give up office (12.27). The church has no right to invoke the practice "in the name of antiquity" while retaining adulterers and fornicators among its priests. Of the Church Fathers, no one other than Jerome impugns the status of marriage "so spitefully," and Calvin much prefers the view of John Chrysostom who, while admiring virginity, also highly commends marriage (12.28).

Calvin discusses vows — in particular, vows of celibacy in book 4 of the *Institutes* under the chapter heading, "Vows; and How Everyone Rashly Taking Them Has Miserably Entangled Himself" (chapter 13, paragraphs 1–21). His first precaution in making a general vow is that it not be a rash decision (13.2); his second is to keep in mind that all things that we offer to God are purely God's gifts to us. Jephthah is an example of someone making a rash vow and being "punished for his own folly." In this category also fall priests, monks, and nuns who think they are "surely capable of celibacy." They shake off for life the "general calling" to marriage, when "the gift of continence is more often given for a limited time" only. By doing so they dare tempt God (13.3). His third precaution about vows is the intention and the end toward which they are directed. There are four intentions that make vows "lawful," two of which refer to the past, such as exercises of thanksgiving or repentance, and two to the future. Vows whose intentions refer to the past involve our response, for example, for when the Lord has snatched us from some calamity or trying illness; or our abstaining from dainty foods for a time to restrain our intemperance (13.4). Vows whose intentions refer to the future are precautionary measures or those that arouse us to our pious duty when we grow lazy toward it (13.5). Excess in making vows is to be avoided for it tends to lead to superstition and cheapens the vow. Calvin believes that vows should be temporary, rather than perpetual, for the latter type invites "great trouble and tedium" or the eventual breaking of it (13.6). People have devised "perverse" vows, i.e., the abstinence from wine or meat on certain days, fasting, pilgrimages to holy places under adverse conditions, and construed them as "worship pleasing to God." These practices are but "empty and fleeting" and full of impiety (13.7).

In discussing monastic vows, Calvin cites Augustine, who said that the monasteries usually supplied the clergy for the church, so that in them pious men customarily "prepared themselves for greater tasks" (13.8). But things are different now, Calvin says. By quoting Augustine's description of the monks' life at Milan at length, Calvin identifies as the most glaring difference the fact that present-day monks lack brotherly love and are not content with the simple piety Christ desires of all (13.9–10). Today's monks have dreamt up "some new sort of piety" so as "to become more perfect than all other people," while leaving "that restraint of theirs buried in a few books" and using people's admiration of monasticism for "the most profitable commerce" (13.11). Since present-day monasticism is founded upon the notion that "a more perfect rule of life can be devised than the common one committed by God to the whole church," it cannot be called anything but "abominable" (13.12). Moreover, the argument in favor of surrendering one's earthly goods is based on a faulty interpretation of Jesus' encounter with the rich young man (Matt. 19:21). What Jesus really intended here was "to compel the young man, pleased with himself beyond measure, to feel his sore," so he could realize how far removed he still was from obedience to the law. Even the fathers have falsely interpreted this passage, so that from it arose "the affectation of voluntary poverty" (13.14). What is certain, though, is that the fathers would have "abhorred the blasphemy" that developed from it, that is, the presumption that declares monasticism "a form of second baptism." Present-day monks have "erected a private altar for themselves." By despising the ordinary ministry, they have "excommunicated themselves from the whole body" and become "a conventicle of schismatics." It is an "injustice to Christ" when some call themselves Benedictines, Franciscans, or Dominicans, "instead of Christians," thus implying their difference from "ordinary Christians" (13.14). Current monasticism departs from ancient example by saying he who breaks the vow of celibacy and marries sins more "heinously" than if he were to "corrupt body and soul by fornication" (13.17).

About the widows (1 Tim. 5:12) who had taken the vow of celibacy, Calvin says they did so only upon entering public ministry. By breaking their vows, they not only sin in their pledge given to the church, but they cut themselves off from "the condition of pious women." The sole reason they professed celibacy, says Calvin, is "that marriage did not agree with the work which they undertook" and was prompted by "the necessity of their calling" (13.18), much as in the case of nuns. For the office of deaconess was not created "to appease God with songs or unintelligible mumbling," but to carry out "the public ministry of the church toward the poor" with zeal, constancy, and diligence in the task of love. The only reason these women vowed celibacy was to be "thus freer to perform their task." Also, they entered the office at age sixty (1 Tim. 5:9), not age twelve, twenty, or thirty (13.19).

Those who break their vows are now "gravely accused of broken faith and perjury" and the breaking of an "indissoluble bond." But, says Calvin, this bond was the bond of ignorance and error, so that once they are set free by the "knowledge of truth," they are "free by the grace of Christ." For those whom Christ illumines with the light of the gospel, he also releases "from all halters which they have taken upon themselves through superstition." Moreover, those who break the vow have the defense that they were not fit for celibacy and had not been "endowed with that special gift." But those who persist in their vows assuming they can conquer "the disease of incontinence" and who "against nature covet what has been denied them," while being "contemptuous of the remedies which the Lord has put within their grasp," will surely be punished by God (13.21).

In his commentary on Genesis,[67] probably given as lectures at the Academy between 1559 and 1565 and taken down by students and later revised, Calvin discusses marriage. When God said that it is not good that the man should be alone and made a helpmate, God meant that "the human race could not exist without woman," so that "no bond is more sacred than that by which husband and wife unite to become one body and one soul." As a general rule, solitude is not good, except for the one "whom God exempts as a matter of unusual privilege" (357).

God has decreed marriage not for a person's "ruin but for his well-being." Not only worldly people advise those who "desire happiness" against marriage; Jerome crammed his book against Jovinian "with petulant insults by which he tries to make sacred marriage hateful and to disgrace it." Despite proofs to the contrary, says Calvin, and the proverb that woman is "a necessary evil," we ought to listen to the voice of God, which asserts that "woman was given to man as a companion and partner to help him to live really well." The reason that "God's blessing as here described is not often seen" is because of "the present corrupt state of the human race." Without this corruption, man would look to God and woman would be his helper and both would cherish "an association no less holy than friendly and peaceful." Fortunately, marriage cannot be totally "spoiled by man's sin," so that there remains in marriage "a residuum of divine good," much like with "a fire which is almost smothered," but where "some sparks still glow" (357–58). In our corrupt state "marriage is also a remedy for lust." Thus marriage represents "a double gift from God," but the second gift is "incidental" (358–59).

Chapter 6

Theological Developments on Celibacy II: The Reformation until Today

The Reformers: A Summary

Martin Luther had attacked the abuses inherent in the power structure of the Roman Catholic Church and their effects upon its members. These abuses included the claim to a centralized interpretation of Scripture by papal authority; the exploitation of the superstition of the masses — especially in the context of the sacramental system of penance and indulgences; the misinterpretation of the role of good works in God's act of salvation; and the dichotomy between the clergy and the laity, and between members of religious orders and nonmembers. Central to his reforms was the issue of celibacy and the celibacy requirement for clergy and members of religious communities. A celibate clergy was set apart from, and above, the laity by the sacrament of holy orders, which appeared to exempt them from the obligation to abide by moral standards and encouraged civic authorities to close their eyes to ecclesiastical extortion and abuse of the privileges of power. Likewise, members of monastic orders appeared to enjoy privileges because of their monastic vows — of celibacy, poverty, and obedience, that placed them in their own minds and in the minds of the laity on higher ground before others and God, without having actively to contribute to the common good and the work of the church. In the case of the clergy, celibacy came to be regarded as imbuing priests with sacramental powers and authority in scriptural and doctrinal interpretation. In the case of monastics, celibacy ensured them a livelihood, an education, financial security not available outside the monastery walls, and a

191

qualification for the priesthood. Since the separate and elevated status of clergy and monastics had as its common denominator the celibacy requirement, Luther attacked it in hopes to expose and shatter the abuses and doctrinal distortions.

Nuns played only a small role in Luther's reforming activity, mostly because they did not significantly shape theological and ecclesiastical doctrine. Since they were ineligible for priestly office nor could they preach in public, as did their male counterparts and mendicant friars, there was little risk that nuns might abuse ecclesiastical privileges. Furthermore, they largely lived in clausuration without significant contact with the outside world. The worst these celibate women could do was contrive for themselves celestial crowns, imagine themselves as brides of Christ, leave their husbands for the cloister, and regard themselves as superior to the married. If their rank within the community permitted, they could also enforce moral conduct and rigorous discipline among those girls and women given into their charge — which occasionally included some male monastic communities — and make life miserable for them. Although Luther was sympathetic to the plight and forced seclusion of nuns of his time, it was largely the celibacy of men that he attacked. The missile he used was the doctrine of justification by faith, not works. According to this doctrine, the works employed in living the celibate life could not and would not convey any privileged status, either before civic authorities, other believers, or God.

In contrast, John Calvin, as a second-generation Protestant, was benefiting from the partially implemented reforms in the Protestant churches. He was less concerned with the dichotomy between clergy and laity — mainly because the priesthood of all believers was already beginning to take shape in Protestant churches. Instead, Calvin focused on the practical implementation of a new church order of presbyters (pastors and elders) and deacons, along with the proper worship of God and the ground of salvation. To him, the celibacy requirement of the clergy was not a core issue in reforming the church, nor a major contributing factor in perpetuating ecclesiastical injustice and extortion. Priestly celibacy was largely to be rejected because it was forced, deprived the church of good and fit (married) pastors, and led clergy who either struggled with it or blatantly violated it into misery and despair. Clerical celibacy was rejected not for the large-scale abuse facilitated by people's adulation of the clergy or the clergy's elevated status among them, but because of the practical problems it incurred, such as a shortage of pastors, internal scruples, and sexual transgressions. The theoretical argument Calvin advanced, almost as an afterthought, was that the Roman Catholic Church's requirement was based on the practices of antiquity and tradition, not on Christ's injunction or what prevailed in the early church. Similarly, monasticism was held in disdain, largely because it was no longer what it used to be in the days of the Church Fathers. The monasteries used to serve as seminaries for clergy and prepared men "for greater tasks"; now they held monks who thought themselves better than other Christians, separated from the rest of the church, and used their celibacy and its concomitant respect for commerce. Moreover, monks lacked brotherly love and humility, and their vow of poverty was based on a faulty interpretation of Scripture. As with the clergy, Calvin argued that monastic communities and vows were not found in Scripture, except for the order of widows.

According to Calvin, the sole reason widows in the New Testament vowed celibacy was because marriage would not have agreed with the work they did. In addition, they had to be sixty before they committed to the order, while present-day nuns could vow celibacy at age twelve, twenty, or thirty. In former days, celibacy for men was a way to prepare them for greater tasks, for women the only way to carry out certain forms of ministry. While the issue of celibacy was not central to Calvin's theology, the practical implications were. Moreover, making a lifelong commitment to the celibate life was now affiliated with the rash and unreflected taking of vows that enslaved people and dared God.

Arguments in Favor of Celibacy

Luther sees the celibate life as a most worthy endeavor for those who have the gift for it. Because celibacy lends itself to abuse, self-elevation, and class thinking between the celibate and the married is no reason not to hold it in high esteem. Its rewards are temporal, not eternal, and provide freedom for undivided Christian service. People should guard this state and restrain their curiosity, instead of deliberately challenging it. Since celibacy is not a command from God, no specific divine and heavenly rewards result from it, other than a sense of personal freedom, happiness, and the ability to serve God and neighbor more freely.

Calvin admits that celibacy is worthy of praise, but only to the degree that it does not induce inequality between single and married Christians. He mocks the admiration of the celibate life so prevalent in antiquity and among the Church Fathers, particularly Jerome, and associates it with superstition. While Calvin appears to reject any institutionalized commitment to the celibate life because of its lifelong vows, he seems to advocate it as a quiet personal expression of piety; as such, he himself is a representative of this form of piety, since he appears to have been celibate before and after his nine years of marriage.

Arguments in Favor of Marriage

Luther says that people can serve God well in any station of life and no particular station is superior to another. What is most pleasing to God is the person's pure disposition of the heart and character, not the amount or nature of works performed in service to God. It is wrong to assume that an unmarried person is automatically more spiritual than a married one simply because the former abstains from sexual intercourse. In fact, the married may have to rely on God more, hence exercise greater faith than monastics because the latter are provided for, while the former continually have to fret about how to eke out a living for themselves, their spouse, and their children.

According to Luther, the proverbial saying that marriage is brief joy and long disgust is true. Marriage involves much labor and trouble here on earth, including anger and dissension between the partners, and inevitably distracts from giving focused attention to God's word. Since Christians are both flesh and spirit, they have no need of marriage according to the Spirit, but they do according to the flesh. Marriage has been instituted as the proper medicine for those to whom it has not been granted to restrain the desires of the flesh, for it is better to find relief from the tortures of the flesh through the married state than to be single and unchaste. Moreover, an unhappy marriage is better than unhappy celibacy, because there is at least some earthly benefit deriving from an unhappy marriage — i.e., increased dependency on God, while none results from an unhappy celibate state.

Calvin agrees with Luther that marriage does not make for happy days. But in contrast to Luther, Calvin believes that the main reason for marriage is people's need for community, not their inability to conquer lust. God said that it is not good for a man to be alone, and so God created woman as a companion and helpmate, which foreshadows marriage. From the beginning, God instituted marriage as a sacred bond. Thus, a woman is to be with a man and a man with a woman that together they should live "really well" on friendly and peaceful terms. The reason that most married people do not exemplify a blissful state is because of sin; yet even their sin and corrupt disposition cannot completely extinguish the residuum of divine good inherent in the marital state. The fact that marriage functions also as a remedy of lust is only an added benefit and merely incidental.

Celibacy for the Few

Luther says that celibacy is a special gift from God granted only to a few. In comparison, the gift of marriage is much more common and is given to many more. Those who have the gift of celibacy will experience only transitory temptations of the flesh, while those who do not will be unable to rid themselves of these temptations even if they do not act on them. The great number of monks and nuns living in monastic communities gives the false impression that there are many who have the gift, but Luther's personal experience of living with monks has made it evident that they do not. External evidence then belies internal truth, for the number of those with the gift is far smaller[1] than outward appearance, i.e., cowls and tonsures, and monastic enrollment suggest. Only those who are certain they have received, or will receive, the gift of celibacy should take these vows.

Calvin also regards celibacy as a special gift granted only to a few, but holds that it may be given only for a limited time, and not for life. Therefore, monastic vows suggest that people are capable of something they may not be, thereby tempting God.

Celibacy and Faithful Discipleship

To Luther, faithful Christian discipleship involves the constant aware-ness of being made righteous before God by grace, through faith in Christ, not good works. Works are the outgrowth of the believer's grat-itude for God's forgiveness and the divine act of salvation, but are meaningless as a way of salvation and do not generate divine rewards. Faithful discipleship also involves improving one's character, and re-sponding to one's particular calling and the responsibilities inherent in one's station in life. Everyone can practice faithful discipleship, re-gardless of age, gender, marital status, and economic and educational background, and no one is better than another before God in Christ.

Celibacy, according to Luther, is a way of life, a tool and "technique" employed by those gifted for it in service to God's word. When em-ployed in faith it is "pure radiance" and nothing done on earth can be "more beautiful" or more highly respected. But when used for personal gain, merit, and credit before God, it is earthly, worldly, heathenish, and ungodly.

Luther says that celibate living also enables people to be of much comfort to others, to become freer here on earth, and to be more attentive to God's word. But instead of using it for liberation, people employ it as self-chastisement or as a way to control others, to set themselves above them, and to induce pain and suffering. Those who do so rob others of the freedom that Christ purchased by his death on the cross; and, by raising their own works above faith, they make Christ out to be an accuser and condemner, thereby crucifying him all over again in their hearts.

Calvin's view on faithful Christian discipleship is complex. He in-tegrates Luther's doctrine of justification by faith, the ideas of other contemporary theologians, such as Erasmus and Melanchthon, and the writings of the Church Fathers, most prominently Augustine, and also enlists historical and literary sources. No common theme emerges from his writings that would clearly identify his view on the nature of faithful Christian discipleship, but a pastiche can be composed. Calvin agrees with Luther that faithful Christians know they are not justified by works, but by faith through the grace of God in Christ, and recognize that all are equal before God, regardless of outward acts of piety and their station in life. Faithful disciples are not proud and pleased with themselves, but recognize they fall short of proper obedience to the law and hence stand in continuous need of grace. Finally, faithful disciple-ship in Christ consists in furthering the unity of the church, helping the poor and oppressed, and treating one's neighbor with dignity, love, and respect. To Calvin, celibacy plays only a minor role in living the life of a Christian. Its positive effects remain largely a thing of the past and are confined to the ecclesiastical, institutionalized structures. In monaster-ies, men could prepare themselves for the greater tasks of priest and bishop; in the order of widows, women could carry out responsibilities that they could not do if they were married. While Calvin admits that celibacy allows people to give more attention to the Lord's service, the negative connotations he attaches to this form of commitment, in the context of priestly office and religious orders, far outweigh the benefits. Calvin does not distinguish between celibacy and religious orders, as does Luther. This collapsing of both into one relegates the practice of celibacy among Christians in general to a temporary matter expected of the unmarried, rather than an intentional, long-term commitment that serves as a source of altruism, equibalance, and personal autonomy in one's service to Christ.

Other Developments

Freedom of Choice

Both Luther and Calvin say that celibacy cannot be imposed from without, but needs to be freely chosen by those who have the will and inner desire for it. Luther says that the ability to remain single does not come by command, vow, or intent, but only by the grace of God. While this way of life is not for everybody and cannot be willed, Christians still are obligated to give it a fair try, restrain their curiosity, and refrain from deliberately seeking out the marriage bond.

Luther opposes the practice of placing children, particularly girls, in convents and monasteries and keeping them there by force and often against their will. While Luther admits to parental rights, he reproaches parents and guardians unwilling to respect the wishes of their children and charges.

He also says that just as no one should be forced to remain single, no one should be forced to remain married if differences arise between the partners pertaining to coercion in faith matters or adultery. Even remarriage following divorce is permissible for those without the gift of celibacy — provided they do not bear the main guilt in the divorce — so that no one is driven into unchastity because of the fault of another. Furthermore, couples may practice temporary sexual abstinence with mutual agreement, but it is wrong of a partner to withdraw sexually as a way to coerce the other into converting to the Christian faith.

Calvin emphasizes freedom of choice, too, though not in choosing celibacy but in choosing to break one's celibate vows. Once people without the gift of celibacy examine why they took these vows and can recognize them as empty, fleeting, and prompted by superstition, they are released from them by this knowledge of truth and by the grace of Christ. Those who persist in them though aware they lack the gift of celibacy will be punished by God for going against their nature.

Celibacy Requirement for Clergy

Luther argues against the requirement that priests remain single and celibate on three grounds. First, Scripture affirms that in the early church bishops and priests were married, and so were some of the apostles, including the Apostle Paul. Second, since the church regards both marriage and priestly ordination as sacraments, they should be reconcilable and priests be allowed to marry. And third, since sexual licentiousness and fornication run rampant among priests without intervention by ecclesiastical authorities, the priestly celibacy requirement appears a farce.

Calvin opposes the celibacy requirement for priests and pastors with a long list of arguments. First, Scripture as the "will of God" attests that marriage is honorable to all, regardless of ecclesiastical office; it affirms that bishops in the early church were married; and it shows that the apostles nowhere make mention of such a requirement and were married themselves. Therefore, Scripture as the "will of God" overrules the tradition of antiquity. Second, the Council of Nicaea (325) declared such a law intolerable, while the Council of Gangra ruled that there be no distinction regarding dignity and worthiness between a priest who is married and one who is not. Third, priests are coerced into committing to it by vow regardless of whether or not they have the gift for it, so that their consciences are strangled. Fourth, the Roman Catholic Church regards a priest who marries as committing a capital crime while condoning or only mildly penalizing fornication and other truly callous crimes and iniquities among its priests. Fifth, Scripture (1 Tim. 4:1, 3) warns of those who forbid marriage and calls such teachings a doctrine of demons, while the early church called them heretics. Sixth, the requirement is unjust and oppressive. Seventh, the clergy is to be distinguished from the laity not by external marks, such as marital status, but by internal convictions and a greater piety in adhering to the teachings of Christ. Eighth, ritual purity through sexual abstinence for priests was a requirement in Old Testament times and does not apply to the New. Lastly, the requirement robs the church of good and fit married pastors.

The Status of Celibate Women

As part of his doctrine of the priesthood of all believers, Luther affirms the equal footing of both sexes before God. This equal standing before God did not necessarily translate into equal standing in church and society. With the closing of most convents in Saxony and the northern regions of Germany, the opportunities for women to serve in active ministry diminished; women were either forced to return home, find employment, or marry. Luther's push for the freedom of Christians to be allowed to marry granted men — priests and monks — the freedom to do so and to become pastors in Protestant churches, while at the same time leaving many women — abbesses and nuns — no other choice but to marry out of economic necessity or for reasons of status. In writing against those who view women as temptations who needed to be banned from sight, Luther argues that it is sinful even to ponder whether "women ought to be married or not," when the answer is as self-evident as a person's need for food.

Calvin maintains the view that woman was ordained to be man's help-mate. In fact, in the ideal model, man looks to God while woman looks to be man's helper, so that both live on friendly and peaceful terms. One may only surmise what Calvin might have thought of women who refused marriage because they claimed to have the gift of celibacy, instead of agreeing to become man's helper in the context of the matrimonial bond.

The Post-Reformation and Subsequent Developments

The abolition of celibacy in Protestant areas affected men differently than women. Women whose convents had been forcibly closed were left to find employment — usually menial labor and domestic service, return to their homes, or enter into marriage as a last resort. Men who were forced out of their monasteries, on the other hand, could find skilled employment easier than women or they could continue their religious vocation through the pastorate in a Protestant church, and marry besides. Single, celibate women not only lost their religious vocation in the church, but often were driven by economic necessity into relinquishing their vows. Rosemary Radford Ruether's theological history on women and redemption[2] has shown that some noticeable trends emerged for single women for the period from 1500 to 1700. Even prior to the Reformation, she says, single women in Western Europe had been losing economic opportunities and legal status. For example, while guardianship for adult single women had been abolished in the late Middle Ages, the Renaissance revival of Roman law in the fifteenth century required single women to have a male guardian[3] — be it father, brother, or another male. Accordingly, the power of rulers over their citizenry was paralleled with that of male heads of households over their wives and their children. Protestant Reformers saw female rule as inherently unnatural, unlawful, and contrary to Scripture, despite the women who ruled their own territories and had favored the Reformation. The most notable tract on the subject was John Knox's *First Blast of the Trumphet against the Monstrous Regiment of Women* (1558), written against Mary, Queen of Scots, and Mary Tudor. The Middle Ages (roughly from 476 to 1453) did not differentiate between economic activity and the household, so that women were involved in a wide range of work, from baking, brewing, keeping pharmacies, printing, and making textiles.[4] A case illustrating such vigorous household activity of a former nun and married woman is Katherine von Bora, who as part of her responsibilities in the Luther household tended to an orchard beyond the village; netted fish from their fish pond; brewed beer; fed, sold, and slaughtered barn animals, including pigs and cows; planted the fields; and ran a farm at Zulsdorf where she spent several months out of the year.[5] With the arrival of the modern era by the late fifteenth century, paid work became increasingly separated from domestic work, and women were forbidden to engage in work in the paid economy. With the forming of male-only workshops, women's work became unpaid work and remained largely confined to the home or to an informal economy of low-paid piecework. Moreover, licenses and educational requirements for skilled labor excluded women who had been previously trained in the family trade. While low-paying drudge work was always available for women without male support, the better-paying skilled work became increasingly difficult for women to secure.[6]

The Protestant rejection of monastic life during the Reformation then, along with the changed definition of paid work outside the home, affected women more adversely than it affected men. Not only was skilled work severely limited for women, but women whose convents were closed also lost the option of a full-time religious vocation apart from marriage. This meant that in Protestant areas, women's only valid religious vocation and socially acceptable calling was to be wife and mother. In addition, the closing of convents in Protestant territories meant the end of institutions that had provided education not only for the nuns themselves but also for women boarders who graduated and went on to marry.[7] Furthermore, the Protestants' removal of the devotion to Mary and women saints — nearly all of whom were celibate — deprived women of the comforts of female advocates in heaven and of revered role models for gender identity in their Christian faith.

The study of women's response to the closing of their cloisters and religious houses is fairly new, and until recently, histories of the Reformation made little distinction between the closing of men's and women's houses.[8] In her analysis of Catholic and Protestant nuns responding to the Reformation, Merry Wiesner-Hanks[9] examines the fate of monastic women in Germany, which differed little from that of women in other countries in Western Europe that had become Protestant. In England and Ireland, where all monasteries and convents were taken over by the Crown,[10] most nuns received small pensions and were expected to return to their families. Many Irish nuns fled to religious communities on the continent or continued to fulfill their religious vows in hiding while waiting for a chance to emigrate. Upon the closing of convents and the liquidation of their assets in several cities of the Netherlands, women had their dowries returned in the form of a small pension. In most Protestant areas of Germany, convent residents were ordered to move to a Catholic area, or, when allowed to remain living on a small part of the property, ordered not to accept novices. Convent lands and buildings were subsequently confiscated, and the buildings often converted into hospitals or schools.[11]

In light of the options for women religious whose houses were threatened with closure, it is not surprising that many women resisted the Reformation. Studying their response to the Reformation in Germany is particularly crucial since it was there that the consecrated or celibate monastic life was threatened with suppression and outlawed on a large scale for the first time in more than a thousand years. In Germany, women religious often made up as much as 5 to 10 percent of the population in a given city. This high number cannot simply be ascribed to male guardians forcing single women into convents, but must also have been the result of women's own desire to join based on the advantages of monastic life.

One of the most prominent examples of a German nun who fought to remain in her convent was Charitas Pirckheimer, the abbess of St. Clara convent in Nuremberg. To Pirckheimer, the abolition of celibacy was an assault not only on her congregation, but on the religious vocation, Christian autonomy, and educational and leadership opportunities. In one of her writings, she describes in vivid detail the ways in which nuns were violently dragged out of the convent by their parents with city residents hurling insults at them. "We don't want to be freed of our vows," the women shouted, "rather we want to keep our vows with God's help."[12] Other convents that opposed the Reformation were those open only to members of local noble families, who were generally well educated and whose abbesses controlled vast property and had jurisdiction over many subjects. Not only was their religious vocation threatened, but also their economic and intellectual independence. Becoming a pastor's wife, for example, constituted a compromise on both counts. The view of Katherine Zell, who married former Catholic priest and reformer Matthew Zell in Strasbourg and who in a tract praised marriage as uniting ordained ministry (for men) and married life,[13] was incompatible with that of the well-educated monastic women of noble status. Although these women had a priest available to say mass and hear confessions, since these functions were not allowed to be carried out by women, all other administrative, educational, and pastoral duties — including the spiritual counseling of residents and novices — were carried out by women.[14]

Another group of women religious opposing the Reformation were canonesses who lived in canoness houses (*Kanonissenstifte*). This group, which had a less prominent male counterpart, was organized like a convent with an abbess as head, followed the Aachen Rule of 816 rather than the Benedictine or Augustinian rules, and offered women an alternative to monastic life. Members performed a variety of liturgical and charitable services outside the convent walls, owned personal property, employed servants, had their own quarters or small houses, were not cloistered, and took no solemn vows[15] though they practiced celibacy. By the time of the Reformation, these houses had existed for at least seven centuries in various cities of Switzerland, France, and Germany, claiming as their ancient roots the orders of virgins and widows of the second through the sixth centuries. In the ninth century in France there were at least eighteen of these houses, and between the tenth and eleventh centuries another thirty-eight houses were added.[16] The opportunities for service, freedom, contact with the outside world and friends and family, and retention of property rights made these houses attractive, especially for members of the upper classes.

Some houses survived for centuries as Catholic establishments within Protestant territories. When Duke Ernst von Brunswick, who had been educated at Wittenberg University, began to introduce the Reformation in his territories in the 1520s, almost all the male monasteries agreed to disband and relinquish their property, while nearly all the female convents refused even to listen to Protestant preachers. When personal pleas failed with two of them, Walsrode and Medingen, the duke had the gates forcibly opened and a hole bashed in the choir loft for his preachers to speak through.[17] In another convent in Lüne, the nuns disrupted the sermons with singing and lit old felt slippers to smoke the preachers out. When forbidden to hold public mass, they held it in private quarters or the convent granary. The nuns at Heiningen refused to feed the Protestant preachers and turned down the duke's sizeable offer of dowries. In bishoprics that had become Protestant, such as Magdeburg and Halberstadt, half the female convents survived, but only one-fifth of the monasteries. The survival of these convents was ensured not only by the women themselves, but also by their relatives. The cost of a dowry for an equitable marriage was higher than the cost of entry into the convent. Since it was more convenient and less controversial for families to allow women to stay in convents than marry them off to partners from lower classes, relatives beseeched the dukes to keep the convents open, saying, "What would happen to our sisters' and relatives' honor and our reputation if they are forced to marry renegade monks, cobblers, and tailors?"[18]

Still other houses survived by accepting Lutheran or Reformed-Calvinist theology while retaining celibacy and the general rule of religious life. In the Nassau region, several canoness houses accepted either a Lutheran (1548 and 1567) or a Reformed-Calvinist rule (1594). When Duke Johann I, who was Lutheran, became a staunch Calvinist, he prescribed for the canoness house at Keppel compliance with the Heidelberg Catechism, so that the 1567 Lutheran rule he had ordered was altered and adjusted in 1594.[19] Other canoness houses adopted Lutheran theology. Anna von Stolberg, the abbess of the free imperial canoness house of Quedlinburg, governed a sizeable territory which included nine churches and two male monasteries. When she became Protestant in the 1540s, she made all priests swear to Luther's Augsburg Confession, and turned one of her former monasteries into an elementary school for both boys and girls. At least fourteen convents in the relatively small territory of Brunswick/Lüneburg survived into the nineteenth century by becoming Lutheran; most of them are still Protestant religious establishments for unmarried women today.

Evidence from Brunswick and Augsburg indicates that Protestant and Catholic women lived together for decades protected by the walls of their convent,[20] so that the denominational distinction was less important than the ability to preserve their communal living, religious autonomy, and celibate vows.

One of the Catholic responses in the period of the Counter-Reformation was the founding of new religious orders. Among them was the Society of Jesus, founded by Ignatius of Loyola (1491–1556), whose members called themselves Jesuits and were dedicated to active service to the world in schools and hospitals, while earning their own living. Women who wanted to model a religious order along the same lines experienced opposition from church authorities — largely because of the clausuration requirement for female nuns — and by the Jesuits themselves. Nonetheless, Angela Merici (1474–1540) founded the Company of St. Ursula, or Ursulines, in Brescia, Italy, and, nearly twenty years later, received papal approval in 1535. Angela modeled her order after the early church, with pictures of Paula and Eustochium in her meeting room and a division of the order into two tiers: virgins, usually from the lower classes; and matron widows, each with her own superior, who often had been recruited from the groups' outside female benefactors and local female nobility. Her concern was for women driven to prostitution by poverty and, hence, had contracted diseases — mostly syphilis, which had newly arrived in the West. In her ministry, she combined practical Christian instruction and education to protect young women from immorality and destitute conditions.[21] Most Ursulines continued to be poor women closely connected with those they served, including the orphaned and war victims, while members earned their own living by teaching or weaving. The Ursulines soon spread to Milan, throughout Italy, and into France and began to focus completely on the education of girls. Originally founded as a society for virgins and widows living under one common rule and ministering outside their houses, similar to the canonesses in Germany, the Ursulines were eventually forced to accept clausuration, take solemn vows, and place themselves under the direct authority of the local bishop, thus preventing any movement or cooperation between houses. They were still allowed to teach girls, but could only do so in the confines of the convent.[22]

The forced clausuration of nuns and canonesses and the push to have them take solemn vows was a result of the Council of Trent (1545–63), which sought to redefine Catholic doctrine, liturgy, and discipline in the wake of the Reformation. The Council reinforced the church's institutional structure and tightened clerical control. But during its nearly twenty years, the fathers barely considered the situation of the besieged German nuns fighting so bravely for their rules. It was not until December 3, 1563, as they were leaving the final meeting, that the prelates hastily decreed that nuns were universally to observe strict clausuration unless they had specific episcopal approval, and were to live in accordance with the papal bull *Pericoloso* ("danger") issued by Boniface VIII in 1298. Until the Council's decision, the 1298 bull that had ordered strict clausuration for nuns had been infrequently enforced, so that nuns were allowed to leave the walls of the convent. In 1566, Pius V ruled that the law of clausuration be applied to all professed nuns, even third-order nuns (tertiaries) who had only taken simple vows of celibacy and were lowest in the hierarchy of female monastics. Moreover, those who had taken simple vows were instructed to take solemn vows or else have their communities closed, while women who were not nuns were forbidden to form new communities.

Opinion differs as to why Council members saw the need to revive strict clausuration for women monastics. Between 512 and 534, clausuration for women had been formally stipulated in the *Rule for Nuns,* drafted by Caesarius of Arles in collaboration with his sister Caesaria for the first women's order of the West. Several advantages for nuns might have guided the authors in recommending the practice at that time. Clausuration eliminated distraction and worldly temptations, protected the women's reputation, reduced conflicts of interest with wealthy donors or the powerful elite, increased physical and mental focus, and provided security against invasion. Also, the *Rule* may have been a response to political, social, and cultural changes, whereby male monastics implemented the vow of stability — remaining in the same monastery for life — while female monastics opted for clausura-tion.[23] With the 1566 clausuration requirement for nuns, the Council of Trent had revived a tradition conceived a thousand years earlier. Following the 1566 ruling, three subsequent papal bulls were produced over the next ten years that insisted on the clausuration of women. In commenting on the measure, Patricia Ranft concludes that the papacy "was more serious than ever about women religious being en-closed" without offering a rationale for it.[24] On the other hand, Jo Ann McNamara views the decree of clausuration as a pure issue of cleri-cal control. The restriction on religious women who had previously been left free to do charitable work outside the convent walls fitted into a larger pattern of restriction on private social enterprise. This measure was congruent with those of Protestant rulers, who outlawed confraternities in their territories because they — along with Catholic monarchs — viewed them as potentially disruptive of the social order. Moreover, clausuration for religious women was generally supported by secular magistrates and by the families of nuns who did not want to see inheritance patterns disrupted or the social order threatened by "undefined single and ill-placed women."[25]

The papal decrees of the sixteenth century and Tridentine canon law could have struck a death blow to the creation of new active re-ligious orders of women and, in time, could easily have extinguished women's religious orders altogether. That it did not may be attributed to the women's creativity and adaptability. Moreover, it may be a tes-timony to their sense of calling to active ministry, their courage to pursue this vocation, and the education and independence that re-ligious life offered women in contrast to the institution of marriage. Rather than disbanding, existing Catholic communities of single, celi-bate women adjusted to the new restrictive conditions of enclosure. The Carmelites, for example, who experienced reform and redirection in 1562 under the leadership of Teresa of Avila (1515–82) in Spain, adopted strict poverty as a means to liberate women from slavery to fashion and dependence on donors, patrons, and to some extent even dowries. New sisters were recruited on the basis of spiritual qualifica-tions, instead of dowry, social status, or even racial background. Since her own Jewish background made her vulnerable to the Inquisition,

Teresa bound her rule closely into the existing ecclesiastical structure. She prescribed frequent confession for her congregations — which included two houses for men — coupled with contemplative practices, spiritual disciplines, mental prayer, and contemplation of the Eucharist and the divine mysteries. Teresa adapted her congregations to the clausuration requirement by developing for her Carmelite sisters an internalized, mystical form of piety, patterned after the Jesuit *Spiritual Exercises*, but distinctly her own as set forth in her *Way of Perfection* (1566) and *The Interior Castle* (1577).

Other women's orders continued their services to the outside world by bringing the outside world to them. The Ursulines, for example, brought the sick, destitute, or those to be instructed inside the convent walls. Their initial focus on caring for sick and underprivileged women transformed into one of educating girls and women in the boarding schools located within convent walls. Unfortunately, their commitment to the poor suffered from the cost of boarding students, so that to a large degree only girls from wealthy families found entry into their schools. Still other women began forming so-called secular sisterhoods. The idea may have originated with Mary Ward in the early seventeenth century in England, who wanted for her group of nuns, called the English Ladies, to be uncloistered without a distinctive habit, bound together by their vows and common rule, and living under a superior general with authority to transfer the sisters. But Pope Urban VIII issued a Bull of Suppression for them in 1631, which argued that the women "went freely everywhere, without submitting to the laws of *clausura,* under the pretext of working for the salvation of souls; they undertook and exercised many other works unsuitable to their sex, their capacity, their feminine modesty, and above all, their virginal shame."[26] Still, the sisterhood survived and later became known as the Ladies of Loretto. Based on the same model, the Daughters of Charity were founded in 1633 as a secular sisterhood by Vincent de Paul and Louise de Marillac and later came to be known as Sisters of Charity. Other sisterhoods formed at the time were the *filles seculières* ("secular girls") in France, and the Sisters of Notre Dame, founded by one of the externs of the *filles,* Marguerite Bourgeoys, in Canada in 1671. The name change from "nun" to "sister" was introduced during this period, and set apart those religious orders of sisters who had not taken solemn vows and hence remained free for full-time Christian service outside the convent walls. The reason that new Catholic sisterhoods were allowed to form at all was that they, as their founders insisted, were not religious but "secular" orders. The secular image was underlined by the fact that the sisters wore no habits and owned no common property and land, as did their cloistered and often wealthy counterparts. While bishops sought to retain close oversight of these sisterhoods and continued to put their own priorities over the interests of the orders they oversaw, in America and in Europe the popularity of "secular" service nuns for a variety of tasks — mainly teaching and nursing — grew quickly and continued well into the nineteenth century.

In addition to the restrictions imposed on women's religious orders by the Council of Trent, the image of celibate women living in convents and sisterhoods began to suffer. With the Enlightenment of the eighteenth century, the view rose that nuns lived frivolous, idle, and superstitious lives. Many of the leading writers of the period, such as Diderot, Voltaire, and Rousseau, presented women's vows as "forced"; convents and sisterhoods were believed to confine "healthy" young women to an "unnatural" life of celibacy. They also believed that convent life and the practice of celibacy resulted in madness. McNamara says that these depictions were drawn by men to whom enlightenment meant the pursuit of the sweetness of life, which included a free run in a garden of women. The king of France, Louis XV, aptly called the "well-loved" king, epitomized an age whose citizens considered a choice of bed partners essential to living the good life. In addition, writers such as Casanova and his fictional counterparts, such as Don Giovanni, cultivated a reputation for sexually subduing women by seduction, fraud, or rape, and discerned an erotic component in flagellation. Lesbian behavior and ill-treatment of girls were suspected to run rampant within the convent walls. To many of the writers of the Enlightenment a system that withheld women from male sexual ambitions was naturally abhorrent.[27]

By the end of the eighteenth century, as a result of the Enlightenment and the French Revolution (1789–99), monasticism was nearly eliminated in several countries of Europe. Monastic communities —

often supported and populated by members of the aristocracy — had literally been stamped out in France, Spain, Portugal, and other parts of Europe. Also, convents that withdrew desirable women from the marriage market and endowed them with tax-exempt property had become a growing irritation to the money-hungry states of the eighteenth century. As Napoleon's armies swept across Europe, they imposed de-Christianization laws. In 1792, the Paris government decreed the final dissolution of monastic houses, except those used for hospitals, and by 1810 the French suppressed all the monasteries. In Belgium, no convent was spared. In Germany, the princes were encouraged by Napoleon to repay their wartime losses with ecclesiastical property, so that eighty-three convents were closed. In Italy, French troops took over convents as military headquarters or turned them into prisons. The number of nuns expelled from their communities at this time ranges from 30,000 to 55,000. Only 6,700 former nuns still living in 1800 resumed their vows. Some 356 nuns are known to have married, mostly priests, thereby combining their own poor pension with the equally poor ones of their husbands. Another 700 are known to have found secular employment or settled as single people and asked to be relieved of their vows between 1800 and 1808. Of the rest, little is known. Many of the older nuns died almost immediately after the expulsion. Some of the youngest were seduced or raped. Those who could took refuge with their families, but older ones had none left and others found their families had emigrated or would not take them in. When their pensions were not paid, some starved; others died of exposure and violence.[28]

By 1802, survivors began to return to some of the Italian and Belgium convents. In 1828, religious orders returned to Austria, German, and Holland. In France, at least one third of the old religious communities survived clandestinely. But reconstitution of the former religious order was difficult since the convents' endowments and even their household furnishings were gone.[29]

In America, the number of sisters grew rapidly during the early nineteenth century. As soon as Roman Catholic sisters from Europe and Canada were admitted to the mission field, they volunteered to serve in America and the rest of the world. In America, their numbers grew from under forty to more than forty thousand during the nineteenth century. They outnumbered male church workers in the last half of the century, and there were almost four times as many nuns as priests by the century's close. The sisters' main focus was teaching and nursing. By 1900, nearly 4,000 parochial schools were in operation, most of them run by sisters, and 663 girls academies, compared to only 102 Catholic academies for boys. Nursing work was done by sisters in private homes, almshouses, and hospitals. Sisters administered at least 265 hospitals during that century, and worked in military hospitals and provided pastoral care and spiritual counsel to hospital patients during the Civil and Spanish-American wars. In addition, they ran daycare centers, infant and maternity homes, homes for the aged, mental institutions, settlement houses, residences for single working women, and homes for delinquent girls and unwed mothers. The large numbers attracted to the sisters' way of life and ministry led to complaints that too many women of marriageable age from the countryside were joining the urban convents.[30]

Despite their growth in numbers on American soil, the sisters had to face two other major forces of opposition. One involved sisters whose communities were divided into two classes: choir sisters — those who possessed education and chanted the divine office, the official prayer of the church, and lay sisters — who had less education, came often from the lower classes, and performed manual labor. This distinction, outwardly visible in the color and detail of their habits, had been imported from Europe and offended American sensibilities because of its lack of equality. The other force of opposition came from anti-Catholic sentiment in American society — particularly in the South, and including American Protestantism. The sisters' foreign language, customs, and methods, along with their celibate communal life, made them prime targets for abuse, so that many went about their work in contemporary dress. Between the 1830s and 1850s, pamphlets, books, and newspapers flooded the country purporting to reveal what "really" happened behind convent walls. Tales of secret tunnels, rape, seduction, infanticide, prison cells, and exaggerated and absurd penances were reinforced by sermons from Protestant pulpits that enlarged upon the "Catholic threat." Prominence was given to reports from ex-nuns and ex-priests and the revelations of "escaped nuns." People giving credence to these reports organized mobs to attack convent property, tried to undermine the sisters' schools, and proposed convent inspection laws with the intent of freeing nuns from their prisons. In 1834, the flourishing Ursuline academy in Charlestown, Massachusetts, was destroyed; other attacks on convents took place in Philadelphia, Baltimore, Frederick, St. Louis, Galveston, and elsewhere.[31]

By the end of the nineteenth century, the canon laws for nuns of the thirteenth century, initially formulated under the papal bull *Pericoloso* of Boniface VII and reactivated at the Council of Trent in 1563, were still in effect. Clausuration of nuns who had taken solemn vows was required and the forming of new "religious" orders prohibited. The sisters' constitutions inherited from Europe reflected a monastic regime of prayer and fasting, but in America this was combined with full-time teaching, domestic work, farming, and other self-support projects. Their heavy clothing, often unsuited to the weather, along with inadequate sleep, food, and medical care, contributed to a high mortality rate. Adjusting to the American context was often found in a complete break with the European motherhouse.[32] While Rome had established the practice of giving approval to new constitutions, many superiors spent years struggling to gain independent status for their communities.

The sisters were an important influence in the American Catholic community and controlled most of the church's charitable institutions.[33] But while from 1900 to 1950 the number of Catholic sisters still continued to increase, their freedoms and roles narrowed. In 1900, U.S. Catholics gained permission from Rome to organize as a church with a recognized hierarchy. At the same time, the Vatican classified the third-order sisters as a true form of religious life, thus imposing on its members partial clausuration and monastic rules. Strict control limiting activity outside the convent or contact with the world became normative for nuns. Teaching in parochial schools became the nuns' primary role. The meager annual salary of two or three hundred dollars paid directly to the superior and not to the individual nun widened the gap between educational and professional opportunities available

to nuns and those of laywomen. Concerned about their inferior training compared to that of lay professionals in nursing and teaching, nuns
struggled to complete their education through summer and weekend
classes.[34]

It was not until the Second Vatican Council (1962–65) that the
clausuration requirement for nuns was lifted. Several reform movements preceded this ruling. In 1947, secular sisterhoods were recognized by the pope as an approved form of religious community, even
though they did not require common life and stressed service in the
world.[35] In 1950, Pope Pius XII took the first steps toward modern-
izing religious orders of women. And in 1951, the First International
Congress of Religious Teaching Sisters met in Rome, where the pope
advised them to adjust their apparel, do away with outmoded customs
and rules, and pursue professional training that corresponded in quality
and academic degrees to that of their lay contemporaries. According
to Joseph H. Fichter, the pope was simply affirming what many of the
sisters themselves had been trying to accomplish for decades. In the
United States, some of them had already received doctoral degrees
from universities. More than anything, the sisters wanted to perform
the good works they had been called to do more efficiently by de-
mocratizing their structures and diversifying their work.[36] Among the
sixteen major documents issued by the Vatican Council, the principal
one pertaining to the modernization of the sisterhoods was the 1965
decree on "The Appropriate Renewal of the Religious Life" (*Perfectae
Caritatis*), which recommended renewal of spirituality and adaptation
of ministries. The norms for the implementation of change were formulated by an apostolic letter, *Ecclesiae Sanctae*, the following year,
which required each congregation to convene a general chapter within
three years for extensive and open consultation among its members.
The period of experimentation was completed when the religious orders submitted their revised constitutions to Roman authorities, which
most of them did by 1970. Response from Rome was deliberately de-
layed until new Canon Law was promulgated in 1983. This meant that
the process of renewal, begun in the 1950s, was still without papal approval. With the arrival of the new Pope John Paul II in 1978, whose

conservative preferences soon became known, the sisters' renewal process came to a halt. One of the decisive events occurred in 1983, when the programs worked out by the sisters for the reform (*aggiornamento*) of their communities were repudiated by the Vatican. According to the 1983 document from the Sacred Congregation for Religious and Secular Institutes, titled "The Essential Elements in the Church Teaching on Religious Life," the sisters were once again to wear religious garb, observe a common life by returning to their convents, pronounce their public vows of poverty, celibacy, and obedience, and restrict their apostolic ministries. Since many sisters had been living and working outside their religious communities and over a third of them no longer wore a habit, they viewed the "Essential Elements" as a repudiation of their lifestyle. Some complied and some left their religious communities; others responded in ways least expected by the Vatican: they donned street clothes, took positions on public university campuses, stood on picket lines, or ran for public office.[37]

Another source of conflict between the Vatican and women religious was the official organization and activities of Catholic nuns in the Leadership Conference of Women Religious in the 1970s. One of the goals of the organization was the education of women religious in feminist consciousness. They sponsored a series of study packets on feminism to enhance members' awareness of their spiritual and social formation.[38] The groundwork for these changes had been laid twenty years earlier when the pope advised a revamped social organization of the women's orders and members' increased academic preparation. Many had followed the papal advice, so that the decade before Vatican II saw a sharp increase in academic achievements among American sisters. By the 1960s, women religious had become "too educated" to keep silent about patriarchal discrimination and episcopal whims. When bishops sought to force changes upon the sisterhoods or interfered with their renewal efforts, many of the members left their order. This happened in 1965, when Archbishop Karl Alter legislated for the lives of the Glenmary Sisters; half of them left and formed an independent lay group. It occurred again in 1968, when 400 of the 450 Sisters of the Immaculate Heart of Mary in Los Angeles chose the same alternative rather than allowing Cardinal James McIntyre to overrule their chapter decision.[39]

Conflicts between U.S. Catholics, both lay and religious, heightened in the 1980s under Pope John Paul II. A major display of this conflict appeared on October 7, 1984, when ninety-seven prominent Catholics, including twenty-six nuns, signed a *New York Times* ad that stated that a diversity of opinion existed among Catholics on the morality of abortion. The Vatican saw this statement as a direct challenge to its teaching authority and insisted that the nuns who signed the document either recant or leave their orders.[40] In the meantime, some bishops were beginning to realize that the church could only lose by conflicts with some of its best-educated women and, in light of the dwindling number of priests, would have to depend more and more on nuns and laywomen for ministry. A three-year dialogue (1978–81) between the Women's Ordination Conference and the Catholic Bishops' Committee on Women resulted in an effort to write a pastoral letter on women. The attempt went nowhere; each draft became more problematic than the last, exposing the profound inability of the Catholic hierarchy to accommodate feminist critique without admitting that it had erred in the past. By 1992, the attempt was dropped with bishops merely urging the church to spend more time listening to women.

In the United States, many Catholics were grateful for the heightened feminist awareness and social activism emerging within the church, but others were not. Beginning in the 1980s, some Catholic lay women regarded feminist ideas as evidence of a deep spirit of infidelity and even "paganism." They believed that dissidents either had to be purged from the church or reformed in order to save both the church and society. Echoing the conservative ideology that had been standard in the pre–Vatican II era — only with a sharper edge that polarized the Catholic Church from within — the women formed interest groups to organize against contraception, abortion, and feminist theological goals, such as inclusive language.[41] These groups include Women for Faith and Family, Catholic Daughters of America, and the National Council of Catholic Women. In their efforts to bring recalcitrant women to their senses and put them back in their place within the pre–Vatican II hierarchy of church, family, and society, members linked up with other conservative Catholic and Protestant groups whose goal it was to restore and further the "sacred value of the family." One of these Protestant groups is Presbyterians Pro-Life (PPL) — a lobbying organization not supported by or affiliated with the Presbyterian Church (U.S.A.) — whose mission is to establish anti-abortion, anti-feminist, and anti-gay agendas in mainline denominations. Board members have collaborated with national Catholic groups — including Priests for Life and the Catholic League for Religious and Civil Rights, and U.S. cardinals and bishops. In a dramatic move in 1988, PPL attempted to reverse the pro-choice stance of the denomination by featuring Mother Teresa during a pre-Assembly event of General Assembly, the annual national convention of the Presbyterian Church (U.S.A.).[42] Board members of PPL are also affiliated with the Council on Biblical Manhood and Womanhood, an organization that espouses "male headship" in family life and the church, and asserts in its mission statement that "wives should forsake resistance to their husband's authority and grow in willing, joyful submission to their husbands' leadership."[43]

Celibacy in Protestantism

Since their formation during and after the Reformation, Protestant mainline denominations have expected celibacy of their single members prior to and outside of marriage. In the early nineteenth century, several movements arose that either directly or indirectly discouraged members from marrying and expected of them a lifelong commitment to celibacy. Some of these became part of the mainline denomination, and celibacy was expected of members in some offices or in certain forms of ministry. Examples are the deaconess movement, which had been adopted by most Protestant mainline denominations, and denominational missionary societies that expected their female foreign missionaries to remain single while in service. Other groups severed their ties with mainline Protestantism and formed separate religious communities that required lifelong celibate commitment for full membership.

The Deaconess Movement

In the early nineteenth century, the deaconess movement combined celibacy and charitable Christian service within mainline Protestant denominations. It was begun in 1833 in Kaiserwerth, Germany, by the Lutheran pastor Theodore Fliedner (1800–1864) as an outgrowth of his prison ministry. Deeply concerned about the rehabilitation of discharged female prisoners, he offered his garden house to train them in Christian service and to have them assist in his ministerial work. He and his wife taught the women nursing, social work, Bible, and Christian doctrine. When the garden house became too small, a larger house was purchased from donations, and the Rheinisch-Westphalische Deaconess Society was founded as a hospital and training school for unmarried women. By 1840, seventeen deaconesses were in training, caring for thirty-three patients. The following years saw the addition of an orphanage, a shelter for epileptics and mental patients, and a motherhouse. In 1847, a deaconess house was established in Berlin. By 1850, Fliedner was sending Kaiserwerth deaconesses to start orphanages, hospitals, and schools overseas, including in Jerusalem, Constantinople, Cairo, Beirut, and Alexandria. Based on this model, the Moravian church founded a deaconess center in Niesky in 1842. The German Methodists opened their first motherhouse in Frankfurt in 1876. The German Baptists founded a home in Berlin. France, Switzerland, and Holland followed suit. At the twenty-fifth anniversary of its founding, twenty-seven deaconess institutions were at work all over Europe and Scandinavia. The model was brought to England by the Episcopal priest William Pennefather in 1860 and promoted by others, including one of Kaiserwerth's former students, Florence Nightingale, who opened the Nightingale School for Nurses at St. Thomas Hospital in London.[44]

Supporters were intent on distinguishing the deaconess movement from any association with Roman Catholicism. "The deaconess," a magazine article read, "is not a Protestant nun as she takes no vow of celibacy or of any other kind." Her dress is not to be confused with "the habit of a nun," in the same way the "clerical cut" coat worn by a preacher cannot be confused with a "priest's cassock." She is not a church beggar, "haunting the stores and public places"; and the deaconess home is not like a "nunnery," for it is usually "a frame cottage where several womanly women live a simple home life, with possibly one of mature years and experience to advise and guide."[45] The life of a deaconess resembled in most ways the "secular" sister or the canoness who took only simple vows. Deaconesses, according to one of the constitutions, were to be single and celibate or widowed, at least twenty-three years of age, and willing to give themselves fully to Christian service, work long hours, and receive no salary. After a probationary period of usually two years, they were duly consecrated into service, frequently by a bishop. They spent daily time in worship, prayer, and singing. They wore habits and were addressed with the title "sister." They were not clausurated, retained personal property and their own rooms, and could leave the order at any time or be married without sanctions.

The idea of training women for home mission, Christian social work, and nursing was adopted first by the Methodist Episcopal Church in Germany. Its members took the model to England,[46] Canada,[47] and, in the 1840s, to America, where it initially faltered, but saw great success in the 1870s. Within the next three decades, more than 140 deaconess homes were established in America. They represented almost every Protestant denomination, and some interdenominational, and were often combined with hospitals, orphanages, nursing homes, and schools. By 1894, the thirty-three Protestant foreign mission societies had sent abroad more than one thousand female missionaries, most of them trained in deaconess homes of Protestant denominations. They served as teachers, evangelists, and physicians in schools, churches, and hospitals on every continent. Women saw in the dedication of the deaconess a reflection of the ministry of Christ. Most deaconesses were daughters of ministers or leaders in women's society. Normally they were young women from strong church backgrounds who responded to a call of Christian commitment, just as their brothers might have chosen to be ministers.[48] Under the leadership of Lucy Rider Meyer, a trained teacher and Methodist, the first American deaconess house and a training school for single, female church workers were established in Chicago in 1888. The School reached its highest enrollment of 248 in 1912. By 1917, the all-female Chicago Training School became affiliated with the all-male Garrett Biblical Institute, which is now Garrett-Evangelical Theological Seminary.[49] In 1934, the Chicago Training School moved to the Evanston campus, adjacent to Northwestern University. Other schools followed, including the Dorcas Institute in Cincinnati; it opened in 1910, and united with the Cincinnati Missionary Training School to become the Cincinnati Training School in 1931.[50] Three hospitals still operating today were started by deaconesses in Cincinnati alone: Christ Hospital, founded by the Methodist Episcopal house; Bethesda, built by the German Methodist branch; and Deaconess, an initiative of several other Protestant denominations in the city. In the United States, the deaconess organization still operates in several Protestant denominations, most prominently in the United Methodist Church, though with varying success because of the other venues of full-time Christian service now open to women and their admittance to diaconal and pastoral leadership. In Europe, particularly in Germany, several hospitals and nursing homes are served and run by deaconesses. Their numbers have been dwindling, possibly again because full-time ministry in the diaconate or the pastorate have become available to women in most Protestant churches of Germany.

Female Foreign Missionaries

By the late nineteenth century, female foreign missionaries were authorized to serve by most Protestant mainline denominational boards in America. In the early twentieth century, the ratio of women to men in the mission field was in some areas as high as two-to-one. Generally mission boards encouraged their male missionaries to marry prior to service abroad, but they discouraged women from marriage — by giving preference to single women in their selection and missionary assignments and by penalizing them when they married in the mission field. The selection process based on marital status resembled the celibacy requirement for priests in the Roman Catholic Church: Protestant women only qualified for appointment and continued service in full-time mission work abroad if they were not married and practiced celibacy. Though most of the single women missionaries had made no vow or commitment to singleness and celibacy, the female mission boards that sent them did.

Two factors probably prompted women's missionary boards to do so. First, the Victorian era viewed men and women largely in traditional roles with the man as head of the family and the woman as his helper, assisting to accomplish his goals. This view, shaped by the Reformed tradition and Calvinism, presumed that men in the mission field needed a wife as a helpmate, while women could fulfill certain forms of ministry only if they were not impeded by marriage and children. Second, the celibacy requirement was certainly influenced by the preparatory training the women received at the missionary schools. According to Rosemary Skinner Keller, before going abroad most female missionaries were trained in one of the 140 deaconess homes. These single and celibate women had become the female role models of devout Christian service among Protestants. Since among their major tasks was the Christianizing and evangelizing of immigrants crowding the inner cities, they were ideal teachers of those intent on serving in similar ministries overseas.[51] The result of the implicit requirement for women to remain single was that nearly the entire women's missionary movement was built upon a celibate order of life-career missionaries, who were maintained on a subsistence level.[52] In the event that a woman did marry during her first term, which typically lasted from five to seven years, she was required, by a signed pledge, to return her travel and outfit allowance and sometimes her salary on a prorated basis.[53]

Other missionary organizations were less covert about the celibacy requirement of the women they sent. One of them was the Sisters of the Common Life, which had been founded by Amy Carmichael, an English missionary to India; membership required celibacy. During her more than fifty years in India, Carmichael wrote thirty-five books which were widely read in both England and America. The work of her sisters was directed at educating girls and women and preventing them from becoming subject to temple prostitution. Many times the sisters — and other Christian missionaries — intercepted infant girls whose families, in the belief they were gaining redemptive privileges with the gods, handed them over to the temple authorities to be raised as temple prostitutes.[54] Eventually a home and a school for these girls were built in Dohnavur, Southern India, which attracted other women who felt called to this form of Christian service. By 1952, there were nine hundred sisters working as missionaries in various parts of India.[55]

The founding of the deaconesses in Germany by Theodore Fliedner is linked to two existing movements in the Netherlands that Fliedner may have become aware of during his visit there in 1822. The two movements, the Beguines and the Damsels of Charity, afforded single women the opportunity to serve in full-time Christian ministry. The latter was a product of the Reformation and arose in 1559, when Henry de la Mark, sovereign prince of Sedan, The Netherlands, became Protestant and founded institutions of learning and charity. These charitable institutions were placed under the Damsels of Charity, which later came to be regarded as the first Protestant deaconess association.[56] The second group, the Beguines, were of Roman Catholic origin and had been founded by Lambert de Begue, a Belgian priest, in 1184 to offer single women an opportunity for full-time Christian service and ministry apart from a monastic rule. Women lived in small Gothic brick houses surrounding the church, did not take vows, and had as their ministry the care of the sick and the poor. Within fifty years, the movement had spread from Belgium to France, and into the Low Countries, Italy, and Germany. The Beguines related their ministry to the deaconesses of the early church, with their emphasis on works of mercy and nursing, so that a hospital was frequently attached to the community.[57] Charges brought against the movement by the 1260 Synod of Cologne and the 1312 Council of Vienne offer a glimpse of certain characteristics that foreshadow the future Protestant stance of the movement. They suggest, for example, that the women did not practice regular confession to a priest nor engage in eucharistic adoration, had doctrinally perfectionist and antinomian tendencies, used a Bible that had been translated into the vernacular, and preached and read vernacular commentaries in public.[58] Beguine spirituality may have also influenced the *devotio moderna*, a lay movement focusing on liturgical prayer, spiritual accountability, and scriptural interpretation that had arisen in the Low Countries in the fourteenth century, and in which Erasmus (1469–1536) was raised. Since the hundreds of beguinages that sprang up in the Low Lands and Germany had no single leader, rule, or congregation, the movement remained spontaneous and amorphous. By the fifteenth century, the first phase of the movement was spent; beguinages began to resemble houses for single working-class, poor women rather than those of women religious. In the seventeenth century, however, the Beguines experienced a revival of their religious ministry and devotional practices that lasted well into the twentieth century, and again offered single Christian women a *via media,* a life between that of a nun and a lay woman.[59] Houses of Beghards, the Beguines' male counterpart, were few in number. In Belgium, some Beguine houses continue to operate to this day.

Other Celibate Communities

So-called utopian societies[60] based on Christian principles were also formed. Rosemary Radford Ruether observes that most of these communities, both Christian and secular, sought to modify the private family in one way or another, largely by introducing celibacy.[61] These communities flourished in America during the second quarter of the nineteenth century. Some of the Christian utopian communities had origins in Reformation radicalism, including the German communities of the Rappite Harmonists, the Zoarite Separatists, and the Amana Inspirationists. The pietist and spiritualist movements of the seventeenth and eighteenth centuries, shaped by mystical and theosophist philosophers such as Jakob Boehme (1575–1624) and Emanuel Swedenborg (1688–1772), heavily influenced these communities. Others, like the Shakers, were an English Quaker sect that came to America at the time of the American Revolution. Still others were born on American soil, including the Oneida Perfectionists, which arose out of a revolt against New England Calvinism, and the Church of Latter-day Saints (Mormons), which was in response to the revival atmosphere in Western New York and developed communal structures as the group moved west. Ruether says that most utopian communities — with the exception of the Mormons — stressed a spiritual androgyny that was linked with celibacy. These groups believed that the separation of human beings into male and female was a result of the Fall, so that the desire for carnal union was associated with the Fall, hence with sin. This sin manifested in a male-female dualism was eliminated and spiritual androgyny restored as members transcended their sexuality. Moreover, spiritual reality was divided into male and female principles, representing the complementary aspects of truth and goodness; the union of these two principles of male and female constituted the apex of spiritual development.[62]

While several utopian movements favored celibacy as a means for spiritual growth, others — most notably the Shakers — made celibacy a condition for membership. The Shakers, also called the United Society of Believers in Christ's Second Appearing, grew out of a sect of "shaking" Quakers in 1747 near Manchester, England. In 1758, the founders, James and Jane Wardley, were joined by Ann Lee, a twenty-two-year-old mill worker. She eventually became the leader of the group and took it to the United States. Following a series of physical attacks on her and members of her sect, she emigrated to America in 1774, accompanied by her husband and seven followers. From their settlement near Albany, New York, the Shakers conducted preaching tours to nearby towns, where they began to draw converts, mostly from Methodists and New Light Baptists, as part of the religious revivals that swept the region. Because of their millennialist views, female leadership, celibacy, and pacifism, the Shakers often met with hostility and violence by mobs and local authorities who suspected them of witchcraft and political and religious subversion. Both Ann Lee and her husband, William, received violent beatings from angry mobs, causing his death in 1784, and hers a few months later. Ann Lee's work was carried on by James Whittaker, one of her original followers from England, who continued the preaching tours and the founding of societies. Following his death in 1786, the work was continued by Joseph Meacham, an American convert from the New Light Baptists. He gave the Shaker societies a three-court structure divided along distinct degrees of celibate commitment. The inner court was composed of mature believers, who had consecrated themselves and their property to the community. The second court was composed of young people in formation or those who still had worldly obligations. The third court consisted of members who carried on the business of the society in the world. Based on their view that the church must be led by a complementary male and female leadership, representing the dual parentage of Christ as Father and Mother, each local society had equal numbers of elders and deacons, i.e., two male elders and two female eldresses, and two male deacons and two female deaconesses who shared in the responsibilities of spiritual leadership and the diaconate. Meacham shared his own role with Lucy Wright, who virtually led the whole movement alone for twenty-four years after Meacham's death in 1797.[63]

In 1808, Benjamin Seth Youngs published a comprehensive work that placed Shaker beliefs in the context of biblical and Christian history and theology. The work became the so-called Shaker bible and was entitled *The Testimony of Christ's Second Appearing*. Central to the *Testimony* are celibacy and four successive dispensations of revelation and salvation. According to the *Testimony*, the remedy for human lust is celibacy practiced in mind and body. People who give in to lust allow their rational soul to succumb to their animal instincts. Since lust corrupts not only human relationships, but also the proper order of all creation, it is at the root of all sin, including war, oppression, slavery, pride, and gluttony. The *Testimony* outlines four historical stages or dispensations that have contributed toward helping people overcome lust, particularly sexual lust. Since the Fall did not eradicate people's capacity for sinless sex, only made it more difficult and infrequent, a new dispensation was needed — first through the patriarchs, then through Moses — so that people could control their animal instincts. In time, another dispensation was needed; it was ushered in through Jesus, who transcended the natural, material creation and pointed to the final end of humanity toward spiritual regeneration and immortal life. In this dispensation there would be no marrying or giving in marriage. Jesus modeled this new celibate and lust-free life through his own sexless birth and the celibacy of the true disciples among his early followers. But the full power of the spiritual life was not made available until the second coming of Christ as a woman. This woman was Ann Lee, who complemented the male image of God in Christ, functioned as revealer of the Mother or Wisdom side of God, and disclosed God's feminine nature. Only when people subscribe to both the father and mother side in Christ can they overcome lust, give birth to children of regeneration, and grow into a community through which the mass of fallen humanity can be transformed. All men and women are to take up the cross of Christ: crucify the flesh, become transformed into the new humanity of celibacy, and share in communal living, gender equality, and peace.[64]

As their numbers began to dwindle by the end of the nineteenth century, the Shakers abandoned the notion that redemption could not come until the majority of people had been transformed to their way of life. Consequently, Shakers began to see themselves as a planted seed that had to take root in various other movements. Some adopted an ecumenical stance toward the world and involved themselves in social and political movements, such as feminism, vegetarianism, anti-racism, and socialism. Others, like Anna White, eldress of the Society of New Lebanon, became involved in the peace movement. Under her leadership, several delegations of Shakers attended meetings of the Universal Peace Union. White also associated herself internationally with the Alliance of Women for Peace, obtained hundreds of signatures for the Petition for International Disarmament, and was appointed New York vice president of the Alliance. According to White, any female reformer looks to Ann Lee "as the one who taught and through her followers teaches still perfect freedom, equality and opportunity to woman." Her female followers "rejoice in true freedom, not alone from the bondage of man's domination," but "from the curse of that desire 'for her husband,' by which, through the ages, he has ruled over her."[65]

It is frequently assumed that the Shakers died out because of their celibacy. But their death, which came in the twentieth century after more than two centuries of survival, is more likely a result of several other factors. For one, the American fascination with millenarian, communitarian, and utopian social experiments was replaced in the early twentieth century with an interest in the class struggle in an increasingly industrial and urban society. For another, industrialization made a life of severe simplicity less desirable, and also made Shaker crafts, one of their main sources of income, obsolete.[66] Celibacy may have played only a small role in making the movement less attractive to new members; historically, celibate communities generally lasted longer than those that accepted the nuclear family.[67] This may have been the case because adult converts constitute a more stable and committed community than those merely born into a certain way of life and faith. One may conclude that the Shakers died out not because they had no natural progeny — as do the Amish, for example — but because they failed to attract the next generation to their way of life and religious beliefs.

Marriage, Celibacy, and the Church Today

The church's direct involvement in the marriage rite was a fairly late development. For the first thousand years, the church paid little attention to developing a distinct Christian marriage ceremony, while it had quickly produced its liturgy for the Eucharist, baptism, and confirmation. The first detailed account of a Christian wedding in the West dates from the ninth century, and was identical to an old nuptial service of ancient Rome, except that the names of the Holy Spirit and Christ were substituted for names of two pagan gods.[68] Until the Renaissance, people married by mutual agreement in the presence of witnesses; they had sex at once — often in the presence of these witnesses, and there was no need to wait for the church's blessing. This practice is illustrated by the 1525 marriage "ceremony" of Luther and Katherine von Bora on June 27, in which Luther appeared with his bride at the portal of the Wittenberg parish church — not inside — before a number of his friends as witnesses. There he and his bride were blessed by the former priest Johann Bugenhagen — who himself had married in 1522. Later that day, the couple consummated the marriage in front of witnesses. Since the marriage bond had already been established by the betrothal — the public announcement of the marriage that took place June 10, the ceremony was merely a social event.[69] This social custom, known as spousals, existed until the eighteenth century.

The Council of Trent designated marriage as a sacrament in the sixteenth century. The marriage ceremony, and with that the institution of marriage, was now given increased attention by the church; eventually both Catholics and Protestants placed it under ecclesiastical auspices. In the Catholic tradition, clandestine marriage was now rejected and the validity of a marriage came to depend on the public announcement of banns and vows of consent before a priest and two witnesses. Among Protestants, the rituals and celebratory preparations surrounding marriage that were largely derived from folk traditions were seen as sinful waste. The Reformers rejected the canonical view that consent of the couple alone was essential for a marriage's validity, insisting on parental consent for the young and a formal joining of the couple in church before the minister and the congregation. The nuptial mass was replaced by a sermon in which the minister emphasized the scriptural doctrines of marriage in the Old Testament accounts of Creation and the Fall. Both Catholics and Protestants shared the view that the marriage bond was essentially hierarchical, a matter of male headship and female submission, an ordering that was the foundation for all other hierarchies of church and society.[70]

Beginning with the French Revolution, the Catholic and Protestant churches' view of marriage as hierarchical fed into a changing definition of family. Historically, the Roman *familia* had included slaves and servants, as well as relatives by blood or marriage. The first English usage of the term "family" did not occur until the beginning of the fifteenth century, when it still included the servants of a particular household. Not until the late seventeenth century did the contemporary meaning of family as a group consisting of parents and their children come into usage, and it was not fully developed until the Victorian era.[71] According to Rosemary Radford Ruether, the ideology of the family and its crucial importance in social well-being intensified in the late eighteenth century as many productive, educational, health, and religious activities shifted to institutions outside the family. Language borrowed from monastic communities and evangelical crusades invested the family with new salvific significance as a place of refuge from the fallen world. By the end of the nineteenth century, Victorian thought had cast the home as a benevolent realm of godly, uplifting nurture, providing refuge from the outside world. It was a woman's job to create a dreamworld of a home where men could come to rest and recuperate. An ideology of true womanhood developed that not only domesticated women but feminized religion. With the American separation of church and state, the family and private life emerged as the sphere of religion. In turn, the church and its ministry became an auxiliary to the home and its private piety and morality.[72]

The arrival of the industrialized age in the late nineteenth century threatened to undo this newly created family ideology, and social critics raised concern about the future of marriage and family life. In an attack on the popularity of celibacy among women in England, and its negative effect on the family and the nation, Walter M. Gallichan blames the industrialized age. "The great influx of women into the field of industrial labour and business," he wrote in 1914, "is a grave problem." The increase of women workers "tends to augment the celibate army" in two ways: first, it relieves women of "dependence upon their sex, or marriageable value, as their only asset"; and second, it causes them to postpone marriage so that they come to be content with the single life.[73] As a "remedy" for this inclination toward celibacy — which had become popular among the lower and the upper classes but not the middle class — Gallichan suggests "a finer, broader education of the young in the dignity, beauty and sacredness of love and marriage." He also suggests that owners of capital be "relieving the lot of the woman-worker" and accept their share of responsibility for facilitating the marriage of "sound men and women."[74] Since "love and marriage should be esteemed as the destiny of all," "remedies" for female celibacy could be introduced by the legislature, by economic reforms, by the adjustment of industrial wages, by housing schemes, and by educating girls for marriage in the way boys are trained for labor or business.[75]

In America, the fight to preserve and further the family has largely been fought by the Christian Right, which has aligned itself with the political right. The Christian Right originated with Protestant fundamentalism in the late nineteenth century. In the early twentieth century, emerging Protestant fundamentalist leaders began to rescue what they perceived as the only true Christian faith by doing battle against the evils of evolution and the Social Gospel movement. They viewed it as their failure when mainline Protestantism increasingly accommodated its theology to social changes, such as by adopting the historical-critical method in studying the biblical texts, and when Prohibition failed. These trends led to what historians have called the Great Reversal, in which fundamentalists and other evangelicals dissociated themselves from social reform movements and fled from the political scene. Many left mainline denominations to form their own groups, with schools, seminaries, and publishing houses. During the 1930s, radio evangelists issued warnings against various social and political forces, including communism, socialism, labor unions, immigrants, and ecumenical organizations, like the World Council of Churches. By the 1950s, the Christian Right was back in the political arena in the fight against communism. In the 1960s, it fought the struggle for civil rights, then secular humanism and feminism in the 1970s, and relativism, abortion, and gay rights in the 1980s. All but communism are of concern to the Christian Right today.

Among the first organized efforts of fundamentalists to restore, protect, and advance the traditional family in America was the founding of the Moral Majority by Jerry Falwell in the 1970s. In an effort to undermine a liberal power base in government, he urged pastors to have members of the congregation write letters during church services to be sent to state representatives. The goal was to protest the 1972 Equal Rights Amendment, which would have given women equal legal standing with men, and would have cleared out many obsolete laws regarding a woman's right to choose her own domicile apart from her husband's or to retain control of her property after marriage. In addition, Falwell urged that further action be taken against those who might pose a threat to the family and to America, a group that included homosexuals, abortionists, pornographers, atheists, secular Marxists, and feminists.[76] Women of the Christian Right joined their male counterparts in asserting that feminism was responsible for the deterioration of the American family. They founded coalitions, such as Concerned Women of America (1979), started by Beverly LaHaye, to fight passage of the Equal Rights Amendment, which they believed would destroy the male-female roles mandated by Scripture, and the American family, which made up the backbone of a healthy, godly nation. Pat Robertson, founder of Christian Broadcasting Network, televangelist, and host of *The 700 Club*, captured much of the feeling of the Christian Right on feminism. "The feminist agenda," he says, "is not about equal rights for women.... It is about a socialist, anti-family political movement that encourages women to leave their husbands, kill their children, practice witchcraft, destroy capitalism, and become lesbians."[77]

In 1977, James Dobson, a psychologist, founded Focus on the Family, which was organized around a broad spectrum of family-value issues including the battle against abortion and gay rights. In 1984, when invited with others by President Ronald Reagan to discuss the problems facing the family, Dobson suggested the following measures: increase government support for the economic survival of marriage; introduce an amendment to the Constitution to give the institution of the family its own standing; cut federal funding of advocacy groups with a purportedly anti-family stance; and review all agencies of the federal government to assess their impact on the institution of the family.[78]

In 1982, the Equal Rights Amendment failed to achieve the required ratification by two-thirds of the states. But efforts of the Christian Right continue to this day. Pro-family issues have remained a constant. According to Ruether, three issues are viewed by the Christian Right as the most pressing needs in the battle to preserve the traditional family. The first is parents' rights to protect their children from secular humanism, public schools, and government agencies that might intervene against parents who are deemed abusive or neglectful. The second is outlawing abortion from conception, while, in the interim, critically limiting women's access to the procedure. The third is fighting homosexuality by blocking legislation to protect gays and lesbians against housing and employment discrimination and grant them legal rights of marriage.[79] The Christian Right has built a sophisticated infrastructure to promote its agenda. In 1997, there were 1,648 full-time Christian radio stations and 257 full- or part-time television stations, with programs also available on cable systems.[80] Christian TV networks, such as Trinity Broadcasting, the Family Christian Broadcasting, and Christian Broadcasting Network, along with Christian radio promote the pro-family agenda. The Christian Right also publishes didactic tracts, magazines, and books for every age group, and provides devotional, teaching, and homeschooling resources for Christian bookstores. Today, the Christian Right counts among its number some thirty million Christians who have become active political organizers and voters. Although it claims victimization in the struggle against the evil forces of feminism, homosexuality, and secular humanism, it is thoroughly system-supporting in its pro-capitalist commitment to traditional class hierarchies.[81]

In the 1990s, the deep cultural split between liberals and progressives on the one hand and the Christian Right on the other was reflected in a sharp polarization within mainstream Protestant denominations and within Catholicism as well. According to Ruether, conservative and liberal Christians now have more in common with their counterparts in other denominations than with fellow communicants whose views differ from their own.[82] With the promotion of the traditional family by conservative factions within both Protestantism and Catholicism, other forms of relationship outside of traditional marriage are perceived as contrary to nature and a threat to the Christian faith and the future of America. According to Anne Bathurst Gilson, the emphasis of the Christian Right on family values has romanticized marriage, cast it as the only acceptable Christian form of relationship, and supported the myth that there is one, and only one, person of the opposite gender who is predestined to complement and complete the other in fulfilling one's longings. Such an understanding of marriage propagates a theology of ownership, reinforces an ideology of control, and fosters exclusion rather than inclusion, and law rather than spirit.[83] More important, it leaves little room to theologically affirm Christians who have chosen to remain single, who enjoy their single life, or who even consider it a liberating and empowering way of living out their Christian mandate to discipleship and service in Christ.

The prominent voice of the Christian Right within both Protestantism and Catholicism and its pro-family stance has called into question the place of single people in the church and a Christian theology of the single life. Within the Roman Catholic Church, this stance questions the self-worth and identity not only of single lay people, but more prominently of members of religious communities, who have pledged themselves to Christian service by their lifelong vows of obedience, poverty, and celibacy. In addition, the changes instituted by the Second Vatican Council (1962–65) have significantly contributed to a lack of self-definition and identity among members of Catholic religious communities, and particularly women religious. For example, when the Council was convened by Pope John XXIII in 1962, no member of a women's order or congregation was permitted to participate in, or even attend, the first two sessions, although a limited number of sisters were admitted as auditors in 1964 and 1965. Of prime importance to religious communities were the two documents *Lumen Gentium* and *Gaudium et Spes.* The former emphasized that all members of the Church had received an equal call "to the fullness of the Christian life and the perfection of charity," simply by virtue of their baptism. According to Patricia Wittberg, this seemingly innocuous statement nullified the basic ideological foundation for eighteen centuries of Roman Catholic life, which had postulated a three-tiered hierarchical ranking of the clerical, religious, and lay states. Now all baptized Catholics were called to holiness, so that religious life was no longer a middle way between clerical and lay conditions of life.[84] This meant that since sisters were not ordained clerics — and did not have the prospects of becoming ordained clergy, unlike their counterparts in male religious orders — they must be laity, hence equal in their call to holiness with all other Catholics. The second document, *Gaudium et Spes*, or "The Church in the Modern World," proclaimed that the Church was to be in solidarity with the very world its female religious orders had been told to shun, thus contradicting the cloister emphasis that resulted from the Council of Trent. The removal of boundaries between the cloister and the world left these communities struggling to maintain their distinctive identity in ministry and remain protected from competing secular ideologies.

It was hoped that the Council might further clarify the role and theology of religious life. But when the long-awaited decree on religious life, *Perfectae caritatis*, was promulgated by the Vatican in 1965, members of religious communities were disappointed. In their eyes, the document did not advance the same kind of groundbreaking theology in redefining the role of sisters and male religious in the Church that *Lumen Gentium* had done for the role of the laity.

Disappointment with *Perfectae caritatis* translated almost immediately into opposition. Patricia Wittberg has examined issues of the bimonthly Jesuit trade periodical *Review for Religious,* founded in 1942 and considered "the most pertinent" periodical for the study of the renewal of religious life during the past four decades.[85] In 1967, one writer, a priest, characterized *Perfectae caritatis* as "somewhat routine or uninspired," and pointed out that it had completely ignored the orders' fundamental ideological frames, namely, that the Holy Spirit had been active in their foundations. The author also complained that "religious women have not had a word to say about all the legislation that concerns them." Criticism continued in subsequent decades. A 1991 author called it merely "a revamp of the theology of the vowed life outlined by St. Thomas Aquinas in the thirteenth century." When the 1983 "Essential Elements" reiterated the traditional definition, writers were forced to depend on *Lumen Gentium,* the very document that had denied religious women any distinct place in the Church. Between 1963 and 1991, a few writers continued to maintain that the religious state was different from that of the laity, but a larger number denied that it was superior in any way. This latter trend left them with the task of devising a new definition and legitimization of the very lifestyle their readers had taken for granted for so many years. By the mid-to late 1980s, an alternative definition was proposed, namely, that all Christians were indeed called to the same holiness, but that religious were called "to an increased level of visibility" in living out this call serving as "prophets or public witnesses" to the rest of the Church. But the various authors differed about what exactly the prophetic religious were supposed to be witnessing to the rest of the Church. The new definition failed to receive the Vatican's approval as the word "prophetic" never appeared in the 1992 "Lineamenta."

By the mid-1980s belief in the superiority of a religious vocation over that of the average lay Catholic had largely dissolved and a replacement had not been realized. Accompanying this lack of theological identity was a sharp decline in membership in religious orders. In the thirty years since the 1960s, membership in Catholic religious orders had dropped by nearly 50 percent to below 100,000. According to a major survey funded by the Lilly Endowment and conducted between 1989 and 1992 among 9,999 religious priests, brothers, and sisters, the prognosis for the future of religious life was not good. "Without significant change," the study reported in a wide range of secular and church-related newspapers, "religious life in the United States will continue to decline, and, more important, those who most need the help of these orders will not be cared for."[86]

The lack of clarity about their role among members of religious communities also affected adherence to the three vows of obedience, poverty, and celibacy. According to Wittberg, the least of these three vows affected or altered by Vatican II was the vow of celibacy. While peripheral observances, such as definitions of appropriate reading material or modest behavior may have changed, its basic external observance did not.[87] But even here the ideological framework after Vatican II left its traces. While in the 1960s some *Review* articles still asserted the "objective excellence of virginity over marriage," others were beginning to deny this claim. Furthermore, an increasing number of authors took the stance that a celibate lifestyle might be psychologically unhealthy, or even impossible. By 1968, 65 percent of the respondents to the so-called Sisters' Survey (1966–68) — commissioned by the Conference of Major Superiors of Women and conducted by Sister Marie Augusta Neal among its entire professed membership of 157,000 sisters — said that the traditional way of presenting celibacy in religious life "has allowed for the development of isolation and false mysticism among sisters." Religious found themselves defending the one aspect of their lives still readily identifiable. One author said that "if formerly marriage was considered a second-rate vocation, it is clear that the atmosphere of sexual fulfillment as a necessary ingredient for maturity and personality growth has left the celibate vocation almost in need of a 'singles lib' movement." Another said that while "formerly, religious assured the laity that, even though they were married, they could still attain true sanctity, now the laity have to assure religious that, even though they are celibate, they can still achieve true personhood and first-class citizenship as human beings."[88]

The question remains why anybody would choose celibacy at all if marriage is just as holy and if celibacy might even be dangerous to one's psychic and spiritual health. Based on the *Review* articles since Vatican II, Wittberg observes that authors have largely identified four reasons for being celibate. First, consecrated virginity is a prophetic sign of God's love for the Church, or of the end times when all will attain perfect union with the divine. Second, the reason for vowing celibacy cannot be readily explained, for it is largely based on an individual, personal experience of the love of God. Third, celibacy is a useful by-product or a side effect of one's dedication to ministry or service. And fourth, celibacy is superior to marriage because it allows for one's single-hearted focus on God. Interestingly, the concept of a mystical marriage with Christ was considered to be an embarrassing and outdated metaphor.[89] Of the four reasons for celibacy, only the first is abstract or theoretical in orientation; the other three are in some way related to personal experience. Two of the four reasons are directly related to ministry, either as a by-product or a way of increasing its focus.

Within the Protestant tradition, lifelong celibacy is frequently regarded as a result of circumstance. If the "right" partner has not appeared and since sexual activity is reserved for the married, celibacy is an involuntary result. Learning to accept this involuntary turn of events and even regarding it as gift is one way in which Protestants are encouraged to reflect theologically on celibacy. According to Herb Anderson and Freda Gardner — Anderson is Lutheran and married, Gardner Presbyterian and never-married — living alone and being single is a particular gift that allows people to be and do what those who live with others find more difficult, if not impossible. Instead of exploring the possibilities for personal development and ministry and its subsequent joys and sense of fulfillment, the authors emphasize the difficulties of living the single life and the "challenge" of seeing it as gift.[90] Even those who adopt the view that celibacy is a gift still have to suffer the loneliness of certain hours of the day or night and "those agonizing times when one feels that no one knows or cares." While the authors grant that living alone is a way "for some to live with integrity and purpose, even joy and fulfillment"[91] and that it is an appropriate way in its own right, their argument lacks conviction. The word "celibacy" has been carefully avoided in their discussion of the single life, and sexuality is only briefly touched on. The authors uncritically presuppose "the human need for sexual gratification," at the same time warning those who decide against genital sexual activity not to ignore "what is missing."[92] Their emphasis on the absence of certain things in the life of someone who lives alone and is celibate depicts celibacy as an outside force, making it other-determined rather than freely chosen. The single, celibate life emerges in their writing as the result of necessity defined by lack, a life to be endured rather than enjoyed.

Another way to reflect on the single life in the church is to redefine family. According to M. Craig Barnes, pastor of the National Presbyterian Church PC (U.S.A.) in Washington, D.C., Jesus established a new spiritual family composed of those intent on doing the will of God. This means that Jesus' model of family is "much more radical than most Christians want to admit," for it has little to do with "a loyalty to the two-parent, two-child model we now assume is the all-American family."[93] Jesus' model is one of church as family, composed of brothers and sisters in Christ, with God as Father. Barnes says that families in his congregation that don't look like the all-American family are comforted by this concept, because it means that "they are no longer destined to go through life as failed approximations of families." Others, however, are discomfited, because they may be under the illusion that church is a place where they can learn "the secrets to a better marriage." While the model of spiritual family is a helpful reminder especially for single people that the spiritual family allows for the formation of more intimate and spiritually deeper bonds than those forged by blood and descent, the tone of the language used to describe it is hierarchical and patriarchal, as reflected in the view of God as Father, Christians as children, and Christ as the older and wiser brother — all of which suggest submission, especially to male authority, and the concept of ownership.

Single people may long to "have" a spouse and to "have" children and to "have" a family of their own. Barnes illustrates this dilemma by the example of a never-married woman in his church, Mary. Mary was determined to "have" it all, both a career and a family. While invested in her work, she continued "to wait on the Lord's timing for marriage," but the Lord's timing was slow. Now, at age forty-five, past the age of being able to have children of her own, she is grieving the death of her dream of family and "a great sadness" has settled into her life. While she has continued to go about her work and her many activities at church, Barnes noted that "the gleam that used to be in her eye faded." She began to see a counselor, spent considerable time in therapy, and eventually concluded that her problem was not depression or anything clinical, but was "more like despair and the loss of hope,"[94] caused by her notion that without a partner and children a person is incomplete. Mary's example illustrates how the ideology of ownership has permeated the traditional model of family, so that a person's worth is defined by whether or not one has a family of one's own. Thereby, self-worth is based less on one's connectedness and relationship with God in Christ and others, but on "having" a spouse or a child or both.

A theological discussion of the single life that shirks the issue of sexuality is both evasive and incomplete. Perhaps it is indicative of the discomfort among Protestants with an open discussion of sexual issues that the one person who in recent years has written most personally about the single and celibate life and its sexual challenges from a Protestant perspective is not a pastor or theologian, but a writer and poet. In her autobiographical reflection *Cloister Walk*,[95] Kathleen Norris, a Presbyterian, describes the benefits and challenges of the celibate life as they relate to sexuality and sexual desire. Ten years earlier before she wrote *Cloister Walk*, Norris had become a Benedictine oblate attached to St. John's Abbey in Minnesota, which involved pledging to abide by the Rule of St. Benedict insofar as her personal situation permitted. Because Norris is married, she observed her vows by frequent visits to the monastery, by contemplative readings of the Scriptures, and by learning from and recording the wisdom shared by the members of St. John's religious community. In *Cloister Walk*, Norris discusses her deepening friendship with a male member of the monastic community and the evolving sexual attraction. "The danger was real, but not insurmountable," she writes, but "our respect for each other's commitment — his to celibacy, mine to monogamy — would make the boundaries of behavior very clear." As a result, "we had few regrets, and yet for both of us there was an underlying sadness, the pain of something incomplete." It was not until both faced a personal crisis — he lost his mother, she experienced a betrayal — that she was able to place the relationship in its proper, religious context. Instead of channeling their energies into acting upon sexual desire, they were channeled into a deepening friendship. From Norris's perspective, "this was celibacy at its best, a man's sexual energies so devoted to the care of others that a few words could lift me out of despair, give me the strength to reclaim my life." The sense of incompleteness had turned into a sense of abundance.[96]

According to Norris, celibacy rightly practiced is not a hatred of sex, as is commonly assumed, but has the potential to address the sexual idolatry of our culture. Celibates who are fully aware of themselves as sexual beings manage to sublimate their sexual energies toward a purpose other than the culturally conditioned, highly prized end of sexual intercourse and procreation. The constraints of celibacy are transformed into an openness that exudes a sense of freedom. Rather than equating sublimation of sexual drives with repression, Norris suggests that sublimation, when conscious, is a normal and healthy part of adulthood that fosters spiritual development, intimacy, and a "holy simplicity" in friendship and relationship, including marriage. The celibate practice is countercultural in that it rejects the consumerist model of sexuality. Instead of reducing woman, for example, to the sum of her parts and regarding her as object and possession, monks give up the idea of possessing anything, including women. By sublimating the desire to possess toward developing and fostering friendship among equals, celibates are freed up to listen without imposing themselves, and to make themselves available to others both in body and soul.[97]

A theological definition of celibacy is no substitute for personal encounters with those who practice this way of life. In theological terms, says Norris, one dedicates one's sexuality to God through Jesus Christ. But this concept is "extremely hard to grasp," so that in the end one is left to experience it personally through "people who are doing it, incarnating celibacy in a mysterious, pleasing, and gracious way." Celibacy then is a form of ministry and a subtle form of service and hospitality to others. We can experience this ministry when coming in contact with celibates and finding ourselves attracted to them for "the thoughtful way in which they converse, listening and responding with complete attention," and making us feel "appreciated, enlarged, no matter who we are."[98] Coming to understand and appreciate celibacy is less a matter of detached theological reflection than the result of experiencing the fruits of those who practice it. Moreover, the decision to adopt the celibate life and continue in its practice may less depend on an act of the will than on the extent of our personal contact with those who can model for us celibacy's benefits and allow us to experience this form of Christian ministry.

Celibacy may be defined differently by women than by men. Norris recounts her conversations during directed retreats with members of St. Benedict's, a neighboring community of Benedictine women. The women discussed the experience of falling in love.

According to one sister, men tend to define celibacy as not having sex. Women, on the other hand, define celibacy as a way to "govern affective relationships." For men, the worst offense against celibacy is engagement in sexual acts, while for women the offense extends to having sexual feelings for another person. Both celibate women and men need to remind themselves that celibacy is not a vow to repress their feelings, but a vow "to put all our feelings, acceptable or not, close to our hearts and bring them into consciousness through prayer." The experience of falling in love is "celibacy at work," an invitation to "experience ego collapse" and then to "move beyond projecting unto another person" toward seeing "them as they really are," which makes "us more aware of who we are." Norris says that the experience of falling in love teaches "to accept my need for love" and "my ability to love, as great gifts from God." But it also serves as a reminder "that my vows were made to another person, the person of Christ" and that "all of my decisions about love had to be made in the light of that person."[99] A sister who works in formation said if another sister comes to her saying she has been masturbating because she has fallen in love, "the questions she'll need to ask herself, if she wants to remain a nun, are: How does Christ's love show through this person she loves? How can she best show her love in return — for the person, for the community, for Christ? Chances are it's not by masturbating."[100] Celibacy, according to these women religious, is an invitation to increased consciousness, to honestly own and acknowledge unconscious feelings and sexual desires, to accept them as part of the long conversion process of a lifetime, and to place them in the context of their relationship with God in Christ.

Norris notes that the aspect of freedom is among the most frequently mentioned values of celibacy; freedom to keep one's energies focused on ministry and communal living, freedom to love many people without being unfaithful to any of them, freedom to donate the self as a gift to others. Instead of focusing on "what I gave up," the focus is "on what being freed by what I gave up has allowed me to do in service to the church and other people." This freedom entails making a commitment to grow both intellectually and spiritually, to engage in regular prayer and worship, to be active in some form of meaningful ministry, to take care of the body, to seek out solitude at regular intervals, and to take increased pleasure in beauty. One sister Norris conversed with remarked that celibacy is "a good way to integrate my sexuality with my spirituality" since the goal of both is union with God and with others.[101]

Conclusion

Toward a Theology of the Single Life

In this study I have examined how the church through the centuries has viewed Christians who are not married and live the single life. I have done so by primarily focusing on the stories of women's experience as single and celibate in the church's structure and hierarchy, and the theological arguments and context surrounding the experience. The guiding question I have asked was, Why did women choose to remain single and celibate when this choice often placed them on the economic fringe and did not give them formal access to leadership positions in the church, as it did their male and single counterparts? My contention is that if the motivating factors can be unearthed, they can aid in the construction of a theology of the single life that applies equally to both men and women.

From nearly the beginning of the Christian movement, the defining element of the single life was the practice of celibacy. The apostles, especially Paul, and later church authorities required that members who were not married abstain from sexual relations. Sexual activity was acceptable only in the context of marriage, and even then only under the provision that intercourse be directed at producing children. Both artificial methods of birth control and the termination of pregnancies were viewed as interfering with the natural results of the sex act, which meant interference with the will of God, so that these acts were considered sinful. The mode of marriage recommended by the early theologians of the church, most notably Augustine, Jerome, and Ambrose, was the state of "wedded chastity," by which couples mutually agreed on sexual abstinence, except for the purpose of procreation.

Reading such recommendations may sound strange to modern ears; it is not surprising that modern commentators have frequently concluded that the church as a whole condemned sexual activity, was afraid of it, and regarded it as dangerous. Theologians up to the fifth century were subsequently accused of fearing sexual behavior or being out of touch with their own sexuality, prompting them to prescribe total sexual abstinence for those who wished to be faithful members of the Christian community. The monastic movement in the Western church during the Middle Ages was regarded as a case in point, with its clausuration requirements for women and strict separation of male and female monastics that apparently sought to quell any opportunity for sexual stimulation or transgression. Subsequent commentators made the writings of these theologians subject to psychological analysis and examined the lives of Paul all the way up to the Reformers of the sixteenth century, who had relied heavily in their scriptural interpretation of sexual matters on their predecessors and fathers of the church. Invariably, the psychological analyses detected early childhood deprivation and sexual repression on the part of their subjects. The argument ran that since Paul, Augustine, Jerome, and Luther were sexually repressed, their views on sexual conduct or celibacy were of little relevance for today. Furthermore, since all the formulators of the faith were men, they had little to say to women and their sexual practices within the structure of the church. To remedy the situation, some modern commentators have suggested that the church needs a more updated theology on matters of sexual behavior, including the area of the single life. The church, they argue, would have to formulate a more integrated view of sexuality among Christians, one that would overcome the presumed mind-body dualism of ages past.

While the church has undoubtedly had trouble integrating the mind and the body in its theological framework, it would be a mistake to label early theologians and the reformers as simply prudish on matters of sex. The high regard for celibacy among Christians for the first five hundred years of its existence, followed by another thousand years of flourishing monasticism during the Middle Ages, cannot be simply ascribed to the fact that the church's leaders were out of touch with their sexual identity, viewed the body as in opposition to the mind, and sought to repress the body's, hence all sexual, desires. Reading the detailed discussions of sexuality and sexual behavior by the early theologians of the church and the reformers, one may wonder whether these are indeed the abstractions coming from the sexually repressed. The emergence of the celibate practice in the first and second centuries and its wide and lasting appeal, particularly among women, leads one to suspect that something more substantial and life-giving than fear of sin or an attempt to repress were at work.

One has to go back to the beginnings of the celibate movement in Christianity to retrieve the motivating causes. The study of both Old and New Testament references to the single life shows that Christianity, in contrast to Judaism, offered the early Christians an alternative to marriage. Theologically speaking, they were freed up to consider a way of attaining eternal life other than by procreation and one's living on through offspring. This new way was the choice of remaining celibate and to dedicating one's being to God in Christ, the bestower of eternal life. Christians could now procreate in the spirit, instead of the flesh. To be sure, the choice of the early Christians to remain single and celibate was dangerous, since it stood in plain opposition to the state, the Roman Empire, which demanded marriage of its citizens to ensure a steady supply of taxpaying citizens.

Nevertheless, it was a choice, and one that apparently many Christians made, though their numbers were small in contrast to those preferring marriage. It is unlikely that this choice was motivated by a sudden distaste for sex among the leading classes, particularly noblewomen, who emerged as the pacesetters in the celibate movement and catapulted celibacy into popularity among the rest. The attraction had to be grounded in something deeper and more enduring. Clearly it did not have economic advantages, for people did not significantly benefit from remaining in the single station of life. Men would have had their inheritance claims questioned as they only had themselves to support, in contrast to their married siblings with families. Women, unless they were rich and widowed, were most likely forced into remaining at home while trying to make themselves useful by caring for siblings or aging members of the extended family living under the same roof, and sharing in the servants' duties. Neither men nor women choosing to remain single had the prospect of enhancing their social and economic status by doing so, and neither could hope to be taken care of in old age by their children when, in fact, there would be none. What constituted the attraction to the single life, and eventually consecrated virginity, had to be an inner faith conviction and the believer's relationship with Christ. While other religions knew of the practice of celibacy, it was the Christian faith that uniquely provided an intimate relationship comparable to that of marriage by presenting a God who could serve as viable "marriage" partner in the person of Christ, the "groom." Christians refrained from marriage and sexual intercourse so as to remain holy and virginal for their union with Christ in the last days. The marriage metaphor was a fit image that turned celibacy into a prophetic sign, suggesting the impending return of Christ and his union with his virginal bride, the church. This metaphor was subsequently extrapolated from the Scriptures and explored at length by the Church Fathers in treatises and sermons to encourage in their congregations wholehearted weddedness to Christ, particularly among single members. It is true that the metaphor was highly suited for women, who now could conceive of themselves as brides of Christ and become consecrated to him for life. Though on the surface the marriage metaphor appeared less fitting for men, they, too, underwent a similar consecration process, which may suggest that the imagery and symbolism of nuptial union underscored their experience of an intimate relationship with Christ, who demanded their all.

Central to a theology of the single life then is the believer's relationship with Christ in what approximates the marriage bond. In this relationship, the believer, whether male or female, is defined as living in a reciprocal relationship.[1] As in a marriage, there can be discord or harmony, infidelity or fidelity, withholding or the unreserved giving of oneself. To carry the metaphor further, it also means that each partner has rights and responsibilities, the right to be heard and the responsibility to listen, the right to be protected and the responsibility to protect, the right to share and the responsibility to receive. Above all, each partner has a right to the body of the other. The believer has a right to the body of Christ, which one partakes of in the Eucharist and in community with other Christians, while Christ has a right to the body of the believer, which He receives in the context of the believer's service to Him. Such a reciprocal relationship in Christ excludes abuse, hierarchical possessiveness, and selfish withdrawal. It fosters loving respect, mutuality, and self-giving.

This view, however, is only a short step from first suggesting and then demanding that Christians surrender their bodily desires, along with their sexual cravings, unto the marriage partner, Christ, instead of taking them elsewhere, as into a marriage relationship. Suggesting leaves the Christian the freedom to acknowledge and wrestle with the sexual temptations and desires and continually invites one to seek God's sustaining grace. Demanding, however, leaves the believer no room but to take refuge in a hypocrisy that pretends to know no sexual temptations and desires, and feigns a marital fidelity to Christ he or she does not have, while disavowing the need for God's sustaining grace.

The single life calls believers continually to evaluate the nature of their marriage relationship with Christ. It suggests that the believer's body be Christ's, which means that Christ places exclusive claims on it, hence requests sexual abstinence in form of the celibate life. Conversely, demanding celibacy of the Christian infers blind obedience to the exclusion of the individual's freedom to choose the beloved. Therefore, Christians cannot be forced to practice celibacy. Instead they are to be encouraged to view their celibate life as a by-product of an intimate and overflowing love for Christ and the exclusive claim their "partner" places on them.

In the Old Testament, women were often considered chattel and their husbands' possession, needed for procreation and the continuing of the male lineage. With the arrival of a God one could marry, women were liberated from being owned by anyone other than God. They were freed from the necessity of giving birth and were no longer owned by a human being, neither were they made subject to their husband's or a suitor's wiles, oppression, and violent rage. The stories of the Apocryphal Acts, in particular, illustrate what such husbands or suitors were capable of, pointing to the much gentler, more even-tempered, and, in fact, perfect partner to be found in Christ and in the community of other believers. Initially then, the freedom from being owned by a spouse was probably a major motivating factor for women to join the Christian movement and to remain single and celibate. This would mean that the aspect of possession is crucial to a theology of the single life. Single and celibate Christians are no longer owned or subject to any single human being, though they continue to depend on other believers for nurture, growth, and support. Their loyalties are not divided between their spouse, on the one hand, who has a significant influence on their livelihood and day-to-day routine, and their faith convictions and connection with Christ, on the other. They need not compromise who they are, at least not on account of a marital relationship. In comparison, Christ emerges as a low-risk and high-returns spouse, who does not interfere with the partner's growth, and, in fact, who will do what is best for the beloved and be the most ideal spouse one could ask for.

The issue of possession comes into play for single, celibate Christians also in form of the desire to possess. Single people may long to "have" a spouse, "have" children, "have" a partner, so that they can "have" a home and a family. This longing to own and possess is a longing for wholeness. It may find expression in the romantic attraction to someone with the very qualities we lack and wish to have. Hope arises that by engaging in relationship with the other, one will "own" these qualities by affiliation and somehow be made whole. After the infatuation subsides, however, this hope is dispelled or at least called into question. As flaws and annoyances emerge, disillusionment sets in and the quest begins anew. Instead of continuing the cycle of attraction and disappointment, single people might ask themselves in the early periods of romantic involvement, What is it that draws me to this person? In what areas of my life do I hope to be made whole by him or her? The answer will point to a weakness or insecurity that begs to be visited, tended to, and healed, and the recognition that healing cannot come from the outside but begins within. The early Christians recognized that neither other people nor possessions could provide them with the longed-for wholeness. Jesus' disciples showed this recognition by renouncing their possessions, which included their home, their children, and their spouse. Several hundred years later, the monastic movement translated this recognition into the vows of poverty and celibacy. Central to these vows was that Christians recognized that no external asset, either in the form of material goods or through marriage and children, could lead to a full and wholesome life. In theological terms this means that poverty, like celibacy, is not a form of self-negation, as is frequently assumed, but rather the recognition that the kingdom of God is within.

Throughout its first fifteen hundred years, and particularly in its first five centuries, the church was tempted to equate the celibate life with faithful Christian discipleship. In principle it was believed that if Christians were taking their marriage to Christ seriously enough, they would not be tempted to engage in sexual activity or to get married. Marriage was only for the weak, for those who could not curb their sexual appetites and needed an acceptable outlet, which marriage provided. Remarriage after the death of a spouse or following divorce was frowned upon, particularly if children had been born. Christians who had already experienced sexual activity in a marriage should have had their curiosity satisfied sufficiently. Why would they seek out another worldly engagement and not channel their affections exclusively toward Christ, unless their faith was weak? It was believed that the married and remarried were weak in their faith, while the celibate and widowed, and even the divorced, were strong, or had to be because the church expected it of them. It was a belief that had become well entrenched by the late Middle Ages, inviting hubris among members of religious communities and the male clergy, which in turn opened the doors to abuse of power and privilege.

With the Reformation, the church split into the Roman Catholic and Protestant churches, and the class system that had formerly divided the celibates and the married population was either called into question or downright abolished. Unfortunately for the Protestant churches, in which the class distinction was replaced by the concept of the priesthood of all believers, it also discredited the believer's gift of and call to celibacy as an expression of faithful Christian discipleship. This meant that in Protestant circles, the word "celibacy," as well as the doctrine, fell in disuse, and celibates had to mask their call either under the guise of not having found the right partner or under the inimical conditions marriage might impose upon their single-minded devotion to their ministry.

While Luther still could sing the praises of the celibate life, extolling its virtues and its resulting freedom for Christian service over marriage, Calvin found at least in theological terms little use for it. He believed that lifelong celibate vows forced upon Christians a way of life that ran counter to what God ordained. It is surprising how readily the Protestant tradition accepted this fear of vows, apparently without noticing the parallel to the vows made in the marriage covenant. Fortunately for the Protestant tradition and for Protestant Christians, it was still granted that some had the gift for the celibate life and could be so-called eunuchs for the kingdom of heaven. But these people were considered the exception, and there were so few of them, mostly women, that it was hardly worthwhile for the church to formulate an adequate theology for them. Also, their celibate commitment was largely clandestine, made in private perhaps or perceived of as a practical necessity for the freedom to serve in ministry, and unencumbered by marital or childrearing responsibilities. At any rate, Protestant celibates carefully denied that their commitment had any resemblance to lifelong vows, in order to dispel the dreaded Calvinist notion of constraint and force. Apart from a few Protestants who were members of religious utopian societies, such as the Shakers, and apart from deaconesses and single women missionaries serving in urban centers or abroad, Protestant churches became the arenas of the married and those hoping to be.

Today, many Roman Catholic monastic and religious communities are struggling with survival because of declining membership. At the same time, dioceses worry about the increasing priest shortage. In both cases, the argument is that celibacy is the stumbling block as people are no longer willing to sacrifice the comforts and advantages of married life. It is probably true that celibacy is a stumbling block, but not because it is as difficult to practice and as rare a gift as is commonly believed but because the church has failed to give recognition to this charism in its life and ministry. For example, the church is not a convincing witness to the charism of celibacy when only one representative of the celibate life is leading public worship in the person of the priest, and when the church even here makes exceptions for deacons and clergy members entering the priesthood from other denominations. It is not a convincing witness when the church extends a special sacrament to the married (marriage) and those consecrated to priestly office (holy orders), while withholding sacramental validation from those who have chosen to be consecrated to virginity and lifelong celibacy. And it is not a witness to the charism of celibacy when from the pulpit and in catechesis are advanced the virtues of married life and the family without due recognition of the single, widowed, and divorced believer. What then needs to change? Rather than lifting or compromising on the priestly celibacy requirement, the church might reintroduce members to, and educate them, on the charism of celibacy. This could happen in adult spiritual formation and new member classes (Rite of Christian Initiation for Adults), in the context of the homily, and during lay ministry and seminary training. In addition, the church might offer venues of visibility to those called and committed to the celibate life, which means making provision not just for celibate men but also for celibate women to assume visible leadership positions in public worship and in the wider church.

Protestant churches, on the other hand, pride themselves on allowing their clergy to marry. Calvin had argued that lifting the celibacy requirement for clergy would stem the pastors' shortage, and so it did, at least initially. Today, five centuries later, churches, and smaller ones in particular, struggle to find a pastor — whether married or single, male or female, that will shepherd them. In my own denomination, some presbyteries, which consist of about a hundred churches, have as many as thirty churches looking for a pastor. Still other churches find themselves embroiled in conflict over pastors found guilty on charges of sexual impropriety, marital infidelity, or sexual harassment. As a result, church members have become disenchanted with the institutionalized church and question its effectiveness, role, and value in guiding their moral and spiritual development and that of their children. Some churches hardly ever recover from what they perceive as a betrayal; others seek to cover up misconduct and persist in a state of dysfunction and denial. At the root, however, lies a sense of confusion over Christian standards of sexual activity and conduct. This confusion is deepened when pastors find themselves officiating at the wedding of a couple who, as all the guests know, have been living and sleeping together prior to marriage. By doing so, pastors may appear to condone the couple's behavior, when they themselves would hardly expect to do likewise and retain their ministerial position. While pastors, and in some denominations ordained officers, are expected to meet one sexual standard, members of the congregation are given latitude to meet another. This double standard has reintroduced a separation between ordained clergy and the laity — a separation Luther worked so hardily to dispel — and reopened the discussion of sexual chastity, as some would call it, or the issue of celibacy. To mend this gap and to lift the confusion in matters of sexual conduct Protestants will need to recognize the spiritual gift of celibacy. They will need to embrace the metaphor that views Christians as being wedded to Christ by affirming the possibility that the believer's intimate relationship with Christ may lead to a voluntary, lifelong celibate commitment. And they will need to educate on sexuality and celibacy as call and gift in the context of adult education and confirmation classes, along with seminary training, and make provisions for affirming those so called in a public service or private liturgy.

Both Roman Catholic and Protestant churches share common ground on the issue of the single life. Both have many single members, sometimes as many as half the congregation. Both offer singles ministries and educational and fellowship programs, often graded by age. And both largely cater to the traditional family, a two-parent household with children, in their programming, liturgy, language, and staffing patterns. Activities are family oriented or family friendly, including mother-daughter banquets, Valentine's dances, long-term marriage recognitions, and family picnics, to the exclusion of the single and childless. The churches' emphasis on the family as the locus of salvation for the children, parents, and even the entire nation, leaves single people wondering where salvation might be found for them. As much as we know the importance of the family unit for the well-being of the child and its religious formation, just as little can it serve as the messiah on whom depends the well-being and prosperity of our souls or our nation. Church leaders will need to address the idolatry involved in vesting an organization with salvific powers, even one as beneficial as the healthy family. These powers are reserved for the one who equally is Lord of the family, the couple, and the single person, and who can be found and who can find us only as we personally open up to him in engaged relationship in the context of a community of faith.

As did the early church, both Roman Catholic and Protestant churches today expect their members to practice sexual abstinence outside marriage. This means one is likely to find two types of celibates there: those who comply with the doctrinal expectation, not because they want to but because they feel morally obligated, while they wait for the right marriage partner to come along; and those who have made a conscious commitment to being wedded to Christ and have stopped anticipating marriage at some time in the future. The first group is presumably the larger one, and could be best described, to use the title of Jean Sheridan's book, as "the unwilling celibates."[2] The second group are the "willing celibates," all those who have "willingly" committed themselves to a form of consecrated celibacy, either by taking vows as part of a dedication or commissioning service, or in private. Both Roman Catholic and Protestant churches would benefit if they were able to draw on each other's traditions in encouraging their single members to consider the life of the "willing celibate." The "willing celibate" would not be expected to take vows for life, but would make an initial commitment for a set time, to be extended later; he or she would be consecrated and commissioned in a worship service or private liturgy; and those who break the commitment and marry would not forfeit ministry opportunities that are normally open to the married.

There are several theological presuppositions concerning celibacy and the role of the church underlying this form of entry for the single Christian into the life of the "willing celibate." First, the Christian may receive the gift of celibacy for life or for a time only. By setting an initial time limit for consecrated celibacy, the believer has an opportunity to explore the commitment. This phase may be comparable to a time of dating and becoming acquainted with the potential marriage partner, Christ. It may lead to a renewal of the commitment or to a consecration for life resembling the perpetuity of the marriage vow. Second, through its faithful proclamation of the gospel and the rightful administration of the sacraments, the church is in a position to call forth, equip, and send out those who might have the gift of celibacy. The public "sending" ceremony serves as an affirmation to the celibate that the church recognizes the gift, holds the believer accountable by expecting obedience, and encourages the gift's use in conjunction with other gifts to enhance the life and ministry of the church at large. Third, the church serves as an instrument of Christ's healing presence in the world by extending forgiveness to those unable to continue the celibate commitment, instead of penalizing them with stigmatization and exclusion from ministry.

Both traditions stand to benefit from identifying, recognizing, and empowering potential "willing celibates." Apart from mobilizing a larger number of believers energized to serve in single-hearted devotion, churches would also give a prophetic witness to Christ's presence and his return. Protestants would need to create a liturgy of commissioning and consecration, and make provisions for the founding and nurturing of communities of consecrated celibates. The Roman Catholic Church would have to reinstitute a third rank — in addition to the ranks of clergy and laity — whose celibate members would have leadership functions in the various areas of the church's ministry.

Both willing and unwilling celibates will need to develop intimate friendships and community among one another. Developing and nurturing such a circle of friends calls for discernment, energy, and perseverance. Ideally, it involves establishing ties with other celibates, both male and female, who can be entrusted with confidences and are willing to listen and to share their own struggles. Other forms of community may evolve by affiliating with a group of religious and participating in their monthly activities. Regular meetings with a spiritual director will expand critical dimensions of one's faith walk. A group of like-minded fellow Christians, under the leadership of a mentor, may open up forums to discuss and help clarify issues of loneliness, romance, sexual desire, and temptation, while affirming the call to wholehearted discipleship and the gift of celibacy that results from an intimate relationship and union with Christ.

Meanwhile it is crucial that Christians learn to differentiate between sexual identity and sexual activity. Sexual identity defines how we act, interact with, and perceive the world. It guides us in how we address our needs for companionship, intimacy, and acceptance, and is an important part of becoming whole; sexual activity is not. The desire for sexual activity remains throughout life, and we cannot effectively control or repress it. However, as those who have given themselves to Christ in body, mind, and spirit, we can allow for its gradual transformation into a desire of being fully present with others and enjoying the freedom of service that results from the celibate life.

Notes

Introduction: A Personal Journey

1. In twenty years, the number of men and women living alone has more than doubled from nearly 11 million in 1970 to 23 million in 1990.

2. A notable exception to this definition is John R. Landgraf's book, *Singling: A New Way to Live the Single Life* (Louisville: Westminster/John Knox Press, 1990), in which he defines singlehood as "a condition of encouraging, affirming, and maintaining one's integrity as a self," regardless of marital status. Landgraf portrays "singling" as an activity of spiritual growth that leads to individuality within community and the bond of marriage, apart from a state defined by law. "Once a person is fully single," he says, "she or he will strongly tend to maintain singlehood no matter what — even when marriage comes.... Once single, one does not need to abandon singlehood to have a good marriage" (18). In fact, he advises that a good marriage can only be built by people who have attained, and continue to nurture, the mature state of being single, as opposed to being nonsingle and dependent.

3. See, for example, Carol M. Anderson and Susan Stewart, with Sonia Dimidjian, *Flying Solo: Single Women in Midlife* (New York: W. W. Norton, 1994), who present models of single women who have successfully carved out a place for themselves.

4. Many books are advice manuals for women on how to live the single life successfully, i.e., Dorothy Payne, *Singleness: Find Fulfillment as a Single Woman; Explore Opportunities and Overcome Prejudice* (Philadelphia: Westminster Press, 1983); Nadene Peterson and Barbara N. Sofie, *Singleness: A Guide to Understanding and Satisfaction* (San Antonio: Watercress Press, 1987). Others are collections of personal testimonies by women living single and their ensuing struggles and ways of coping, i.e., Anderson and Stewart, *Flying Solo.* For a collection of personal testimonies of single women in relation to their spiritual journeys, see Mary O'Brien and Clare Christie, eds., with a foreword by E. Margaret Fulton, *Single Women: Affirming Our Spiritual Journeys* (Westport, Conn.: Bergin and Garvey, 1993).

5. Herbert Anderson and Freda A. Gardner briefly explore the biblical and theological perspectives of singleness and living alone in their book *Living Alone* (Louisville: Westminster/John Knox Press, 1997), 19–25.

1. Celibacy, Sexuality, and Wholeness

1. " 'Fidelity and Chastity' Amendment Debate Clouded by Imprecise Definitions," *Presbyterian News Service*, December 13, 1996.

2. Ibid.

3. For example, in an article in the May 14, 2001, issue of the *Presbyterian Outlook*, titled "The Sabbatical Is Over; What Will the GA Do with 'Fidelity-Chastity'?" John A. Bolt reports that "as of late April, at least 17 of the 62 overtures facing commissioners deal in one way or another with ordination or with the issues that have arisen out of the debate" on the "fidelity and chastity" amendment.

4. For a complete dismissal of celibacy as a spiritual discipline, see Richard J. Foster, *Celebration of Discipline: The Path to Spiritual Growth* (New York: Harper & Row, 1978), especially the Scripture and subject indexes (180–83), including "marriage," which has subentries on corporate guidance in marriage, prayer for marriage, and submission in marriage; "lust" which is linked with "our pride and arrogance," and sex, which has no entry other than "sexual problems" and sexual deviations and how to overcome them through prayer; also, the Scripture Index does not include 1 Corinthians 7.

5. See A. W. Richard Sipe, *Celibacy: A Way of Loving, Living, and Serving* (Ligouri, Mo.: Triumph Books, 1996), 32–33.

6. See chapter 2 in this book for a more detailed discussion of celibacy as charism.

7. C. Peter Wagner, *Your Spiritual Gifts Can Make Your Church Grow* (Glendale, Calif.: GL Regal Books, 1974), 3–67.

8. The various views on how spiritual gifts develop and their use in context is based on Lynne M. Baab's *Personality Type in Congregations: How to Work with Others More Effectively* (Bethesda, Md.: Alban Institute, 2000), 35–36.

9. See Don and Katie Fortune, *Discover Your God-Given Gifts* (Old Tappan, N.J.: Fleming Revell, 1987).

10. See Gary Harbaugh, *God's Gifted People: Discovering Your Personality As a Gift* (Minneapolis: Augsburg, 1990).

11. Wagner, *Your Spiritual Gifts*, 63–64.

12. Wagner, married with children, says that he does not have the gift of celibacy.

13. Susan A. Muto in Sipe, *Celibacy*, 2.

14. Payne, *Singleness*, 12, 49.

15. James B. Nelson, *Between Two Gardens: Reflections on Sexuality and Religious Experience* (New York: Pilgrim Press, 1983), 106–7.

16. Ibid.

17. Thomas Moore, *SoulMates: Honoring the Mysteries of Love and Relationship* (New York: HarperCollins, 1994), 108–9.

18. William F. Kraft, "Celibate Genitality" in *Celibate Loving: Encounter in Three Dimensions*, ed. Mary Anne Huddleston (New York: Paulist Press, 1984), 69–90.

19. Kenneth R. Mitchell, "Priestly Celibacy from a Psychological Perspective" in *Celibate Loving,* 91–108.

20. Kenneth R. Mitchell, *Psychological and Theological Relationships in the Multiple Staff Ministry* (Philadelphia: Westminster Press, 1966).

21. Evelyn Eaton Whitehead and James D. Whitehead, *A Sense of Sexuality: Christian Love and Intimacy* (New York: Doubleday, 1989), 48–49.

22. Carol Gilligan, *In a Different Voice: Psychological Theory and Women's Development* (Cambridge: Harvard University Press, 1982), 5–23 passim.

23. Lisa Sowle Cahill, *Women and Sexuality* (New York: Paulist Press, 1992), 57.

24. Whitehead and Whitehead, *A Sense of Sexuality,* 175.

25. Virginia Ramey Mollenkott, *Godding: Human Responsibility and the Bible* (New York: Crossroad, 1987), 84.

26. The cover story of the August 28, 2000, issue of *Time* magazine was titled "Who Needs a Husband: More Women Are Saying No to Marriage and Embracing the Single Life. Are They Happy?" The story suggests that women are and that they continue to remain single in increasing numbers. For example, in 1963, 83 percent of women twenty-five to fifty-five were married; by 1997 that figure had dropped to 65 percent, a "huge" 20 percent point change, according to Linda Waite, sociologist at the University of Chicago (48).

27. According to Cahill, "Biology is not destiny. Neither is freedom discarnate." See Cahill, *Women and Sexuality,* 63, 67.

28. See John A. Sanford, *The Invisible Partners* (New York: Paulist Press, 1980); also his *Between People: Communicating One-to-One* (New York: Paulist Press, 1982), 40–43, where he discusses the effects of undeveloped animus-anima awareness in interpersonal communication, particularly between women and men.

29. Landgraf, *Singling: A New Way to Live the Single Life,* 106.

30. For an analysis of this new wholistic approach to leadership in the world of business and management, patterned after recent scientific discoveries of the cosmic and biological worlds, see Margaret J. Weatley, *Leadership and the New Science: Learning about Organization from an Orderly Universe* (San Francisco: Berrett-Koehler Publishers, 1994); for an illustration of an integrated successful female leadership style, see Sally Helgesen, *The Female Advantage: Women's Ways of Leadership* (New York: Doubleday, 1995).

31. This practical suggestion comes from Landgraf, *Singling,* 107.

32. Janice Brewi and Anne Brennan, *Celebrate Mid-Life: Jungian Archetypes and Mid-Life Spirituality* (New York: Crossroad, 1992), x.

33. C. G. Jung, *Psychological Types* (Princeton, N.J.: Princeton University Press, 1971).

34. For learning to read and interpret the Myers-Briggs Type Indicator, see Isabel Briggs Myers with Peter B. Myers, *Gifts Differing: Understanding Personality Type* (Palo Alto, Calif.: Davies-Black Publishing, 1995).

35. Evelyn Eaton Whitehead and James D. Whitehead, *Seasons of Strength: New Visions of Christian Maturing* (Winona, Minn.: Saint Mary's Press, 1995), 105–9.

36. Whitehead and Whitehead, *Seasons of Strength*, 185–91.
37. Ibid.
38. Ibid.

2. Celibacy and the Bible

1. A. Colin Day, *Roget's Thesaurus of the Bible* (San Francisco: HarperSan-Francisco, 1992), 628–29.

2. *The New Brown, Driver, Briggs, Gesenius Hebrew and English Lexicon* makes references to three Hebrew usages of the male form of virgin, found in 5 R (a Cuneiform inscription of Western Asia), in Jerome, and in New Hebrew.

3. While the action of the two women may have been considered heroic by later members of the two tribes of the Moabites and Ammonites, the redactor, J 1, did not share this admiration. Instead, the redactor seems to have regarded the story as a negative reflection upon Moab and Ammon, whose descendants are not admitted to the assembly of the Lord (Deut. 23:3), and especially in Deuteronomy 32:32, where "their" — "our enemies" (v. 31) — refers to Moab and Ammon, with the implication being that incestuous activity was still prevalent among these tribes.

4. See v. 34, where Paul distinguishes between the unmarried woman and the virgin.

5. This is the only occurrence in the entire New Testament of the female form of "disciple" (*mathetria*).

6. Other ancient authorities read "him."

7. In the discussion of Lydia, I am referring to two seminal studies on the subject using the sociohistorical approach concerning purple dyers at the time of the writing of the Acts of Apostles by Luise Schottroff and Ivoni Richter Reimer; especially "Lydia: A New Quality of Power" in Luise Schottroff, *Let the Oppressed Go Free: Feminist Perspectives on the New Testament*, trans. Annemarie S. Kidder (Louisville: Westminster/John Knox Press, 1993), 131–36, and "Lydia and Her House" in Ivoni Richter Reimer, *Women in the Acts of the Apostles: A Feminist Liberation Perspective* (Minneapolis: Fortress, 1995), 71–149.

8. See Reimer, *Women in the Acts of the Apostles,* 108.

9. See Luise Schottroff, "Lydia," 132.

3. Celibacy in the Early Church

1. Select books of the Apocryphal Acts of the Apostles have been trans-lated at different times by various authors and gathered in individual volumes. The most recently published largest body of the Apocryphal Acts, a total of thir-teen, is contained in *The Writings of the Fathers Down to A.D. 325: Ante-Nicene Fathers,* vol. 8, ed. Alexander Roberts and James Donaldson (Peabody, Mass.: Hendrickson, 1995), 477–564; because of its recent publication date and the comprehensiveness of collection, this volume will be used in the present study in hopes that it might serve as a representative sample of the kind of writing and sub-ject matter under consideration. The reader is also referred to *Acts of the Christian*

Martyrs, ed. and trans. Herbert Musurillo (Oxford: Clarendon Press, 1972), which contains the well-known story of Perpetua and Felicitas. For an earlier, smaller collection of the Apocryphal Acts, see E. Hennecke, ed., *New Testament Apocrypha*, vol. 2, Eng. trans. ed. R. McL. Wilson (London: Lutterworth Press, 1963). Also, see a later work, dating from the middle of the third century, titled "The Acts of Xantippe and Polyxena," or "Life and Conduct of the Holy Women, Xantippe, Polyxena, and Rebecca," trans. W. A. Craigie, *Ante-Nicene Fathers*, vol. 9, ed. Allan Menzies (Peabody, Mass.: Hendrickson Publishers, 1995), 205–17.

2. In his introduction to the Apocryphal Acts of the Apostles, Alexander Walker, the translator, contrasts the Apocryphal Gospels with the Apocryphal Acts, saying that the former contain more miracle, the latter more discourse and that, according to Jerome, the Apocryphal Gospels were suited for the *vilis plebecula*, while "the Apocryphal Acts appeal more to the *Academia*" ("Translator's Introductory Notice" in *Ante-Nicene Fathers*, vol. 8, 354).

3. Possibly John, also named Mark.

4. Either Peter was accused by his own daughter of lusting after her or was perceived as doing so by someone else; in either case, the Lord answered Peter's prayer, so that the daughter "had paralysis of her side, that she might not be deceived." This paralysis could mean that she was either punished for her untrue remarks or was unlikely to be attractive to Peter on account of it.

5. The Bodleian manuscript is the same from which Grabe derived the text of the *Acts of Paul and Thecla*.

6. This "seal" is mentioned in the *Acts of Paul and Thecla*, when Thecla says to Paul, "Only give me the seal in Christ, and temptation shall not touch me" (489). The scriptural references in the footnote list 2 Cor. 1:22, Eph. 1:13 and 4:30, all of which deal with the gift of the Holy Spirit that is beginning to be operative in the life of the believer.

7. The Bodleian manuscript calls him Aegeas.

8. The Bodleian manuscript inserts this explanation.

9. The *Acts of Andrew and Matthias*, subtitled "In the City of the Man-Eaters," is contained in the *Ante-Nicene Fathers*, vol. 8, 517–25. In this story, Matthias had been chosen by a lot cast among the apostles to go into the city of the man-eaters, people who neither ate bread nor drank wine, but ate "the flesh of men, and drank their blood" (517). Matthias is captured by the people of that city, who gouge out his eyes, drug him, and throw him in prison. Andrew and his disciples are sent by the Lord to release him and convert the inhabitants of the city. Following great torture, Andrew is able to release Matthias. With the Lord's help and several miracles, the residents repent of their idol worship and wickedness, and are brought to faith in Christ. Subsequently, they are baptized by Andrew and are ordered to build a church. Andrew then leaves the city, despite the residents' pleas to "stay with us a few days, that we may be filled with thy fountain, because we are newly planted" (525). Andrew then is made to return by the Lord "until I shall confirm their souls in the faith." And so he stays with them for seven days, "teaching and confirming them in the Lord Jesus Christ."

10. The apostles have "forsaken" all that belonged to them, including their wives and children. Along with one's wife, children are considered a possession to be surrendered unto God. Children are valuable since they continue the paternal lineage and name, and increase the family income as a labor force. When believers are encouraged to abandon their children, they are asked to do without the benefits resulting from their children, especially the economic and status-related advantages to the head of the family. By implication, this view moves children from objects of servitude for the family's well-being to human beings who are intrinsically valued in the eyes of God. As such, children are free to serve as agents of God. The *Acts of Andrew and Matthias* give hints of this new role of children. In one incident, an old man who had sacrificed his children unto death to spare his own life is reproached by Andrew and condemned to Hades. In another, the children of the city of the man-eaters plead with Andrew to stay in the city and teach them, "weeping and praying" and placing "ashes upon their heads." When Andrew leaves the city, the Lord appears to him and reproaches him for not having "compassion upon the children that followed after thee" (525).

11. In the *Acts of Andrew and Matthias*, Jesus appears to Andrew twice, first "in the likeness of a most beautiful little child" (521) when Andrew is sent on his mission to the residents of the city of the man-eaters, and then "like a comely little child" (525) when he would rather flee the city than stay and disciple the residents for another seven days.

12. According to a footnote by Alexander Walker, the translator of the book, "this double name is in accordance with a tradition preserved by Eusebius (H.E., I 13), that the true name of Thomas was Judas" (535).

13. The full title of the document is *Acts of the Holy Apostle Thomas, When He Came into India, and Built the Palace in the Heavens*.

14. These books are: *Acts of the Apostles Peter and Paul*, where Libia and Agrippina "went away from their own husbands" (479); *Acts of Philip*, where Nicanora gives her husband the ultimatum to "prepare thyself to live in chastity and self-restraint" (498) or else she would leave him, whereupon he tries to kill her; at least twenty-four other wives "fled from their husbands" (509); *Acts and Martyrdom of the Holy Apostle Andrew*, where Maximilla, the wife of the proconsul, had been parted from Aegeates on account of his brutal disposition and lawless conduct and had joined the other believers for a "holy and quiet life" (515); and the *Consummation of Thomas the Apostle*, where both Tertia and Mygdonia were physically pressured by their husbands to abandon their faith, but would not, so that the husbands eventually "granted them their own will" (552), which could mean that they let the women go.

15. These books are: *Acts of Paul and Thecla*, where Paul is accused of "leading astray the souls of young men, and deceiving virgins, so they do not marry, but remain as they are" (488), with Thecla renouncing her impending marriage to Thamyris; *Acts of Philip*, where "all the virgins who believe" are to walk about in pairs for matters of accountability, but are not to have "communication with young men, that Satan may not tempt them" (502); *Acts of the Holy Apostle*

Thomas, where the king's daughter calls off the wedding after she and her fiancé had listened to the Lord, who had sat down on their bed and reminded them to recall Thomas's teaching and to abstain "from this filthy intercourse" and "become temples holy *and* pure" (537); the second part of *Acts of the Holy Apostle Thomas*, where the three stories about the young man killed by the dragon, the demon-possessed young woman, and the young man who killed his lover encourage young single people to refrain from fornication and remain celibate; the *Acts of the Holy Apostle and Evangelist John the Theologian*, where John recounts how the Lord had told him while a youth that He needed John, thus protecting his virginity and allowing him to refrain from marriage.

16. These books are: *Acts of Peter and Andrew*, where Peter and Andrew tell Onesiphorus that if he wanted to do the kind of miracles they did, he had to leave wife, children, and goods (527) just as they had done and live on through those "who come up, and come to the light" (526); *Acts of the Holy Apostle Thomas*, where Jesus enumerates to the bride and groom in the bridal chamber the long list of disadvantages involved in having children, especially parental greed and troubles that continue long after the children are grown; instead, believers should have born to them spiritual and "living children, whom these hurtful things do not touch" (537); in the second part of the *Acts of the Holy Apostle Thomas*, the devil identifies himself as the one who bound men "by the desires of women, that earth-born children might be produced from them" (543); through the power of Christ, the believer is able to "share in that intercourse which is lasting and true, and bring[s] forth true fruits, whose nature is from above" (549); the *Martyrdom of the Holy and Glorious Apostle Bartholomew*, where Mary is the first to offer her virginity to give birth to the Son of God, so that believers may emulate her and become that holy womb that gives birth to sons and daughters of God through "the Son of the Virgin Mary."

17. See *Acts of the Holy Apostle Thomas*, in which Thomas addresses the young man who had been killed by the dragon because the man had had intercourse on the Lord's Day, and had been brought back to life by Thomas.

4. Early Theological Perspectives on Celibacy: The Church Fathers

1. J. L. Fischer, "The Sociopsychological Analysis of Folk Tales," *Current Anthropology* 4, no. 3 (June 1963): 262.

2. Virginia Burrus, *Chastity as Autonomy: Women in the Stories of Apocryphal Acts* (Lewiston/Queenston: Edwin Mellen Press, 1987), 108–9.

3. Stevan L. Davies, *The Revolt of the Widows: The Social World of the Apocryphal Acts* (Carbondale: Southern Illinois University Press, 1980), 96–103.

4. Peter Brown, *The Body and Society: Men, Women and Sexual Renunciation in Early Christianity* (New York: Columbia University Press, 1988), 153.

5. Ibid., 146.

6. For example, in an African church, at Cirta, in A.D. 303, the pagan authorities confiscated thirty-eight virgins' veils, eighty-two women's tunics, and

forty-seven pairs of female slippers, but only sixteen pieces of male clothing. See Brown, *The Body and Society*, 148.

7. Ibid., 63.

8. Ibid., 64.

9. Henry Chadwick, *The Early Church: The Story of Emergent Christianity from the Apostolic Age to the Foundation of the Church of Rome* (New York: Viking Penguin, 1967), 36.

10. Rudolf Bultmann, *Primitive Christianity in Its Contemporary Setting*, trans. Reginald H. Fuller (Philadelphia: Fortress Press, 1956), 206–8.

11. Peter Brown, "The Notion of Virginity in the Early Church" in *Christian Spirituality: Origins to the Twelfth Century*, ed. Bernard McGinn and John Meyendorff (New York: Crossroad, 1985), 427.

12. For an overview of the exegetical methods employed by the Church Fathers, see Sandra M. Schneiders, "Scripture and Spirituality" in *Christian Spirituality: Origins to the Twelfth Century*, 1–20.

13. The rivalry for primacy between Rome as the ancient midpoint of the Empire and therefore of the church, and Constantinople, the parvenu capital of the Empire and second-ranking primatial see, began with the rule of Diocletian (284–305) in the East and Maximian (286–306) in the West; it was more clearly formulated at the Council of Constantinople (381), but did not culminate until 1204 with the vengeful destruction of the Byzantine Empire by the crusaders of the Latin Empire and the confirmation by Innocent III of the Venetian Thomas Morosini as first Latin patriarch of Constantinople. See "Schism, Eastern" in *The Westminster Dictionary of Church History*, ed. Jerald C. Brauer (Philadelphia: Westminster Press, 1971).

14. Brown, *The Body and Society*, 78–79.

15. Ibid., 76.

16. Tertullian, *Treatises on Marriage and Remarriage; To His Wife, An Exhortation to Chastity, Monogamy*, trans. William P. Le Saint in *Ancient Christian Writers: The Works of the Fathers in Translation* (New York: Newman Press, 1951).

17. In recent, particularly feminist, literature, Tertullian is frequently stereotyped for his apparent misogyny when reproving the women at Carthage for their excessive apparel, saying: "And do you not know that you are (each) an Eve? The sentence of God on this sex of yours lives in this age: the guilt must of necessity live too. You are the devil's gateway"; quoted in his treatise "On the Apparel of Women," trans. S. Thelwall, *Ante-Nicene Fathers*, vol. 4, ed. Alexander Roberts and James Donaldson (Peabody, Mass.: Hendrickson Publishers, 1995), 14. Simone de Beauvoir was perhaps the first in the twentieth century to give the "gateway passage" wide public exposure through her book *The Second Sex*, where she alludes to it twice. In defense of Tertullian's alleged misogyny, see F. Forrester Church, "Sex and Salvation in Tertullian" in *Studies in Early Christianity: A Collection of Scholarly Essays*, ed. Everett Ferguson with David M. Scholer and Paul Corby Finney, Women in Early Christianity 14 (New York: Garland Publishing, 1993), 199–217. Church says about Tertullian that "the only liberation he knew

was liberation in Christ from the limitations imposed by this age and the curse of mortality" and that he believed women and men "to be equally capable of that liberation, both while on earth and also in heaven" (216).

18. Tertullian, "On the Veiling of Virgins," trans. S. Thelwall in *Ante-Nicene Fathers,* vol. 4, ed. Alexander Roberts and James Donaldson (Peabody, Mass.: Hendrickson Publishers, 1995), 27–37.

19. *Acts of the Holy Apostle Thomas,* trans. M. B. Riddle in *Ante-Nicene Fathers,* vol. 8, ed. Alexander Roberts and James Donaldson (Peabody, Mass.: Hendrickson Publishers, 1995), 538.

20. Brown, *The Body and Society,* 168–69.

21. Origen, "Commentary on Matthew," trans. John Patrick in *Ante-Nicene Fathers,* vol. 9, ed. Allan Menzies (Peabody, Mass.: Hendrickson Publishers, 1995), 413–512.

22. In his work on Origen, Henri Crouzel maintains "that Origen was the first theologian clearly to teach the perpetual virginity of Mary" and "that those who uphold the contrary are treated as heretics" by him. With this view, the author superimposes his own doctrinal bias and misreads Origen's intent in his Commentary on Matthew 10:17. Again Crouzel misconstrues Origen by forcing into a parallel metaphor two separate themes when saying, "Mary among women is the first fruits of virginity as Jesus is among men"; see Henri Crouzel, *Origen,* trans. by A. S. Worrall (San Francisco: Harper & Row, 1989), 141.

23. This view of Mary as the first person to give birth to Christ on account of her virginity finds its parallel in *Martyrdom of the Holy and Glorious Apostle Bartholomew,* which says that "she was the first among women" saying, "I offer to thee, O Lord, my virginity" and "being called for the salvation of many, observed this," so that "she was the first virgin of whom was born God and man"; in *Ante-Nicene Fathers,* vol. 8, 554.

24. Origen, "Commentary on the Gospel of John," trans. Allan Menzies in *Ante-Nicene Fathers,* vol. 9, ed. Allan Menzies (Peabody, Mass.: Hendrickson Publishers, 1995), 295–408.

25. Origen, "Fragments on 1 Corinthians," ed. C. Jenkins, *Journal of Theological Studies* 9 (1907/8): 500–514.

26. The quote is a translation from the Greek of "Fragments on 1 Corinthians," 370, in Brown, *The Body and Society,* 175.

27. For an attempt to reconstruct Methodius's life and thought based on his writings, see L. C. Patterson, *Methodius of Olympus: Divine Sovereignty, Human Freedom, and Life in Christ* (Washington, D.C.: Catholic University of America Press, 1997).

28. Methodius, "The Banquet of the Ten Virgins," trans. William R. Clark, *Ante-Nicene Fathers,* vol. 6, ed. Alexander Roberts and James Donaldson (Peabody, Mass.: Hendrickson Publishers, 1995), 309–55.

29. *Acts of Paul and Thecla,* trans. Alexander Walker, *Ante-Nicene Fathers,* vol. 8, ed. Alexander Roberts and James Donaldson (Peabody, Mass.: Hendrickson Publishers, 1995), 487–92.

30. The book of Judith was probably written around 135–105 B.C. It is not included in the canon of the Protestant Scriptures, which has followed the Hebrew canon. When in the fourth century Jerome, working from the Hebrew canon, prepared a standard Latin version of the Scriptures (the Latin Vulgate), he called the reader's attention to a separate category of writings, the so-called apocryphal books, which included the book of Judith. Due to a possible misreading of or omissions from Jerome's introduction, the Council of Trent (1546) came to regard the books as part of the canon of the Old Testament, so that later the Latin Vulgate text, officially approved by the Roman Catholic Church and the authoritative version of the Bible to this day, incorporated these books in the sequence of Old Testament books. See "Introduction to the Apocryphal/Deuterocanonical Books," *The New Oxford Annotated Bible*, New Revised Standard Version, ed. Bruce M. Metzger and Roland E. Murphy (New York: Oxford University Press, 1991).

While sending for Judith to join him at a feast, Holofernes comments to Bagoas, the eunuch and personal attendant of his, that "it would be a disgrace if we let such a woman go without having intercourse with her. If we do not seduce her, she will laugh at us" (12:12). And after Judith comes in and lies down, "Holofernes' heart was ravished with her and his passion was aroused, for he had been waiting for an opportunity to seduce her from the day he first saw her" (12:16).

31. The book of Susanna, also part of the Apocrypha, was composed sometime in the second century B.C. It describes how Susanna, married to Joakim, is beleaguered by two elders who had been appointed judges by the people. Both are lusting after her and pry their way into her home while Susanna is bathing. "When the two maids had gone out, the two elders got up and ran to her. They said, 'Look, the garden doors are shut, and no one can see us. We are burning with desire for you; so give your consent, and lie with us. If you refuse, we will testify against you that a young man was with you, and this was why you sent your maids away'" (Susanna 10–21). But instead of surrendering to their sexual demand, she says: "I choose not to do it; I will fall into your hands, rather than sin in the sight of the Lord" (Susanna 23). Right before Susanna is to be executed, Daniel appears and brings the proceedings to a halt. He has the people reexamine the case in court, convicts the two elders of lying against Susanna, and brings about their execution, while Susanna's valor and perseverance is praised. Quoted from *The New Oxford Annotated Bible*, NRSV.

32. The tradition that John's celibacy brought about his death is also recorded in Josephus and Ambrose; see Herbert Musurillo, trans., *St. Methodius: The Symposium: A Treatise on Chastity*, Ancient Christian Writers 27 (Westminster, Md.: Newman, 1958), 238, n. 20.

33. Following Basil's return in 356 to Athens, where he had studied rhetoric, he took on as his spiritual guide Eustathius, an ascetic, who had founded several monastic brotherhoods. Eustathius's concern for the poor caused him to be remembered later as the founder of monasticism in Constantinople. See Brown, *The Body and Society*, 288.

34. Gregory of Nyssa, "On Virginity," trans. William Moore and Henry Austin Wilson, *Nicene and Post-Nicene Fathers,* vol. 5, ed. Philip Schaff and Henry Wace (Peabody, Mass.: Hendrickson Publishers, 1995), 343–71.

35. Gregory is believed to have been married to Theosebeia, possibly Gregory Nazianzen's sister, who died early in the marriage. Evidence comes from two sources, this passage in "On Virginity" and Letter 95 of Gregory Nazianzen consoling his friend Gregory of Nyssa over the loss of Theosebeia, fairest among the brethren, priestess, and yokefellow. Since the word "yokefellow" is commonly translated as "wife," Gregory is believed to have been married to her. But "yokefellow" could also mean co-worker, which makes it inconclusive whether Gregory had been married at one time, or merely had sexual intercourse apart from marriage prior to joining his brother's monastery and writing the treatise.

36. The first recorded use of "Chrysostomos" for John was in A.D. 553 by Pope Vigilius. See Elizabeth A. Clark, introduction to the translation of John Chrysostom's *On Virginity and Against Remarriage,* trans. Sally Rieger Shore (New York: Edwin Mellen Press, 1983), xxix, n. 1.

37. See Elizabeth A. Clark, "Introduction," vii. Among John's writings are homilies on virginity, marriage, remarriage, and choosing a wife; and treatises on virginity, the priesthood, marriage, and remarriage.

38. For example, we know from one of John's comments in Homily 66 that the church in Antioch sponsored some three thousand female celibates, virgins, and widows who would have taken such vows. While there were only a few monasteries for women in Asia Minor, many women had pledged themselves to a celibate life and had banded together in groups or continued to live with their families. See Clark, "Introduction," xii.

39. John Chrysostom, "Homily 19" in *St. John Chrysostom on Marriage and Family Life,* trans. Catharine P. Roth and David Anderson (Crestwood, N.Y.: St. Vladimir's Seminary Press, 1986), 25–42.

40. John Chrysostom, *On Virginity and Against Remarriage,* trans. Sally Rieger Shore (New York: Edwin Mellen Press, 1983), 1–128.

41. Ibid., 129–45.

42. Brown, *The Body and Society,* 347.

43. Ambrose, "Concerning Virgins," trans. H. de Romestin and H. T. F. Duckworth, *Nicene and Post-Nicene Fathers,* vol. 10, ed. Philip Schaff and Henry Wace (Peabody, Mass.: Hendrickson Publishers, 1995), 363–87.

44. Ambrose, "Concerning Widows," trans. H. de Romestin and H. T. F. Duckworth, *Nicene and Post-Nicene Fathers,* vol. 10, 391–407.

45. Jerome, "Letter XXII — To Eustochium," trans. W. H. Fremantle, G. Lewis, and W. G. Martley, *Nicene and Post-Nicene Fathers,* vol. 6, ed. Philip Schaff and Henry Wace (Peabody, Mass.: Hendrickson Publishers, 1995), 22–41.

46. Jerome, "The Perpetual Virginity of Blessed Mary," *Nicene and Post-Nicene Fathers,* vol. 6, 334–46.

47. Jerome, "Against Jovinianus — Book I," *Nicene and Post-Nicene Fathers,* vol. 6, 346–86.

48. Jovinianus (d. 405) was an Italian ascetic who warned against the dangers of asceticism, emphasizing the unrestricted indwelling of God in all baptized Christians. Other claims made by him as cited by Jerome were that those who have been born again in baptism cannot be overthrown by the devil, that there is no difference between fasting and gratefully receiving food, and that there is one reward in the kingdom of heaven for all who have kept their baptismal vow; see "Against Jovinianus," 348.

49. Named after Donatus the Great (313–55), this North African movement was a political protest against Roman rule and influence, particularly by the Latin church under Constantine and his son Constans. Augustine spent much of the first fifteen years of his episcopate in Hippo to repress the movement by his anti-Donatist writings, which eventually were raised from the level of apologetics and propaganda to the level of permanent contributions to theology. Augustine challenged this localized sect with the authority of the church universal, and their rigorist claims with the principle that it is Christ who works in the sacraments, even when they are administered by unworthy ministers; the latter stance allowed him to be able to recognize the baptism and ordination of Donatist converts to the Catholic Church.

50. Augustine. "The Confessions," in *The Works of Saint Augustine — A Translation for the Twenty-first Century*, vol. 1/1, trans. Maria Boulding, ed. John E. Rotelle (Hyde Park, N.Y.: New City Press, 1997).

51. Augustine, "Sermons on New Testament Lessons," trans. R. G. MacMullen, ed. Philip Schaff, *Nicene and Post-Nicene Fathers*, vol. 6, ed. Philip Schaff (Peabody, Mass.: Hendrickson Publishers, 1995), 245–545.

52. Ibid.

53. Augustine, "The Good of Marriage," trans. Charles T. Wilcox, *The Fathers of the Church*, vol. 27, ed. Roy J. Deferrari (New York: Fathers of the Church, Inc., 1955), 9–51.

54. According to Augustine, a "venial sin" is pardonable through the act of confession and does not destroy the believer's relationship with God in Christ; in contrast stands "cardinal sin," such as adultery and fornication, which is worthy of eternal damnation.

55. Augustine, "Holy Virginity," trans. John McQuade, *The Fathers of the Church*, vol. 27, 143–212.

56. Jovinianus did not uphold the perpetual virginity of Mary; see also Jerome, "Against Helvidius."

57. A native of Thagara, Africa, Crispina (d. 304) was a wealthy married woman and the mother of several children who was arrested for her Christian faith during Diocletian's persecution. When ordered to sacrifice before the gods, she refused and was beheaded as a result.

58. Julianus had charged that Augustine and his followers condemned marriage and the divine work by which God creates human beings from men and women.

59. Pelagius (d. 419) was a British or Irish lay monk, known for his strenuous ethical standards and great learning, who had settled in Rome around A.D. 400. After a brief stint in North Africa, where he apparently tried to meet with Augustine, he left for the East, and found considerable support there. His chief followers were Coelestius, a Roman lawyer and later a monk, and Julianus, bishop of Eclanum, a man of exceptional polemic. Pelagius's teachings were not innovations and were in accord with the views of the East in general and with those of many in the West. The controversy around him involved free will and grace, reflecting a moralistic human responsibility. Pelagians denied the concept of original sin inherited from Adam. People had the power of formal freedom and the inherent capacity to do what was right without an absolute necessity to sin. People only needed good examples, given through the grace of God and God's revelations in form of the law and more especially through Jesus Christ.

60. Augustine, "Marriage and Desire" in *Answer to the Pelagians, II, The Works of Saint Augustine — A Translation for the Twenty-first Century,* vol. 1/24, trans. Roland J. Teske, ed. John E. Rotelle (Hyde Park, N.Y.: New City Press, 1998), 28–96.

61. Current Roman Catholic thought has broadened the meaning of concupiscence to include any desire or appetite of human nature that is not brought under the control of the mind and reason; hence, it is viewed as a love of some lesser good that upsets the God-given pattern for human life. Concupiscence is the result of the absence of God's sanctifying grace in the person; while this absence of grace disposes the person to sin, it is not considered a sin in itself.

62. Augustine, "Letter 200 to Count Valerius," in *Answer to the Pelagians, II,* 25.

5. Theological Developments on Celibacy I:
The Church Fathers and the Reformation

1. In Spain, the Council of Elvira, ca. 306, addressed questions about the regulation of virgins living at home, which indicates how widespread the practice was, going even into the westernmost part of the Mediterranean.

2. Tertullian was the first theologian to use the word *sacramentum* to refer to such Christian rites as baptism and the Eucharist. Connected with the word was the taking of a vow and the enlistment into an army of soldiers, though the analogy somewhat failed with the Eucharist. The Roman Catholic Church today commonly recognizes seven sacraments, i.e., baptism, confirmation, the Eucharist, penance and reconciliation, the anointing of the sick, holy orders, and marriage. Of these the sacrament of marriage was the last to be accorded sacramental status, though as an institution it was older than all the others. While Augustine was the first to call marriage a sacrament, it was not officially recognized as such until the Council of Trent (1545–63), which relied on such theologians as Peter Lombard and his *Sentences* of the twelfth century, and Thomas Aquinas of the thirteenth century, who both had included marriage in their list of sacraments.

3. Augustine defined a sacrament as "a sign of something sacred" ("Letters," 138, 1) and saw both baptism and marriage as sacramental in nature.

4. In his Commentary on 1 Corinthians 14 written around 250, Origen severely limits the activity of women prophets, saying that neither in the Old or New Testaments did these women "speak out in an assembly" or delivered "public speeches," but strictly prophesied either to individuals only or to a group of women. See C. Jenkins, "Origen on 1 Corinthians," 4, in *Journal of Theological Studies* 10 (1908–9): 41–42.

5. The *Acts of Paul and Thecla* call Thecla an apostle. The term in this context is derived from Paul, who calls himself an apostle of Jesus Christ, indicating his function of making present by a gift or call from God the activity and person of Christ through his ministry of preaching the good news of salvation.

6. The prophetess Prisca was also known as Priscilla. She is believed to have suffered martyrdom in 170 and was buried in the catacombs of Rome. Prisca was a member of the Christian movement of the Montanists, founded by Montanus about 157 in Phrygia, Asia Minor. Among the movement's features were the emphasis on ecstatic prophecy and spiritual gifts, an endtime expectation, rigorous ethical discipline, and the prominence of prophetesses, of whom Prisca, or Priscilla, Maximilla, and Quintilla were the better known. When by the close of the second century the movement was declared heretical by church authorities, its members and followers — Tertullian became one of its sympathizers in 207 — were considered to be outside the church.

7. For a historical overview of women attaining sainthood through the church's process of canonization, including those who do on account of their willingness to die rather than surrendering their virginity, see Jane Tibbetts Schulenburg, *Forgetful of Their Sex: Female Sanctity and Society ca. 500–1100* (Chicago: University of Chicago Press, 1998). The recording of the lives of the saints, also called hagiography, and their martyrdom had its early examples in the *Apocryphal Acts of the Apostles* and the *Acts of the Christian Martyrs;* of the Church Fathers, Ambrose frequently refers to women martyrs who would rather die than lose their virginity or chastity. The tradition of hagiography continued through the seventeenth century, with the Protestant counterpart being *Foxe's Book of Martyrs* (1563).

8. During this persecution, Origen was bound and tortured; in his *Ecclesiastical History*, Eusebius recounts Origen's treatment whereby "he was tormented with the iron collar and kept in the innermost dungeon of the prison" and "was set in stocks with his feet in the fourth hole and threatened with burning" (6.39). While Origen survived the imprisonment by a few years, there is little doubt that his death was related to the torture, hence approximated a death of Christian martyrdom.

9. This status of celibates in the heavenly realm was then given concrete "earthly" evidence by the church's practice of canonization.

10. The Greek word for overseer or elder is *presbyteros*, which initially denoted the office of bishop; only later did the distinction develop between bishop and priest.

11. Henry Chadwick, *The Early Church: The Story of Emergent Christianity from the Apostolic Age to the Foundation of the Church in Rome* (New York: Penguin Books, 1967), 46.

12. Other church orders stem from the third and fourth centuries, evoking the authority of the apostles, particularly the Twelve, rather than Paul because of his association with the Pastoral Letters that make provisions for female prophecy, and the "apostle" Thecla. For example, in the early third century, the Roman presbyter Hippolytus produced the *Apostolic Tradition,* dealing with the selection, ordination, and duties of the male clergy and establishing a hierarchical distinc-tion of clergy ordination, while setting ordination apart from the "appointment" of virgins and widows; this church order influenced initially primarily the churches in Egypt and Syria. Another church order appealing to apostolic authority is the *Didascalia* or *Teachings of the Apostles,* written sometime during the third century in Syria; the order prescribes that all pastoral and liturgical ministries be organ-ized around the bishop — including the office of the deaconess, while sharply defining the ministry of the order of widows and limiting it mainly to prayer and healing, and even that only at the instruction and oversight of the bishop; by contrast, the deaconess helps with women's baptism, the anointing with oil, the instruction of newly baptized women, and the visitation of the sick. While the deaconess is ordained, her office is clearly that of lay assistant to the clergy and not comparable in responsibility and authority to that of deacon, let alone to that of presbyter or bishop. Both church orders then move women, whether they are "ordained" or "appointed" to specific ministries of the church, to the margin of the ministerial hierarchy. See Francine Cardman, "Women, Ministry, and Church Order in Early Christianity" in *Women and Christian Origins,* ed. Ross Shepard Kraemer and Mary Rose D'Angelo (New York: Oxford University Press, 1999), 300–329.

13. Peter Brown, *The Body and Society: Men, Women, and Sexual Renunciation in Early Christianity* (New York: Columbia University Press, 1988), 86.

14. Apart from the three reasons of the celibacy requirement, a fourth reason may have been that the church wished to protect and retain the property rights to land and estates that had been deeded to a bishop because of his office; with the absence of a legal spouse and children, the church was then the bishop's sole heir. This fourth view, however, does not appear in the councils of the fourth century, and may not have been advanced until the ninth or tenth. Edward Schillebeeckx urges against giving too much weight to the financial implications for the church when children of married clergy were allowed to inherit church property. "Anyone who interprets the law of celibacy" for priests "as an ecclesiastical abuse of power for the benefit of the hierarchical organisation," he says, "makes a caricature of history." See Edward Schillebeeckx, *Celibacy,* trans. C. A. L. Jarrott (New York: Sheed and Ward, 1968), 61.

15. In the decretal, Siricius argues that "he who must be present at the divine sacrifices, through whose hands the grace of baptism is conferred and the body of

Christ consecrated," must preserve sexual continence. See Daniel Callam, "Clerical Continence in the Fourth Century: Three Papal Decretals," *Theological Studies* 41 (1980): 3–50.

16. Siricius argues furthermore that clergy who are more involved in procreating children for the world than for God have no right to preach continence to consecrated virgins, widows, or married couples who were expected to practice continence; in fact, clergy, that is, the teachers in the church are to be like soldiers in the imperial army who were absolutely continent during their service. See Callam, 39–40.

17. David G. Hunter, "Clerical Celibacy and the Veiling of Virgins: New Boundaries in Late Ancient Christianity" in *The Limits of Ancient Christianity: Essays on Late Antique Thought and Culture in Honor of R. A. Markus*, ed. William E. Klingshirn and Mark Vessey (Ann Arbor: University of Michigan Press, 1999), 139–52.

18. For example, at the Spanish Council of Saragossa in 380, the bishops required that a virgin be at least forty before she could be consecrated and take the veil.

19. The Council of Hippo in 397, for example, charged bishops that virgins living at home and whose parents had died be placed with celibate Christian women.

20. In a comparison between the writings of Ambrosiaster, a priest in Rome under Bishop Damasus (304–84) and Ambrose (339–97), bishop of Milan, Hunter explores the differing views on the status of virgins and widows in relation to the clergy and delineates possible underlying motives in establishing greater control over these women. See Hunter, "Clerical Celibacy and the Veiling of Virgins."

21. The ultimate reward for celibate and holy living came with the canonization to sainthood. This canonization or the "making of a saint" sprang up locally and expressed the will of the populace or special interest groups, such as a bishop, an abbot or abbess, or a royal or noble family. Among the more practical requisites the would-be saint needed in this world, however, were ways to achieve visibility, which invariably involved wealth and access to positions of prestige and power within the church and the world. See Schulenburg, *Forgetful of their Sex*, 6.

22. Earl Evelyn Sperry, *An Outline of the History of Clerical Celibacy in Western Europe to the Council of Trent* (Syracuse: Lyman Press, 1905), 16, 22–23.

23. Augustine, "Sermons on New Testament Lessons," trans. R. G. MacMullen, ed. Philip Schaff, *Nicene and Post-Nicene Fathers*, vol. 6, ed. Philip Schaff (Peabody, Mass.: Hendrickson Publishers, 1995), 505.

24. Brown, *The Body and Society*, 342.

25. The history of the ordained office of deaconess is frequently cited in the present-day discussion surrounding the ordination of women to ecclesiastical office in the Roman Catholic Church, so that historical "findings" offer a disparate range of opinion, often depending on the author's view on female ordination. Fairly certain is that an office of deaconess existed by the end of the second century, so that the author of the *Didascalia*, a church order of the early third century,

found it necessary to clearly define and delimit a deaconess's responsibilities in the church. There is consistent reference to her helping women in baptism and acting as doorkeeper with regard to women. She is to be living an exemplary life and to be at least sixty years of age. With the *Apostolic Constitutions*, originating around 380 in Antioch or Constantinople, the office of deaconess is assimilated to that of deacon, yet at the same time ranks lowest in the church hierarchy. The Council of Nicaea (325) mentions deaconesses (Canon 19), and the Council of Chalcedon (451) appears to take deaconesses for granted, requiring that they be at least forty years of age and committed to celibacy (Canon 15). Also in the East, deaconesses head up monasteries of nuns beginning with the end of the fourth century, but the office vanishes by the tenth century. During the first five centuries in the West, the office is not evident in Rome, Africa, or Spain, though criticism against the office of the East is advanced in the fourth and fifth centuries from Rome and Gaul, which might indicate that the office had arisen there. Later centuries either call a deaconess the wife of clerics, or the title refers to abbesses, but the office of "deaconess" as described at Nicaea or Chalcedon had disappeared. See Bruno Kleinheyer, "Regarding the History of Deaconesses," trans. Lothar Krauth, in *The Church and Women: A Compendium*, ed. Helmut Moll (San Francisco: Ignatius Press, 1988), 141–50; cf. Aimé Georges Martimort, *Diaconesses: An Historical Study* (San Francisco: Ignatius Press, 1986).

26. Little is known about the life of Scholastica, except what comes mainly from the *Dialogues*, written by Pope Gregory I of Rome, popularly called Gregory the Great (540–604), who was made pope in 590 and laid the foundations of the medieval papacy. The *Dialogues* popularized hagiography and contain accounts of the lives and miracles of Benedict and other early Latin saints. Among the various definitions of the name Scholastica (i.e., jurist or learned person) is that of a female administrator in a high position. See Mary Richard Boo and Joan M. Braun, "Emerging from the Shadows: St. Scholastica" in *Medieval Women Monastics: Wisdom's Wellsprings*, ed. Miriam Schmitt and Linda Kulzer (Collegeville, Minn.: Liturgical Press, 1996), 1–11.

27. It may be reasonable to assume that many women were forced to join convents as a last resort; others found the intellectual stimulation and independence of convent life more appealing than the prospects of an arranged marriage. See Ruth A. Tucker and Walter L. Liefeld, *Daughters of the Church: Women and Ministry from New Testament Times to the Present* (Grand Rapids: Academie Books/Zondervan, 1987), 142 n. 38; also, Will Durant, *The Age of Faith* (New York: Simon and Schuster, 1950), 805.

28. This redemptive function of virgins on behalf of their families and heads of household is paralleled in the Old Testament stories of Jephthah's virgin daughter who is sacrificed to preserve her father's dignity in light of his foolish oath, and Lot's virgin daughters who sacrifice their virginity and honor by having intercourse with their father for the sake of preserving his honor and male lineage; see chapter 2.

29. Some girls as young as three years of age were dedicated by their fathers to a life in the convent, as was the case with Edburga, a tenth-century nun; see Tucker and Liefeld, *Daughters of the Church*, 141.

30. These dowries included land, monthly rents, or cash, sometimes even clothes and furniture, thereby constituting a barrier to admission of the lower classes and favoring members of the nobility, the gentry, and the class of merchants. See Frances Gies and Joseph Gies, *Women in the Middle Ages* (New York: Crowell, 1978), 70.

31. See Tucker and Liefeld, *Daughters of the Church*, 142.

32. Apart from Roman Catholic monasticism, Christian movements had formed where this ratio was reversed. One of them, along with mysticism, was the *devotio moderna*, popular in the Low Countries and Germany and operating within the bounds of the church yet placing few limits on membership restrictions. Begun in 1380, its members included clergy, nuns, monks, married, and single people. Men and women were organized into informal congregations of brothers and sisters, without vows or intentions of becoming a religious order. Within a century there were some ninety houses for women and forty for men in the Low Countries and Germany alone, with women continuing to outnumber the men throughout its history. The most popular work coming out of the movement was *The Imitation of Christ* by Thomas à Kempis, which became one of the most widely read books in Europe at the time. See Patricia Ranft, *Women and Spiritual Equality in Christian Tradition* (New York: St. Martin's Press, 1998), 190–93.

33. Patricia Ranft has demonstrated in her study of Christian material on the role of women based on Scripture, early Christian writings, the Church Fathers, late antiquity, medieval monasticism in East and West, the high Middle Ages, and up to the Reformation, Counter-Reformation, and the Enlightenment, that "within Christianity there exists a strong and enduring tradition that maintains the spiritual equality of women" (xi). This very fact, along with the contributions of the Church Fathers in promoting this standard, have been overlooked largely, as Ranft says, "because we no longer live in a predominantly religious society." That the concept of spiritual equality should have translated into social equality, yet did not do so, must not lead to the notion that it did not exist (231) and, in fact, was rather prevalently underlying the concept and practice of sexual abstinence. See Ranft, *Women and Spiritual Equality in Christian Tradition* (New York: St. Martin's Press, 1998).

34. The collected works of Luther in English translation, which consist of a selection only, make up fifty-four volumes of about four hundred pages each, and were published in 1958 as *Luther's Works* by Concordia Publishing House, St. Louis; the German edition of his works, the *Weimar Ausgabe*, consists of one hundred folio volumes.

35. The *Church Postils*, which Luther himself considered "the best of all his books," is a compendium of sermons and explanations of the pericopes of the liturgical year for use by pastors. Since the majority of pastors in those days lacked

theological training and were underprepared in working out their own sermons, they mostly read only the Epistle and Gospel lessons to their congregations, or perhaps sometimes a sermon by another preacher, such as Johann Tauler (1300–1361), a Dominican monk, priest, and professor at Strasbourg, whose writings — mostly sermons, Luther read and reread. The *Church Postils* comprises four periods: the first (1520–27) where Luther wrote out his sermons and generally prepared them for the printer himself; the second (1527–35) where Roth served as editor and the third (1540–44) where Creuziger served as editor, both times under Luther's supervision; and the fourth (1544 and after) involving all subsequent editorial work following Luther's death. In 1520, Frederick the Wise had instructed Luther to write a church postil for all the Sundays, especially for the season before Easter, largely so as to redirect Luther's attention from the many disputes he was involved in to the positive teachings of the Scriptures for his own benefit and that of the pastors and their congregations. Luther wrote first the Advent Postil, then in 1521 while at the Wartburg the Christmas portions, finishing the same year up to Epiphany; in 1525, the sermons from Epiphany to Easter were printed, with collections for the summer season appearing earlier; see John Nicholas Lenker, "Editor's Introduction" in the first English translation of Luther's Advent, Christmas, and Epiphany sermons of his Church Postil on the Gospels, in *Sermons of Martin Luther: The Church Postils*, vols. 1 and 2 (Grand Rapids: Baker Book House, 1983), reprinted from a 1905 edition. Another sermon collection was the House Postil, containing sermons Luther had preached at home to his family and which had been taken down, printed, and distributed by Veit Dietrich without Luther's knowledge but much to his delight if they could "please and edify others" as "mere fragments and crumbs"; see Luther's Preface to the House Postil in *Dr. Martin Luther's House Postil* (Rock Island, Ill.: Augustana Book Concern, 1871).

36. The staged kidnapping of Luther's and his custody followed on the heels of the 1520 papal bull that ordered Luther's excommunication pending he submit, which he did not, and the Diet of Worms opening on January 27, 1521. Luther himself was not present until April 17, when put on trial on charges of heresy by Emperor Charles V before the secular tribunal of six electors. In light of Luther's refusal to recant his writings on the church's and papal abuses at two hearings, the emperor announced his decision to proceed against Luther as a condemned heretic on April 19; however, only four of the six electors were willing to sign the emperor's proposal, prompting the request that a committee be formed to examine Luther yet a third time, which was granted. The two that had refused to sign were Ludwig of the Palatinate and Frederick of Saxony, or Frederick the Wise. The reexamination failed again, so that Luther left Worms on April 26, with Ludwig and Frederick leaving shortly thereafter. Hence, the secular edict issued against Luther on May 6 was considered the result of a rump tribunal, regarding him as a convicted heretic, prohibiting anyone to harbor him, condemning Luther's followers, and ordering the eradicating of all his books. With Luther's knowledge,

Frederick had decided to hide Luther and had given instructions to his court officials to make arrangements, so that neither the elector nor Luther might know the exact location of the hideout. By May 4, Luther had been "captured," blindfolded, and taken to the Wartburg, where he would stay hidden until March of 1522. See Roland H. Bainton, *Here I Stand: A Life of Martin Luther* (Nashville: Abingdon, 1950), 167–93.

37. Philip Melanchthon, Luther's colleague at the University and close associate in the Reformation movement, had sent a letter requesting advice from Luther on the matter. See Bainton, *Here I Stand*, 201.

38. In his introduction to the first volume of the series of Luther's Works on the New Testament, Jaroslav Pelikan points out Luther's high view of the Old Testament as "Scripture" in the more precise sense of the word, and of the New Testament as "preaching." This high view explains why fully two thirds of Luther's exegetical work is on the Old Testament. Pelikan affirms what had been said by Heinrich Bornkamm, namely, that if Luther had held a chair at a theological faculty, it would not have been that of New Testament or systematic theology, but that of Old Testament. Thus, Luther read the New Testament as the early church had read it, namely, as an addition to the Scriptures which the church already possessed in the Old Testament, at the same time affirming the unity of the Bible; see Jaroslav Pelikan, "Luther's Works on the New Testament," in *Luther's Works*, vol. 21, ed. Jaroslav Pelikan (St. Louis: Concordia Publishing House, 1956), ix–xv. This interpretation is particularly evident in Luther's view of "flesh" and "spirit," whereby the flesh represents the outward compliance to the Mosaic law and the Commandments, while spirit represents the internal conviction and the believer's clear conscience before God afforded by the Spirit.

39. Martin Luther, *Sermons of Martin Luther: The Church Postils*, vol. 1, "Sermons on Gospel Texts for Advent, Christmas, and Epiphany," ed. John Nicholas Lenker, trans. John Nicholas Lenker and Others (Grand Rapids: Baker Book House, 1983), 255–307; reprinted from *The Precious and Sacred Writings of Martin Luther*, vol. 10 (Minneapolis: Lutherans in All Lands, 1905). The exposition on Anna comprises twenty-three pages, compared to the one on Simeon with twenty-one.

40. Löser, the marshal of Saxony, married Ursula von Portzig at Pretzsch December 1524 with Melanchthon and Jonas in attendance at the wedding.

41. Hilton C. Oswald, "Introduction to Volume 28," *Luther's Works*, vol. 28 (St. Louis: Concordia Publishing House, 1973), ix–x n. 1.

42. Faber had studied theology and law at Tübingen and Freiburg and had become a doctor of civil and canon law in 1509. As vicar of Lindau and the vicar-general for the bishop of Constance, he worked against the Protestant Reform movement and in 1521 presented to the pope his first work against Luther, titled *Opus adversus nova quaedam et a christiana religione prorsus aliena dogmata Martini Lutheri*. Luther's colleague Justus Jonas, who was minister of the Castle Church at Wittenberg and newlywed in 1522, had responded to Faber's treatise in 1523.

43. Martin Luther, "Commentary on 1 Corinthians 7," ed. Hilton C. Oswald, trans. Edward Sittler, *Luther's Works*, vol. 28 (St. Louis: Concordia Publishing House, 1973), 3–56.

44. Erasmus, in his 1526 Greek *Novum Testamentum* with notes, had endorsed this observation. Desiderius Roterdamus Erasmus (1469–1536) was the foremost representative of Christian humanism and Christian philosophy. Educated by the Brethren of the Common Life who were a movement of the *devotio moderna*, he became an Augustinian monk, priest, and professor at Cambridge, later moved to Basel, then Freiburg im Breisgau. The sheer volume of his work rivals that of Luther's and includes the first published edition of the Greek text of the New Testament, the republishing and editing of many of the writings of the Church Fathers, commentaries on the literature of antiquity, and theological treatises. Originally supportive of Luther, he later became highly critical of him. About the passage concerning "yokefellow," Erasmus says: "Some people apply this to Paul's wife.... There are important authorities among the Greeks who think Paul had a wife. And it makes sense here for women to be commended to women"; see *Luther's Works*, vol. 28, 22 n. 11.

45. See chapter 4 on Jerome; in "Letter XXII — To Eustochium," Jerome relates his experience of fasting in the desert where his mind is brimming with "bevies of girls" and his body "burning with desire."

46. What Luther calls *Krönlein* in German is borrowed from the golden border (*corona aureola*) of the table for the bread of the Presence (Exod. 25:25). In the Middle Ages the *aureola sanctorum* was a distinction awarded to virgins, martyrs, and teachers of the church for their victories over flesh, death, and the devil. It was variously represented in the arts by styles called aureole, nimbus, halo, glory, or mandorla; see *Luther's Works*, vol. 28, 48 n. 29.

47. The women were among forty nuns at the Cistercian Convent of Nimb-schem, which enforced strict seclusion. Relatives who visited were separated by a latticed window from the nuns, who were accompanied by an abbess. The regulations forbade friendship between the nuns, silence was the rule (as in Luther's own monastery), and the nuns were required to walk with lowered heads and slow steps; see Richard Friedenthal, *Luther: His Life and Times*, trans. John Nowell (New York: Harcourt Brace Jovanovich, 1970), 437.

48. About the incident, a student at Wittenberg quipped to a friend, "A wagon load of vestal virgins has just come to town, all more eager for marriage than for life. God grant them husbands lest worse befall"; cf. Bainton, *Here I Stand*, 286–87.

49. Several of Luther's own associates were dismayed at Luther's marriage. Justus Jonas, for example, a former priest — but not a monk — and minister at the Castle Church at Wittenberg who had been married in 1522, reported the day after Luther's wedding: "Luther has taken Katharina von Bora to wife. I was present yesterday and saw the couple on their marriage bed. As I watched this spectacle I could not hold back my tears"; see Friedenthal, *Luther: His Life and Times*, 438.

50. Bainton, *Here I Stand*, 286–90.

51. Martin Luther, "Lectures on Galatians 1535, Chapters 1–4," *Luther's Works,* vol. 26, ed. Jaroslav Pelikan and Walter A. Hansen (St. Louis: Concordia Publishing House, 1963).

52. At age twenty-three, Calvin had published his first book, a commentary on Seneca's *De Clementia,* which was a failure.

53. When Calvin turned Farel down, insisting that he was on his way to Strasbourg to pursue his own private studies, Farel pronounced a curse on Calvin, saying that "it would please God to curse my leisure and the quiet for my studies that I was seeking, if in such a grave emergency I should withdraw and refuse to give aid and help"; see Timothy George, *Theology of the Reformers* (Nashville: Broadman Press, 1988), 180; as quoted from "Battles," in *Ioannis Calvini opera quae supersunt omnia,* Corpus Reformatorum series, ed. G. Baum, E. Cunitz, and E. Reuss, vol. 31 (Brunswick and Berlin: Schwetschke, 1863–1900), 33.

54. The couple had a son, Jacques, who died in infancy; Idelette left behind two children from her previous marriage for whom Calvin provided solicitous care.

55. Calvin's aim was to make the city and the church educationally self-perpetuating. Under his "rule" and influence with the city government or the magistracy, the church's consistory introduced stringent disciplines and controls upon all citizens, such as urging regular church attendance, children's enrollment in school, strict building and residential codes advancing personal safety and hygiene, and laws and their enforcement against moral and civic crimes, i.e., adultery, prostitution, theft, blasphemy of the clergy, and burglary. Accordingly, people listened to preaching several times weekly, were trained in Calvin's Sunday school, instructed by his sermons, able to recite his catechism, sing the Psalter, and read the Bible with understanding. Inspired by John Sturm's academy in Strasbourg, Calvin raised money by public appeals and personal canvass for the Academy, which operated on a graded system — whereby the abler pupils were set to study Latin and moved on through the stages. Those students who moved on graduated to academy proper, or *schola publica,* which prepared them for the study of ministry, along with law and medicine as secondary interests. In 1559, the Greek scholar and New Testament theologian Theodore Beza (1519–1605) from Lausanne was appointed the school's president, and it was he who would carry on the leadership of the Geneva church for forty years after Calvin's death. See John T. McNeill, *The History and Character of Calvinism* (New York: Oxford University Press, 1954), 188–96.

56. Erasmus's influence on Calvin as exegete can be seen in the former's insistence on knowing the original languages of the Bible, interpreting obscure passages in light of clear ones, reading the Bible for moral edification in both the historical/grammatical and the spiritual sense, a critical view regarding the authorship of certain books, and an independence in relation to patristic interpreters such as Jerome; see Joseph Haroutunian, "General Introduction," *Calvin: Commentaries,* in Library of Christian Classics 23, ed. and trans. Joseph Haroutunian with Louise Pettibone Smith (Philadelphia: Westminster Press, 1958), 19.

57. Calvin's commentaries and sermon lectures fill forty-five volumes in the nineteenth-century English translation published by the Calvin Translation Society — thirty on the Old Testament, fifteen on the New Testament; Calvin did not write commentaries on 2 and 3 John and Revelation.

58. The *Corpus Reformatorum* contains 872 sermons, while another five volumes have appeared in *Supplements Calviniana.*

59. The table of contents lists the publication date as 1539, while the introduction indicates that the work was finished in 1543, which is more likely.

60. John Calvin, "The Necessity of Reforming the Church," *Calvin: Theological Treatises,* trans. with an introduction and notes by J. K. S. Reid, in Library of Christian Classics 22 (Philadelphia: Westminster Press, 1954), 184–220.

61. Charles V (1500–1558) was Holy Roman emperor (1519–56) and ruler of the Hapsburg Spanish and Austrian territories. Since religious unity was his primary concern, he dealt more gently with Luther at the Diet of Worms (1521) than might have been expected and remained tolerant at the Diet of Speyer in 1526 by allowing the princes autonomy in religious matters. When forced by the pope through an alliance against him to invade Italy and to sack Rome in 1527, he nullified the 1526 tolerance, but restored it at the Peace of Nuremberg (1532) when sensing danger from the German princes who had aligned themselves with the Protestant faith at the Diet of Augsburg in 1530. While attempting a gradual restoration of the Roman Catholic faith, he became discouraged on account of his troubles with Saxony, France, and the pope, so that he gave amnesty to Lutherans at Passau in 1552 and granted equality to Roman Catholics and Protestant princes at the Peace of Augsburg in 1555. Following his abdication to his brother Ferdinand in 1556, Charles retired to a Spanish monastery.

62. Calvin produced eight editions of the Latin text (1536, 1539, 1543, 1545, 1550, 1553, 1554, 1559) and five translations into French (1541, 1545, 1551, 1553, 1560). The *Institutes* consist of four books, addressing the knowledge of God the creator (book 1), the knowledge of God the redeemer in Christ as first disclosed to the Fathers under the Law, and then to us in the Gospel (book 2), the way we receive the grace of Christ along with its benefits and effects that follow (book 3), and the external means or aids by which God invites us into the society of Christ and holds us therein (book 4).

63. John Calvin, "Book Four," *Calvin: Institutes of the Christian Religion,* ed. John T. McNeill, trans. Ford Lewis Battles, in Library of Christian Classics 21 (Philadelphia: Westminster Press, 1960), 1011–521.

64. Montanists, named after their founder Montanus (first appearing around 157 in Phrygia — hence the later name Phrygian heresy), emphasized charismatic gifts and prophecy (especially among women) based upon the Gospel and Epistles of John, an impending end-time expectation, fasting, martyrdom and the refusal to flee from persecution, and celibacy (or at most marrying only once). During the early third century, the movement focused on ethical and ascetic rigors, rather than end-time prophecy, during which time Tertullian became attracted to it. In

its own time, the movement was considered a departure from Christian orthodoxy — largely owing to its claim to a superior revelation than that contained
in the New Testament — and was pronounced a heresy; see also note 6 in this
chapter.

65. Tatian was a Christian apologist, literary critic, and theologian of the second century in Syria. After studying under Justin Martyr at Rome, he returned
to Syria. Two of his writings are the *Diatesseron,* a harmony of the Gospels based
chiefly on Matthew and John which usurped the place of the Gospels until its
suppression in the fifth century; and the lost treatise *On Perfection According to the
Savior,* in which Tatian interpreted Paul as advocating celibacy for all Christians.
According to Iranaeus, Tatian was the founder of the Encratites, a Gnostic group
that condemned the consumption of meat and wine to the extent of having a
"water eucharist" and that considered marriage to be adultery.

66. The term "Encratites" means "abstainers" and initially identified the
Tatians; later it came to be applied to various groups of ascetics in Syria.

67. The Commentaries were translated into English soon after they were published in the second half of the sixteenth century. Most of the Commentaries were
originally delivered as lectures either at the church, where Calvin lectured twice a
week, or at the Academy and then recorded by students. Afterwards Calvin went
over what had been taken down, corrected it, and allowed it to be published; see
Joseph Haroutunian, "General Introduction," *Calvin: Commentaries,* in Library of
Christian Classics 23, 15–17; "On Gen. 2:18," 357–59.

6. Theological Developments on Celibacy II:
The Reformation until Today

1. The ratio of one believer with the gift of celibacy for every one hundred
thousand that Luther offers in his Commentary on 1 Corinthians 7 (26–28),
needs to be understood as hyperbole.

2. Rosemary Radford Ruether, *Women and Redemption: A Theological History*
(Minneapolis: Fortress Press, 1998), 113–16.

3. These male guardians also determined the future education of women,
including whether they were to be placed in a cloister.

4. Ruether, *Women and Redemption,* 114–15.

5. See Roland Bainton, *Here I Stand: A Life of Martin Luther* (Nashville:
Abingdon, 1950), 292–93.

6. Ruether, *Women and Redemption,* 114–15.

7. Ibid., 116.

8. A series of German essays on how women were affected by the Reformation and the Council of Trent is contained in Anne Conrad, ed., *In Christo ist
weder man noch weyb: Frauen in der Zeit der Reformation und der katholischen Reform* (Münster: Aschendorff, 1999); essays also contain bibliographical references
to research in English- and German-speaking publications, most of which were
published no earlier than the 1990s.

9. Merry Wiesner-Hanks, *Convents Confront the Reformation: Catholic and Protestant Nuns in Germany* (Milwaukee: Marquette University Press, 1996), 13.

10. Under Henry VIII (1509–47) the monasteries and convents were suppressed. While during 1535–36, monastic members had opposed the king's supremacy over the church, now they were expelled or closed. Around 1535, there were about eight hundred monasteries in England and Wales. Between 1536 and 1540, all of them were closed by Thomas Cromwell with little resistance from the monks in order to make new sources of income available to the Crown. See Karl Suso Frank, *With Greater Liberty: A Short History of Christian Monasticism and Religious Orders*, trans. Joseph T. Lienhard (Kalamazoo, Mich.: Cistercian Publications, 1993), 151.

11. Wiesner-Hanks, *Convents Confront the Reformation*, 13.

12. In 1962, three books on her life and writings were published in German, which include prayers, reflections, and letters. The quote is from an English translation by Gwendolyn Bryant, "The Nuremberg Abbess: Charitas Pirckheimer" in Katharina M. Wilson, ed. *Women Writers of the Renaissance and Reformation* (Athens: University of Georgia Press, 1987), 300; see Wiesner-Hanks, *Convents Confront the Reformation*, 13–14.

13. The marriage of Katherine Schutz (1497–1562) to the former Catholic priest Matthew Zell caused some controversy, especially since Katherine was well-read, articulate, and knowledgeable in theological and biblical matters, so much so that following the death of her husband she was fully expected to take on his office of preacher and apostle as "Doctor Katrina." When in 1524, the bishop suspended the clerical privileges to all married priests, Katherine defended her own role by arguing that marriage to a priest was a ministry that uplifted the moral degradation of the clergy; see Ruth A. Tucker and Walter L. Liefeld, *Daughters of the Church: Women and Ministry from New Testament Times to the Present* (Grand Rapids: Zondervan, 1987), 182; for her tract, see Paul A. Russell, *Lay Theology in the Reformation: Popular Pamphleteers in South-West Germany, 1521–1525* (Cambridge: Cambridge University Press, 1986), 204–5; also, Ruether, *Women and Redemption*, 113.

14. Wiesner-Hanks, *Convents Confront the Reformation*, 14.

15. Solemn vows were publicly taken vows from which dispensation was rarely granted, which annulled all rights to ownership of money and property, and which were recognized in both civil and canon law. Members of monastic communities who had not taken such vows were legally still members of the laity; moreover canon law could not offer them protection or immunity from secular law or exemption from taxes and dues. Hence, a woman who wished to avoid enclosure took only simple vows, which were privately taken and which could be dispensed with, while her ownership rights were left intact. Once family members and relatives, however, realized the ramifications of feudal inheritance laws, meaning that the women could still lay claim to their inheritance even though they were part of a convent or canoness order, pressure was exerted on them to take solemn

vows and become enclosed. See Patricia Ranft, *Women and the Religious Life in Premodern Europe* (New York: St. Martin's Press, 1996), 97.

16. Jo Ann Kay McNamara, *Sisters in Arms: Catholic Nuns Through Two Millennia* (Cambridge: Harvard University Press, 1996), 176–80.

17. Adolf Wrede, *Die Einführung der Reformation im Lünebergischen durch Herzog Ernst den Bekenner* (Göttingen: Dietrich, 1887), 127, 217; in Wiesner-Hanks, *Convents Confront the Reformation*, 16.

18. As quoted in Johann Karl Seidemann, *Dr. Jacob Schenk, der vermeintliche Antinomer, Freibergs Reformator* (Leipzig: C. Hindrichssche, 1875), appendix 7, 193; in Wiesner-Hanks, *Convents Confront the Reformation*, 14–17.

19. Lucia Koch, "'Eingezogenes Stilles Wesen'? Protestantische Damenstifte an der Wende zum 17. Jahrhundert" in *In Christo ist weder man noch weyb: Frauen in the Zeit der Reformation und der katholischen Reform* (Münster: Aschendorff Verlag, 1999), 203–4.

20. Wiesner-Hanks, *Convents Confront the Reformation*, 18.

21. McNamara, *Sisters in Arms*, 462–63.

22. Ibid., 19–21.

23. Ranft, *Women and the Religious Life*, 20–21.

24. Ibid., 104–5.

25. McNamara, *Sisters in Arms*, 461–64.

26. See Elizabeth Rapley, *The Dévotes: Women and Church in Seventeenth Century France* (Montreal: McGill-Queen's University Press, 1990), 32–33.

27. Ibid., 547.

28. Ibid., 555–66.

29. Ibid., 567.

30. Mary Ewens, "The Leadership of Nuns in Immigrant Catholicism" in *Women and Religion in America*, vol. 1, *The Nineteenth Century*, ed. Rosemary Radford Ruether and Rosemary Skinner Keller (New York: Harper & Row, 1981), 101–3.

31. Ibid., 103–4; also, McNamara, *Sisters in Arms*, 569.

32. Some priest-counselors and superiors from European motherhouses insisted that nuns remain faithful to European monastic regimes, despite their unsuitability to the American context. Other advisers urged sisters to relax their rules of enclosure, monastic hours of prayer, and restrictions on the type of work they could do (such as not teaching boys) in order to become more available to the many needs of the American pioneer church. See Rosemary Radford Ruether, "Catholic Women in North America" in *In Our Own Voices: Four Centuries of American Women's Religious Writing*, ed. Rosemary Skinner Keller and Rosemary Radford Ruether (San Francisco: Harper, 1995), 22–23. Also Mary Ewens, *The Role of the Nun in Nineteenth Century America* (Salem, N.H.: Ayer, 1984), 51–55.

33. Bishops frequently had far fewer workers under jurisdiction in their dioceses than did the mother superiors, and less authority over houses appearing to be directly responsible to the European motherhouse or to Rome; see Ewens, "Leadership of Nuns" in *Women and Religion in America*, 105–6.

34. Ruether, "Catholic Women," 23–24.

35. Only thirty years earlier, the 1917 Code of Canon Law had equated religious life with monastic life and had regularized all religious congregations so that they lost their individual flavor; moreover, it had restricted the autonomy of religious congregations and sisterhoods.

36. Joseph H. Fichter, *Wives of Catholic Clergy* (Kansas City: Sheed and Ward, 1992), 32.

37. See Ann Patrick Ware, ed., *Mid-Wives of the Future: American Sisters Tell Their Story* (Kansas City: Leaven Press, 1985), 1; and Fichter, *Wives of Catholic Clergy,* 32–35.

38. Ruether, "Catholic Women," 19.

39. Fichter, *Wives of Catholic Clergy,* 43–44.

40. See Mary E. Hunt and Frances Kissling, "The *New York Times* Ad: A Case Study in Religious Feminism," *Conscience* (Spring/Summer 1993), 16–23; as quoted in Ruether, "Catholic Women," 30.

41. Ruether, "Catholic Women," 31.

42. Lewis C. Daly, ed., *A Moment to Decide: The Crisis of Mainstream Presbyterianism,* with Anne Hale Johnson and Robert W. Bohl (New York: Institute for Democracy Studies, 2000), 41–53.

43. Harold O. J. Brown is founder of PPL and on the board of the Council of Biblical Manhood and Womanhood; PPL board member the Rev. Timothy Bayly, who left the PC (U.S.A.) and joined the more conservative Presbyterian Church of America (PCA) which denies women any form of ordained office in the church, is currently executive director of the Council of Biblical Manhood and Womanhood.

44. Nightingale never graduated from the school because she was prematurely recalled to lead a group of nurses she had been training to the Crimea to care for wounded soldiers; in the annals of the Kaiserwerth School she is recorded as "Probationer 134." See Elizabeth Meredith Lee, *As Among the Methodists: Deaconesses Yesterday, Today, and Tomorrow* (New York: Woman's Division of Christian Service, Board of Missions, The Methodist Church, 1963), 20.

45. The article was published in *Our Homes* magazine and was based on the Woman's Board of Home Missions of the Methodist Episcopal Church, South, "Minutes of Annual Meeting," April 18–23, 1902, 119; see Lee, *As Among the Methodists,* 52–54.

46. The deaconess order enjoyed great success in England, in part, because unlike sisterhoods, the order was placed directly under the bishop's oversight, was an integral part of the English parochial system, and worked with concurrence of the parish clergy. For a detailed account of the beginnings and early development of the deaconess order in the Church of England, see Jane Grierson, *The Deaconess* (London: CIO Publishing, 1981), especially 16–35.

47. In 1893, the Church of England Deaconess and Missionary Training Home opened in Toronto after a few women had visited the New York deaconess home

and two women had been trained in England at the Mildmay House. The deaconess movement of the Protestant Episcopal Church of the United States began in 1855 when the Bishop of Maryland created an association of teaching and nursing deaconesses. In the Church of England, the movement began when a priest, William Pennefather, started The Missionary Training College for Women in 1860, which became later known as the Mildmay House. In 1862, the Bishop of London consecrated the first deaconess, Elizabeth Ferard. But the bishops as a whole declined to impose canons or other controls over deaconesses, thereby permitting to emerge a decentralized pattern of education, ordination, and deployment. It was not until 1889 that the General Convention of the Episcopal Church in the United States passed a canon that regulated the appointment of deaconesses. In 1890, the first American deaconess training institution in New York opened which combined theology and social work. See Alison Kemper, "Deaconess as Urban Missionary and Ideal Woman: Church of England Initiatives in Toronto, 1890–1895," in *Canadian Protestant and Catholic Missions, 1820s–1960s: Historical Essays in Honour of John Webster Grant*, ed. John S. Moir and C. T. McIntire (New York: Peter Lang, 1988), 171–72.

48. Rosemary Skinner Keller, "Lay Women in the Protestant Tradition" in *Women and Religion in America*, vol. 1, *The Nineteenth Century*, 246–48.

49. Rosemary Skinner Keller served as assistant professor of religion and American culture at Garrett-Evangelical Theological Seminary in Evanston. She is a diaconal minister in the United Methodist Church and was codirector with Rosemary Radford Ruether of the Institute for the Study of Women in the Church at Garrett-Evangelical. Keller has written extensively on the deaconess movement. She is now professor at Union Theological Seminary, New York.

50. Lee, *As Among the Methodists*, 33–35.

51. Rosemary Skinner Keller, "The Organization of Protestant Laywomen in Institutional Churches" in *In Our Own Voices*, ed. Rosemary Skinner Keller and Rosemary Radford Ruether, 71.

52. As in church work at home, women's organizations paid women less than general organizations paid men. Meaningful salary comparisons are difficult because male missionaries were generally married and had to support their families; still the standard of living of single women missionaries, who were mostly housed with local families, fell below that of male missionaries of the same parent board. See Jane Hunter, *The Gospel of Gentility: American Women Missionaries in Turn-of-the-Century China* (New Haven: Yale University Press, 1984), 85; see chapter 3, "Single Women and Mission Community," for an overview of social conditions and coping mechanisms of single female missionaries in China.

53. R. Pierce Beaver, *American Protestant Women in World Mission: A History of the First Feminist Movement in North America* (Grand Rapids: Eerdmans, 1980), 179.

54. Carmichael describes the practice of handing girls over to the temple authorities, saying: "Always the one who is to dance before the gods is given to the life when she is very young. Otherwise she could not be properly trained.

Many babies are brought by their parents and given to Temple women for the sake of merit. . . . Always suitable compensation and a 'joy gift' is given by the Temple women to the parents. It is an understood custom, and ensures that the child is a gift, not a loan. The amount depends upon the age and beauty of the child. If the child is old enough to miss her mother, she is carefully watched until she has forgotten her"; see Amy Carmichael, *Lotus Buds* (London: Society for Promoting Christian Knowledge, 1909), 258.

55. Frank Houghton, *Amy Carmichael of Dohnavur* (London: Society for Promoting Christian Knowledge, 1954), 62; as quoted in Tucker and Liefeld, *Daughters of the Church*, 305–4.

56. Lee, *As Among the Methodists*, 12.

57. Ibid., 12, 17.

58. See Philip Schaff, *History of the Christian Church*, vol. 5, *The Middle Ages, A.D. 1049–1294* (Grand Rapids: Eerdmans, 1979), 490; quoted in Tucker and Liefeld, *Daughters of the Church*, 161–62.

59. Ranft, *Women and the Religious Life*, 71–74.

60. Utopian societies and movements share the belief in the perfectibility of humanity. These groups include millennialists, transcendentalists, and spiritualists, who anticipate and lead the transformation of the world toward a new level of spiritual perfection.

61. Rosemary Radford Ruether, "Women in Utopian Movements" in *Women and Religion in America*, vol. 1, *The Nineteenth Century*, 46.

62. Ibid., 46–47.

63. Ruether, *Women and Redemption*, 148–50.

64. Ibid., 154–58.

65. See Anna White and Leila S. Taylor, *Shakerism: Its Meaning and Message* (Columbus, Ohio: Frederick J. Heer Press, 1904), 256; in Ruether, *Women and Redemption*, 158–59.

66. See *http://religiousmovements.lib.virginia.edu/nrms/Shakers.html*.

67. Ruether, "Women in Utopian Movements," 48; also, Raymond Lee Muncy, *Sex and Marriage in Utopian Communities* (Baltimore: Penguin, 1974), 35.

68. Karen Armstrong, *The Gospel According to Woman: Christianity's Creation of the Sex War in the West* (Garden City, N.Y.: Anchor Press, 1986), 294–95.

69. Bainton, *Here I Stand*, 289–90.

70. Rosemary Radford Ruether, *Christianity and the Making of the Modern Family* (Boston: Beacon Press, 2000), 77–82.

71. Anne Bathurst Gilson, *The Battle for America's Families: A Feminist Response to the Religious Right* (Cleveland: Pilgrim Press, 1999), 124–25.

72. Ibid., 83–104.

73. Walter M. Gallichan, *The Great Unmarried* (London: T. Werner Laurie, 1914), 36–37.

74. Ibid., 91.

75. Ibid., 133, 154, 164; the entire second half of the book, pages 131–220, is dedicated to a discussion of the "remedies" of celibacy. The author concludes that

"the more we learn of the wonders of love and life and the soul of man, the more we discover the exquisite meaning of marriage, and truly realise its sacramental nature" (220).

76. See Jerry Falwell, *Listen America!* (New York: Doubleday, 1980), 15–16; as cited in Gilson, *The Battle for America's Families*, 24–25.

77. Quoted in the *Houston Chronicle*, September 4, 1994, 20–21A; see Gilson, *The Battle for America's Families*, 25–26.

78. Gilson, *The Battle for America's Families*, 54.

79. Ruether, *Christianity and the Making of the Modern Family*, 167–68.

80. See Sara Diamond, *Not by Politics Alone: The Enduring Influence of the Christian Right* (New York: Guilford Press, 1998), 21; in Ruether, *Christianity and the Making of the Modern Family*, 164.

81. Ruether, *Christianity and the Making of the Modern Family*, 164, 177–78.

82. Ibid., 178.

83. Gilson, *The Battle for America's Families*, 122–23.

84. Patricia Wittberg, *The Rise and Fall of Catholic Religious Orders: A Social Movement Perspective* (Albany: State University of New York Press, 1994), 214.

85. Ibid., 226–27, 232–33; Wittberg discusses her findings, based on the *Review* articles, in chapters 13 and 14 of her book.

86. Ibid., 220.

87. Ibid., 249.

88. Ibid., 250.

89. Ibid., 250–51.

90. Herbert Anderson and Freda A. Gardner, *Living Alone* (Louisville: Westminster John Knox Press, 1997), 66.

91. Ibid., 66–68.

92. Ibid., 64.

93. M. Craig Barnes, *When God Interrupts: Finding New Life Through Unwanted Change* (Downers Grove, Ill.: InterVarsity Press, 1996), 106–7.

94. Ibid., 114–15.

95. Kathleen Norris, *Cloister Walk* (New York: Riverhead Books, 1996), 116–23; 249–63.

96. Ibid., 122–23.

97. Ibid., 116–21.

98. Ibid., 121.

99. Ibid., 251–54.

100. Ibid., 256.

101. Ibid., 262–63.

Conclusion: Toward a Theology of the Single Life

1. On the power of the nuptial metaphor of union with God in Christ as it relates to consecrated celibacy, see Sandra M. Schneiders, *Selling All: Commitment, Consecrated Celibacy, and Community in Catholic Religious Life* (New York: Paulist Press, 2001), 179–200.

2. Jean Sheridan, *The Unwilling Celibates: A Spirituality for Single Adults* (Mystic, Conn.: Twenty-third Publications, 2000), 1. The phrase is taken from Dorothy Day's autobiography, *The Long Loneliness*, where she describes the founding of her houses of hospitality, run by "the unwilling celibate," the unemployed, and "willing celibates."

Index